Danette and Pam ▮▮▮▮▮▮▮▮▮▮▮▮▮▮▮▮▮▮▮▮▮ ften knew each other's ▮▮▮▮▮▮▮▮▮▮▮▮▮▮▮▮▮▮▮▮ age. Just that morning, ▮▮▮▮▮▮▮▮ drove together to drop the boys off at the same camp . . .

Danette was at Pam's house within minutes. Once inside, she, too, began to worry. She could see Pam must have left quickly. That wasn't like her. To just leave. Danette bent down close to the red smears on the rug, two streaks, one larger than the other. They were so dark, they didn't look like blood, not bright red blood. But maybe, could it be? Pam could have gone to the hospital. But her van was still in the carport, her keys were left in the door.

Danette looked around the room, at the bed, the closet, the window that opens up onto the patio area. Her heart seized. Several framed photos Pam kept displayed on a long wood credenza were knocked over, lying flat on the table, which also was out of place, as if it had been shoved hard against the wall.

"Call 911." The words tumbled out of her mouth. *Oh God,* she thought, *someone's taken Pam.*

**Stephanie Stanley** is an award-winning journalist and was the lead reporter on this story for the *New Orleans Times-Picayune*.

3 1705 00355 2087

# AN INVISIBLE MAN

## Stephanie A. Stanley

State Library OF Ohio

SEO Library Center
40780 Marietta Road * Caldwell, OH 43724

BERKLEY BOOKS, NEW YORK

**THE BERKLEY PUBLISHING GROUP**
**Published by the Penguin Group**
**Penguin Group (USA) Inc.**
**375 Hudson Street, New York, New York 10014, USA**
Penguin Group (Canada), 90 Eglinton Avenue East, Suite 700, Toronto, Ontario M4P 2Y3, Canada
(a division of Pearson Penguin Canada Inc.)
Penguin Books Ltd., 80 Strand, London WC2R 0RL, England
Penguin Group Ireland, 25 St. Stephen's Green, Dublin 2, Ireland (a division of Penguin Books Ltd.)
Penguin Group (Australia), 250 Camberwell Road, Camberwell, Victoria 3124, Australia
(a division of Pearson Australia Group Pty. Ltd.)
Penguin Books India Pvt. Ltd., 11 Community Centre, Panchsheel Park, New Delhi—110 017, India
Penguin Group (NZ), Cnr. Airborne and Rosedale Roads, Albany, Auckland 1310, New Zealand
(a division of Pearson New Zealand Ltd.)
Penguin Books (South Africa) (Pty.) Ltd., 24 Sturdee Avenue, Rosebank, Johannesburg 2196,
South Africa

Penguin Books Ltd., Registered Offices: 80 Strand, London WC2R 0RL, England

AN INVISIBLE MAN

A Berkley Book / published by arrangement with the author

PRINTING HISTORY
Berkley mass-market edition / June 2006

Copyright © 2006 by Stephanie Stanley
Cover design by Erika Fusari
Book design by Stacy Irwin

All rights reserved.
No part of this book may be reproduced, scanned, or distributed in any printed or electronic form
without permission. Please do not participate in or encourage piracy of copyrighted materials in
violation of the author's rights. Purchase only authorized editions.
For information, address: The Berkley Publishing Group,
a division of Penguin Group (USA) Inc.,
375 Hudson Street, New York, New York 10014.

ISBN: 0-425-20887-7

BERKLEY®
Berkley Books are published by The Berkley Publishing Group,
a division of Penguin Group (USA) Inc.,
375 Hudson Street, New York, New York 10014.
BERKLEY is a registered trademark of Penguin Group (USA) Inc.
The "B" design is a trademark belonging to Penguin Group (USA) Inc.

PRINTED IN THE UNITED STATES OF AMERICA

10  9  8  7  6  5  4  3  2  1

If you purchased this book without a cover, you should be aware that this book is stolen property. It was
reported as "unsold and destroyed" to the publisher, and neither the author nor the publisher has
received any payment for this "stripped book."

# Acknowledgments

This book would not be possible without the willingness of the victims' families and friends to share their stories. All of the women lost to this hurricane of violence were caring, intelligent, and essential members of their families and communities. Their absence is felt in the hearts of so many, including mine. They will never be forgotten.

I was first introduced to the Baton Rouge serial killings in 2002 as a reporter for the *Times-Picayune* in New Orleans. After Derrick Todd Lee was arrested for the murders in May 2003 and the media headlines moved on to other topics, I knew so much was left untold about the case. So many questions still lingered. One of my sources on the story, criminologist Peter Scharf of the University of New Orleans, insisted a book was in order. I thank him for the suggestion.

Thanks also to the many police officers and detectives who agreed to speak about the events covered in this book, especially Attorney General Investigator Dannie Mixon; Kurt Wagner; Zachary Detectives Ray Day, David Mc-David and Lewis Banks; former East Feliciana Parish Sheriff's detective Joel Odom, and West Baton Rouge Parish Sheriff's detectives Ned Horner and Freddie Christopher.

The Baton Rouge Police Department and several members of the serial killer task force declined several requests for interviews to discuss the case. To tell their story, I have relied on interviews with confidential sources, victims' families, and others with knowledge of the investigation, as well as police records and other investigative and court documents. Except for his older sister, Derrick's immediate family also declined to be interviewed. Tenieta Lee

Allen, who shares the same mother as Derrick, granted me several interviews during which she spoke about growing up with Derrick in Saint Franciville, Louisiana. A special thanks to her.

Special thanks also go out to James Odom, Collette Walker Dwyer, Anne Williams, the state crime labs' forensic investigators and all the lawyers, prosecutors, and other investigators who I have not mentioned by name.

Thanks, too, to Bob Mecoy, my agent, a man of tireless energy, and my editor, Tom Colgan, a man of great patience.

I owe a debt of gratitude to my mom and dad, two amazing people who always encouraged my curiosity and supported by ambitions. And a final muchas gracias is for Chris, my hero.

One of the greatest tragedies of this case is the fact that Derrick could and should have been locked behind bars years before he was able to commit so many of his murders.

More than anything, I hope this story can provide lessons for the future. It is a cautionary tale for police as well as a warning for the rest of us. Sometimes the person we most fear is standing in clear sight, yet because of our preconceived notions, we cannot see him. He is an invisible man.

# AN
# INVISIBLE
# MAN

# CHAPTER 1

*"We serial killers are your sons, we are your husbands,
we are everywhere. And there will be more of your dead
tomorrow."*

—TED BUNDY

A silent electric impulse, shooting faster than a bullet through
the wet Louisiana night sky, across miles of copper lines high
above the sleeping suburbs and darkened swampy land, fired
down into a modest two-story brick home on Danny Park
Drive just outside New Orleans, bursting the silence with a
loud, alarming ring.

Lynne Marino jolted awake. The clock said 1:30. The
caller ID read Kinamore. Her daughter Pam's home in Baton
Rouge, sixty miles away. She picked up the phone and heard
her son-in-law's voice. He sounded confused, almost as if he
wished he, too, was still dreaming.

"Lynne, this is Byron."

"What's wrong?"

"Pam is missing."

"What?"

"Pam's missing. She's gone."

At sixty-six, Lynne's mind still worked faster than most,

and it was racing. She could not make sense of those words.

"Did you two have a fight?"

"No."

"Oh, she's probably at the movies with Danette."

Lynne thought of Pam's best friend. Those two loved going to the late movie together. She reassured herself, clung to the idea. In the milliseconds that passed, she told herself Byron was confused, had a miscommunication with Pam, or that Pam simply forgot to tell him where she and Danette had gone.

"No. Danette is here with me." The heaviness in Byron's voice sank into Lynne's chest.

"It doesn't look good," he said. "There's blood on the floor."


**Four Hours Earlier**

After hours of rearranging polished wood tables and side chairs, glass lamps and decorative picture frames, scented candles and age-flecked wall mirrors at her antiques shop, Pam Kinamore was sweaty and spent, her petal-white skin dusted in a coat of grime and her muscles begging for a hot bath. She hurried through the misty summer rain to her Dodge minivan parked just outside the store, Comforts and Joys, undaunted and unconcerned that the streets in little Denham Springs, Louisiana, were already dark, the neighboring shops already locked up and their owners long gone.

She liked her independence, her freedom to make her own schedule, work as long or as little as she wanted. She was a long way from her days in the corporate world, beholden to the office every day from nine to five or six or seven. She had given all that up—the $80,000-a-year position with First Union, the sprawling house in a gated community, the fancy cars—to become a full-time mom for her adopted son, Jacob. But Pam was certainly not the stay-at-home type, especially when Jacob, then twelve, wasn't home, like on that night. She had dropped him off just that morning for a week away at camp. She and her husband, Byron, were supposed to get dinner out and catch a movie—they insisted on honoring regular date nights—but at the last minute, Pam decided to take advantage of Jacob's absence and fix up her store for the onslaught of shoppers who flocked to Denham Springs' antiques row every weekend. She called Byron to cancel about six p.m., promising a rain check. He accepted and he decided to pass the evening alone at a local casino.

That freed Pam to work late, well past nine thirty, when her landlord, Julie Norris, happened to drive by the store. Inside, the lights burned bright, and Julie saw Pam through the picture window, working. Alone. Julie nudged her husband out of the car to check on Pam. He rapped on the glass, startling her.

"Go home!" he said. "It's nine thirty. It's not safe to be here alone."

"OK. OK." Pam laughed and waved her friends off. "I'm just finishing up. I'm leaving right now."

Pam was genetically predisposed to perfectionism, especially when it came to decorating, and she could have stayed all night, making sure every item and piece of furniture was displayed just so. She was born with an eye for design, be it a room, an outfit, or a piece of artwork. She began hustling her skills at the age of six, when she made and sold her own gift cards. She painted through college, majored in art, and for a while scratched by selling her own line of jewelry. When she got tired of the self-imposed poverty, she gave real estate a try and discovered a penchant for sprucing up hard-to-sell properties, sometimes by simply taking better pictures of the house or rewriting the description on the brochures. Her office named her rookie agent of the year, amazed that she could sell as many loser homes as she did. The banks where she brought her clients for mortgages also noticed her sales talents. Soon she was working for the money people, climbing a fast ladder to an executive position. That is, until she jumped off in 1993.

The drive home to Briarwood Estates didn't take long, a quick skip onto Interstate 12 west and a short stop at Jack in the Box for a Diet Coke. Pam lived on the outskirts of Baton Rouge, Louisiana's capital city, in the far reaches of the suburbs among fast-disappearing farm fields, used car dealerships, and nondescript industrial parks. Sometimes she missed their old house inside the city, but she never regretted her decision to move. Downsizing wasn't nearly as bad as some of her coworkers suggested with their stunned faces when she quit. She did not care what others thought. Pam knew, or something in her gut told her, that time with Jacob would be more valuable than any amount of money or prestige.

Her instincts proved right. Her house was smaller, the location more remote, but her life was fuller. She devoted herself to mothering Jacob, taking care of her home, and doting on her husband. She earned a reputation as the Martha Stewart— with a Southern accent—among her circle of friends. Her house seemed never to show a speck of dust. Dinner was home-cooked almost every night. Laundry did not pile up. And Pam always looked like she just stepped out of a beauty salon with her clothes pressed and coordinated, shoes matching the belt and purse. At forty-four, she was still an irresistible head-turner. She was naturally gorgeous, with a face possessed of enviably high cheekbones, full red lips, bright big brown eyes, and an even bigger and brighter smile. Men constantly tried flirting with her, but she was forever stuck on Byron. And he never stopped fawning over her. They delighted in each other's company. They married in 1982. Byron was already in a wheelchair when they met, the result of a car wreck, but Pam didn't care. She knew he was her man.

"Isn't he handsome!" she'd say to friends, combing her hand through his thick, dark hair. "Look at him!"

The best part of accepting the title homemaker, however, was Jacob. She made sure she was always available to him, to tie his shoes, wipe his nose, help with homework or a crisis with friends, or simply to kiss him on the forehead before bed every night. Pam treasured her summer days with him, sneaking off to the afternoon movie, visiting museums, or riding bikes around the lakes at the Louisiana State University campus in Baton Rouge. To her, he was everything, and everything seemed just about perfect.

"I've got it made," she'd say. "I love my life."

Even her professional life was working out well. In her free time, she tended to her antiques shop—something she dreamed of owning all her life—and worked on her interior design business, which was starting to bring in a fair share of extra cash. "I've got the best job in the world," she told her mother. "I get paid to shop and decorate."

The only thing Pam hated was the idea of Jacob growing

up and needing her less and less. She chased away her dread—or rather, avoided it—with plans to expand her business. She was thinking of those plans as she busied herself that day, trying not to already miss her son.

Pam turned into Briarwood Estates sometime after ten thirty p.m. The subdivision is across the street from a golf course and has only one entrance, meaning one way in and one way out, so traffic doesn't just pass through. Pam enjoyed the quiet privacy of the neighborhood, especially the stretch of woods behind her backyard. She felt safe there, so far removed from the city. She felt immune from its typical urban problems.

Just that week, the city was buzzing over the rapes and murders of two women in their homes. Police linked the killings by DNA to the same man, but they had no leads on his identity. Local chatter was tossing around the words *serial killer*. People were frightened because the dead women were not typical murder victims. They did not reside in dangerous neighborhoods or live high-risk lives. They were not prostitutes or drug addicts. They were not killed by spurned boyfriends or jealous husbands. One was a recently divorced nurse, just a few years younger than Pam. Beautiful, smart, savvy. The other was a recent business school graduate, twenty-two, and also a looker, intelligent and independent.

If someone was looking for a profile of the victims, Pam would had made a good candidate. All three women were eye-catching brunettes with lots of spunk. They were undeniably sexy, with flirtatious smiles and tireless personalities. They all stood about average height and weighed somewhere between 130 and 140 pounds. And they each carried themselves with the utmost confidence; they were comfortable in their skins, happy with their success in life, and proud of their strength as women.

Maybe that's why Pam did not feel threatened. She never thought the two Baton Rouge murders were anything but a city problem. She lived out in the suburbs. She was married, a mother. She did not live alone like the other women. She thought she had no need to worry.

Pam parked her van in the carport, gathered up her purse and drink and packages into her arms, and pushed through the gates leading into her backyard. A high fence offered total privacy in the patio area, which was landscaped with giant palms and potted plants. She unlocked the back door and went inside through the kitchen, putting her purse down on the counter. The house was quiet as she walked toward her bedroom.

She enjoyed few things as much as her home, which looked like something off the pages of *Architectural Digest*. She spent years decorating it with her favorite antique armoires and tables and wrought-iron accents. She created a warm, soothing atmosphere within its walls, where she and her family and friends often gathered for good times and memories. Walking into the living room felt like walking into the warmth of a Norman Rockwell painting, and sitting down on the big pillowy sofa she loved was like settling into a dreamy safe haven from the world.

In the bathroom, Pam turned on the water faucet for the tub and began undressing. She put her watch on the counter, slipped out of her bra and panties, and stepped into the tub. At forty-four, her body was still trim and strong. She tried to exercise regularly. The day before, she and her neighbor had walked the subdivision streets before beginning their days.

Pam leaned back in the tub, letting the warm water swallow her body and rise up to her chin as she rested her head against the cool porcelain. She loved her baths. This was how she ended many of her days. She looked at her feet, at the polish on her toes. Time for a pedicure. She grabbed two cotton balls, dabbed them with polish remover, and began wiping the color off her toenails.

Outside among the palms, a shadow passed across the patio. He followed the lights to the bathroom window. He had been watching her. She caught his eye the first time he saw her. He was always trawling, looking for the ones who set his blood rushing. She was perfect. A high-class lady. Real sexy. He could tell by the strut in her walk.

He needed to get closer, see more of her. He placed the side of his hand against the window, shielding the glare from his eyes, and peered in. Directly across from him was a mirror and in the reflection he could see the tub.

He watched Pam from the darkness. She was oblivious to

his stare. He had the advantage: the element of surprise. A familiar thrill shot through him. He looked toward the back door. His head was buzzing. A pressure built inside his chest. Watching used to be enough. He had been doing it since he was a little boy. But now he had to go all the way. He would get some of that bitch.

In the light cast from the living room windows, something glistened in the dark near the back door knob. He moved closer to it. Fate was on his side that night. Pam's keys were dangling from the lock. He pushed open the door and walked inside.

Byron pulled into the carport just before midnight and parked next to his wife's green van. He maneuvered his wheelchair though the gates and could see as he moved closer to the back door that Pam's keys were dangling in the lock. After nineteen years of marriage, he lost count of the times he cautioned Pam about the bad habit, urging her to break it.

"Someone could walk right in after you," he'd say.

"I know. I know. Never again," she'd promise.

But neither one of them was too worried about it. The neighborhood was too safe. Their home was wired for a security alarm, although they rarely used it. There seemed no need.

The lights were on in the kitchen when he went inside, and Pam's purse was on the counter.

"Pam . . ."

Byron was tired. He had spent the evening surrounded by smoke, flashing lights, and drunken gamblers. He was ready for the soothing company of his wife.

"Pam . . ."

He waited to hear her voice. No answer.

He went into their bedroom. Pam was relentlessly neat. She couldn't walk out of a room if something was out of place. She was constantly fluffing pillows, rearranging the family photos, and straightening tabletop magazines. But there, by the couple's bed, the French footstool was knocked askew.

"Pam?"

His gaze fell to the throw rug. At its edge, he saw two red smears. He touched them. *Is that blood?*

He went into the bathroom. The tub was filled with water; a cotton ball with red nail polish was floating on the surface. He dipped in his hand. Still warm. On the tub, a Jack in the Box cup was dripping condensation. The clothes she had on that day were folded and placed in the laundry hamper. Her Rolex watch was on the vanity. Her shoes were on the floor. But no Pam.

He thought perhaps she had fallen and cut herself. Maybe she went to a neighbor's or a friend's house for help, but she had left no note. Pam always left a note. She would let him know where she was going, especially if she was hurt. He called Danette, Pam's good friend, who lived down the street.

"Is Pam with you?"

Danette and Pam talked almost every day, and they often knew each other's plans. Their sons were the same age. Just that morning, the women drove together to drop the boys off at the same camp.

"No, I haven't seen her since this afternoon."

"I don't know where she is." He paused. "And I think there's blood on the rug . . ." He hoped his fears were as ridiculous as they sounded. "Can you come over here and see what you think?"

Danette was at Pam's house within minutes. Once inside, she, too, began to worry. She could see Pam must have left quickly—without her purse, without her wallet and cell phone. That wasn't like Pam. In the bedroom, Danette bent down close to the red smears on the rug, two streaks, one larger than the other. They were so dark, they didn't look like blood, not bright red blood, but maybe, could it be? Pam could have gone to the hospital. But her van was still in the carport; her keys were left in the door.

Danette looked around the room, at the bed, the closet, the window that opens up onto the patio area. Her heart seized. Several framed photos Pam kept displayed on a long wood credenza were knocked over, lying flat on the table, which also was out of place, as if it had been shoved hard against the wall.

"Call 911." The words tumbled out of her mouth. *Oh God,* she thought, *someone's taken Pam.*

* * *

After Byron's call, Lynne dressed quickly. She tried not to imagine the worst. She prayed. *Please, God, don't let anything happen to my child, my Pammie baby.* But a rushing panic was creeping in. She was disoriented. She didn't pack a bag. Why would she need more clothes? Pam would be home soon. That's what she kept telling herself to stay sane, to move forward, to handle this.

With her companion, Richard, driving, they sped to Baton Rouge on Interstate 10, crossing long, uninhabitable stretches of swampland and thick forests. Lynne looked out the window; the mist was still thick in the air. She wrestled with the scenarios passing through her mind. Pam attracted lots of men. She was so nice to everyone. Maybe one became obsessed and let his fantasy go too far. Lynne remembered Pam spoke of guys who stopped by her shop just to flirt. Someone like that, someone with a crush on Pam wouldn't hurt her, right? Would he? She desperately fought off the most horrific, violent images barging into her mind. She would not let herself imagine the sound of Pam screaming.

"If anyone can talk her way out of a kidnapping, Pam could," Lynne told herself.

Lynne remembers Pam was always the feistiest in the family, the hustler. She wasn't book smart, but she was street smart. "My Pam wasn't good with numbers unless they had a dollar sign in front," Lynne says.

In high school, Pam worked two jobs—forging her birth certificate at the age of fifteen—to afford her first car, then earned gas money by charging friends $5 a week for rides to school. One year out of college, she bought her first home, paying the mortgage with rent collected from roommates. Everyone was getting a good deal, but Pam was the one getting the equity. She was a true saleswoman at heart. Pam's tongue was as fast as they come.

Pam would convince the man to let her go, Lynn told herself. She would trick him, get a message out to the police, and find a way to escape. She had to.

Richard got off the interstate at Highland Road, a busy commuter artery for Baton Rouge that makes a straight shot from inside the city limits to its outer suburbs where Pam lived. The four-lane thoroughfare was usually clogged with traffic, but at two thirty in the morning, the roadway was empty. Even the endless series of fast-food restaurants and gas stations were dark and still.

As the car turned into Briarwood Estates, Lynne immediately saw the police cars in Pam's driveway, the second house on the right, just yards from the subdivision entrance. The other homes were dark, their owners peacefully asleep inside. But at Pam's house, a sober white light shone from the windows, a stark reflection of the cruel reality inside.

Danette, Byron, and a few of Pam's neighbors drawn from their homes by the sight of police cars, were gathered outside, barred from the house. Investigators were inside, securing the scene. Danette's father-in-law, a preacher, hovered near Byron, trying to comfort him in the night air. They all looked to Lynne as she stepped out of the car. She went straight for Byron and wrapped her arms around him. He began to sob in his chair. She held him tight and repeated again and again, "Everything's going to be OK. She's going to come home." But Lynne was crying, too. She bargained in between her sobs, aiming her voice at the sky: "Please, God, bring her back. I'll do anything."

Danette struggled for words when she hugged Lynne, thinking to herself, *Her daughter's been abducted. What can be said? Pam's home, her precious haven, is a crime scene. How do you talk about that?*

Danette glanced up at the sky, too. *Where could Pam be? Who could have taken her? Why? How? In this neighborhood?* In the distance, in a lumbering storm cloud moving away from the city, she saw several flashes of fading lightning. A chill passed through her heart: "Something just told me Pam's dying."

•

# CHAPTER 2

# A Mother's Battle Begins

The seconds clicked loudly in Lynne's head as she waited at her daughter's home in those early morning hours. She did not know the statistics, but instinctually she knew the deal. Pam's chances of survival diminished exponentially with each lost minute. Most abduction victims are killed within the first few hours. Pam was taken between 10:30 p.m. and 11:45 p.m. More than three hours had already passed. If Pam was still alive, her only hope would be for police to find her fast.

Detectives from the East Baton Rouge Parish Sheriff's Office had arrived at the house just after midnight, so when Lynne got a moment with them, she needed reassurance; she expected to see their law enforcement hustle, and she wanted to know how they planned to save Pam. What she witnessed only frightened her more.

Detectives were busy questioning Byron and Pam's friends, hoping for information that might explain Pam's disappearance, perhaps spotlight a suspect. A crime scene technician was combing the house for evidence, looking for hints of Pam's whereabouts, rolling up the bloodstained rug for a trip to the police station. The lead investigator, Lieutenant Tommy Rice, ordered his deputies to issue a BOLO, a "be on the lookout" for Pam, which should have gone out to all area law enforcement agencies.

But to Lynne's dismay, there were no bloodhounds sniffing for Pam's trail, no army of police searching the woods behind her house or fields around the neighborhood, and no helicopters or planes with heat-sensing detectors dispatched. No one from the FBI showed up to help. No team of investigators appeared to hook Pam's phone up to a wiretap and wait for a ransom call.

It was nothing like what Lynne had seen countless times on television police dramas. She quickly got the feeling the detectives were not sure Pam was even abducted.

"Where are the dogs?" Lynne demanded.

"None available," she was told.

"What about helicopters?"

"We don't know where to look."

"What about a roadblock?"

"We can't just stop traffic."

Frustration bunched up in her throat. The helplessness she felt was almost worse than the fear. Lynne is not the type to relinquish control of her life. She learned early, in her first marriage, after waking up with four children and a hard-drinking, unemployed husband, that she must depend on herself for survival, to protect her children. Now, when her daughter most needed her strength and determination, Lynne felt she could do nothing.

Lieutenant Rice, a stocky guy who favors Gap T-shirts and speaks with a bit of tough-guy swagger, tried to comfort Lynne, promising her he and the sheriff's department were doing everything they could. They had called Pam's landlord, who checked on the store and found it locked up and no Pam. He sent another detective to search Pam's storage space, a building not far from her home where she kept extra furniture for her store, but again no signs of Pam.

If they hoped to find her, they needed to know more about Pam and her life.

Does Pam have any enemies? police asked. Received any recent threats? Has she been acting strangely? Does she drink or gamble excessively? Use drugs? Has she disappeared before?

The questions struck everyone who knew Pam as ridiculous. Pam's life was blissfully normal. She was an enviably stable, responsible person. She was the type to make casseroles for sick acquaintances. She attended church on Sunday. She volunteered to coordinate fund-raisers for the adoption agency where she found Jacob. If she had any enemies, they were the jealous female type, and Pam usually made it hard for them to hate her because she was so darn nice.

The biggest risk Pam ever took, which she did not consider a risk, was treating strangers as friends. Sometimes, if she needed help lifting a piece of furniture out of her van, she was quick to ask a passerby. And her smile, her effortless rapport with people, always won a willing volunteer.

Is she depressed? The detectives continued. Unhappy with her marriage? Did she show interest in other men? Did she take trips by herself? Keep credit cards her husband didn't know about?

When police respond to a missing person report, they walk in on the unknown. Possible explanations are endless. Most people turn up within a few hours, surprised they were even reported lost. Another set of the missing don't want to be found; they left—some sneaking away, some in a huff—on their own. And sometimes the person reporting an absent loved one is trying to cover up their own involvement in a more ghastly crime.

Lynne knew what the detectives were getting at with their questions about other men, and she didn't want them to waste any more time pursuing it.

"If Pam had a boyfriend, I would be the first to know," she insisted. "And I would be the first to tell you."

But the police were not so confident. Here was a husband in a wheelchair. A beautiful wife who could have her pick of men. The son away at camp. And one of Pam's friends relayed a strange message to detectives from Pam, spoken years before: "If anything ever happens to me, look at Byron first."

"That's ridiculous," Lynne said when she heard it. "Pam

and Byron are soul mates. They love each other more than anything."

Police, schooled in the secrets people keep, believed Pam's disappearance could very easily involve a domestic dispute. Jealously. An insurance scam. A spurned lover. Statistically, those possibilities were more likely than a stranger walking into the home and kidnapping a forty-four-year-old, upper-middle-class suburban mom. That kind of crime just didn't happen in East Baton Rouge Parish.

Yet Danette, Pam's good friend, wasn't so sure. Almost immediately after looking inside the home, she feared Pam had become another victim of the man who killed the two women in Baton Rouge. She and Pam had discussed the murders just days earlier. Danette had been nervous about it. She wondered if they were in danger, if the killer would come after them. Pam seemed unruffled, convinced that the murders were too far removed from their quiet little lives in the suburbs. Danette, who rarely talked to strangers and always kept her car doors locked when she drove, got ribbings from Pam about being paranoid, so Danette tried not to worry either.

But now she was worrying again. Really worrying. When the detectives arrived at Pam's house, Danette was quick to put the question to them.

"Do you think this is related to the Baton Rouge murders?"

"Absolutely not" was the answer she got.

She tried to hope the police were right. Those were city murders, committed miles and lifestyles away. The women were single, not married with a kid. And they were killed in their homes, not abducted. Pam's case, the detectives told her, was too different.

Regardless of whether detectives suspected a link or not that first morning, whether they were simply keeping their thoughts close to their vests, they were not discussing it. Instead, they denied it, distanced themselves from the suggestion. They didn't want any wild speculation spreading among the already skittish Baton Rouge public. Until they learned otherwise, they were treating Pam's disappearance like they would any other missing persons case: cautiously.

When police reports were filed that morning, Pam remained classified simply as a missing person. "Foul play" was not ruled out, as the police spokesman Darrell O'Neal told reporters the next day, but detectives were awaiting more information—maybe Byron's confession, maybe even Pam's return—before they drew any more conclusions about the case.

Before the sun rose on Saturday morning, the police cleared out of the Kinamore home. They had collected all the evidence they hoped to need:

- The bloodstained rug, which was rolled up and driven to the East Baton Rouge Parish Sheriff's Office evidence room.

- Twelve fingerprints from the wood floorboards of the master bedroom next to the bloodstained rug.

- A few hair and fiber samples from the same area of the floor.

- Another print lifted from the outside of the back door just above the lock.

- A letter Pam had dropped on the floor by the tub.

- Pam's hairbrush and toothbrush were also taken for DNA and hair samples.

Nothing else seemed to stand out as evidence, so sometime early Saturday morning the police released the home from its status as a crime scene, and Pam's family and friends were left there to wait it out alone.

Lynne sat by the phone in the living room, comforted in a small way by the warmth and serenity of the room Pam tenderly decorated. No one could sleep. Byron had gone into the bedroom alone, and the rest of Pam's friends were with Lynne, pacing, sitting, and pacing some more, and each one struggling to think of who could have taken Pam and fighting off images of what might be happening to her.

Lynne looked at her watch every few minutes and imagined her daughter walking through the door. Perhaps if she imagined hard enough, her thoughts would become true.

She was practiced at bending reality with her will. She is full-blooded Irish, inheriting a stubborn fiery streak from her parents: a hard-drinking "mean son of a gun" as a father, she says, and an equally hardworking, selfless, saint of a mother. "My mother scrubbed floors to feed us children." Lynne grew up equally selfless and determined in the Irish Channel, a working-class section of New Orleans. She never shied from a necessary battle. When she walked out on her drunken husband, she had little money and just a vague plan: to make a better life for her and her children.

The divorce was just short of scandalous in the 1960s South, especially among her devout Catholic community. But Lynne didn't care. Her husband, Ed Piglia, had laid a hand on her too many times, she says, and that last time, when his fists swung near their son, Eddie Jr., Lynne could no longer ignore his abuse. She knew she had to dramatically change her life, uproot her home, if she was going to protect her children. Out of sheer hustle and will, she created a whole new world for her and her children. She got a job, worked long hours, and earned just enough to afford a small house and keep rice and beans on the table. They didn't have much, but Lynne gave her children the safe, stable, and sober home they needed. Each of them becoming happy, successful people, lifting themselves into higher social and economic levels through the drive and smarts inspired by their mother.

Likewise for Lynne, through the years she worked her way into better, higher-paying jobs, finally retiring just a few years earlier as manager of a large insurance office, a job that taught her the power of her intelligence, strength, and energy. If only she could make that power work for her now.

Before dawn, through the front window of the house, Lynne noticed a car slowing down. She jumped up for a closer look, peeking her head outside the door.

"Miss Lynne . . ." a voice called from the open car window. "It's Jackie."

Byron had called Jackie Badon, Pam's good friend, a few hours earlier with the news, and Jackie could not get back to sleep. She drove over to see if she could help.

Lynne was glad to see her, and when Jackie suggested they start knocking on the neighbors' doors, Lynne was relieved to have something to do, something that would relieve the torturous sense of helplessness.

They crossed the street in the darkness, the sun still hours behind the horizon. Police told her that the neighbors neither saw nor heard anything unusual, but Lynne wanted to ask her own questions. She wanted to be sure. She was surprised to see Pam's neighbors, one after another, several of whom Pam had befriended, if ever so slightly, come to the door with sleep still thick in their eyes and a frightened confusion straining their faces.

"Sorry to wake you," Lynne would begin, "but Pam is missing . . ."

The relief that they were not meeting news of their own loved one's death was matched only by their shock: "What? Pam's missing? Why didn't the police wake us?"

One of the first steps for police in missing person and abduction investigations is canvassing the neighborhood, talking to neighbors, fishing for any information that might help explain the disappearance—maybe she was seen arguing with a gardener that day. Or provide a lead to follow—maybe an unfamiliar van was parked in the neighborhood or a stranger was seen knocking on doors. Witnesses often don't know they might have pertinent information until they are asked. And if they aren't asked, the information is lost and usually forgotten.

Standing there as the sun began to peek above the horizon, as horrid images of what might be happening to her daughter flashed before her mind's eye, Lynne began to realize police investigations are not like what she had seen on television. She did not spend much time wondering what else the police were not doing. She and her family just got busy.

By sunrise, Pam's home was gearing up as the War Room, run not by the police but by Pam's friends and family. Lynne made the difficult calls to Pam's siblings, Eddie Jr., Ellen, and Nancy, who sped with their spouses from their homes in the New Orleans area.

Jackie, still hoping to find that one witness, a blessed set of eyes that saw something essential, stood at the subdivision entrance, stopping every car going in and out, asking for any information they might have. A flier with Pam's photo, the joyful smile on her face juxtaposed harshly against the thick black word: MISSING, was printed and passed out and posted by the hundreds, their desperate message traveling as far west as Texas and east to the Mississippi coast.

Several phones were going at once as the army of Pam's hopeful saviors called all of Pam's friends and acquaintances and business associates and customers, anyone who worked for her or with her, gardeners and carpenters and deliverymen, asking for any information, anything that might help the investigation.

They fed police every shred of information they thought might provide a lead. They called Pam's credit card companies and her bank, looking for something suspicious, any charges after July 12. They pieced together her whereabouts for the last days of the week. They called pharmacies throughout the Baton Rouge region, hoping Pam, who needed thyroid medicine every day, had called in a prescription. During their own search of Pam's yard just after the sun came up, they discovered a set of footprints in the wet grass leading from the vacant house next door to the line of woods in the back. They called for the detectives, and Sergeant Hodges arrived about seven thirty a.m. to investigate. But after examining the woods, he told the family he saw no disturbances in the woods and that several unbroken spiderwebs suggested no one had walked back there recently. What he did find, however, in a renewed examination of the house, was another print on the outside of Pam's bathroom window, the one that looked in on her tub.

Throughout the day, as more and more people began to hear of Pam's disappearance, the offers of help poured in. They compiled lists of people for the detectives to call and investigate. They provided information on a few suspicious people in Pam's life, including one man who frequently visited Pam's shop just to flirt and another, a man with a criminal record, who she had encountered on decorating jobs. Police promised to check everything out, although the family rarely heard anything back about the results of their suggestions.

After repeated unmet requests for the sheriff's office to conduct an aerial search, one of Byron's friends conducted a search in his own helicopter on Saturday. He found nothing, adding to the increasing sense of dread. The day was passing slowly, but also too fast, without any promising leads. No news was not good news.

Frustrated, Pam's family thought maybe the FBI could help, but their requests through the sheriff's office were rebuffed. Pam's brother-in-law, Ed White, contacted a relative in the U.S. Marshals Service and made inquiries on his own about getting the FBI involved.

By the end of the day, the best hope for Pam seemed to be prayer.

Her church, Parkview Baptist in Baton Rouge, hosted a candlelight vigil. More than sixty people attended. A photographer from the Baton Rouge paper, the *Advocate*, showed up, snapping a few pictures. On Sunday, a photo of Pam's sister-in-law and niece ran on the front of the metro section, but there was no story; just a detailed caption, 127 words, about the vigil and the barest of details about Pam's disappearance. The police department had placed so little emphasis on the case that the paper barely noticed it as a story. The East Baton Rouge Parish Sheriff's Office continued to call Pam a "missing person." They did not tell reporters about the blood on the rug, the overturned footstool, and the other signs of a struggle. What the police did not say, however, came from Lynne's lips: "We're sure she's been abducted," she told the *Advocate*. But few people were listening.

On Sunday, with still no signs of Pam, the East Baton Rouge Parish Sheriff's Office finally got the help of U.S. Coast Guard's airmen, who flew over Pam's neighborhood and surrounding areas with an infrared heat indicator. But again, the search turned up nothing. At the urging of family members, police towed Pam's van in to comb it for evidence. More people were called, more interviews conducted, and more dead ends were met.

Hope was running thin among the people still gathered in Pam's home. The wait was torture, a constant battle against imagining horrific images of Pam's suffering. Sleep was impossible without the aid of body-numbing pills. Nancy and

Ellen clung to each other and tried to convince themselves Pam was going to survive, she was going to come home. They talked about her return, how she would be so traumatized that she would need a good psychologist, but she would be OK, she would be alive.

Sunday came and went with scant attention from the media. On Monday, another small article, 202 words on page five of the metro section, provided little more information about Pam's disappearance. This was not big news yet. Pam was simply a missing woman. No word about an abduction, no details about the signs of foul play in her bedroom. Her picture wasn't getting broadcast on every station at the top of the hour, urging people to call a tip line if they had seen anything.

Lynne could not understand why police would not tell the reporters and the public that Pam was abducted, that she disappeared from her home after an obvious struggle. Lynne wanted the world to know. She thought the world might help.

But the detectives told the family to avoid the media. The police suggested in stern tones that reporters would twist the facts and could damage the investigation. Lynne heeded the warnings at first, but by Monday afternoon, she was losing patience. She was chomping at her muzzle.

The family asked a young officer now stationed at the house what he would do.

"Frankly," he told them, "if it was my wife, I would talk to every reporter who would listen. I would get her picture on every news show and in every newspaper as often as possible."

Emboldened by the young man's plainspoken honesty, the family changed course. They welcomed reporters into their lives. They began sharing their memories of Pam. They spoke of her spunk and fighting spirit. They tried to humanize her, make people pay attention, look at her picture, think about whether they saw her.

Perhaps it was Pam's family's efforts to gain exposure for the case, or maybe it was just the full news staffs were back on the job after a weekend of skeleton crews, but finally on Monday, the story picked up steam. Police, however, remained tight-lipped. The sheriff's spokesman, Lieutenant Darrell O'Neal, continued to call it a missing person case. During questioning by reporters, he said every available officer was working on the case. He confirmed Pam's disappearance was suspicious, but he stayed away from the terms *abducted*, and *kidnapped*.

Even behind closed doors with the family, the police refused to use the word *abduction*.

Whether the police said it or not, the speculation was already beginning. Until she saw it in print, Lynne did not realize what was really on the minds of every reporter in Baton Rouge, what Danette had already asked police: Was Pam's disappearance related to the two Baton Rouge murders?

Lynne was unaware of the other murders. She was so surprised by the suggestion that Pam was a victim of the same man she quickly dismissed it. No one in the family wanted to even consider it, partly because they still hoped to get Pam back alive, but also because the police had never mentioned it to them. When Lynne asked, detectives declined to speculate, saying they had no evidence of a link, stressing the differences in the cases. The man who killed the two Baton Rouge women left the bodies in their homes. Pam was missing from her home. No one could even say she was dead.

Still without other viable suspects on Monday, the police showed more interest in Byron than the man who committed the two Baton Rouge murders. Detectives asked him to meet them at the police station Monday for more questioning. When he arrived—his entrance caught by all the local news cameras—the detectives ushered him into an interrogation room. They began nicely enough, repeating some of their earlier questions from days before. "Tell us again how you and Pam met. How long were you married?" But soon the tone changed. The detectives insinuated they had heard things . . . That his marriage wasn't as great as everyone said . . . They wanted him to take a lie detector test.

Byron was enraged. He never imagined the police were "stupid enough," he said, to suspect him. But here they were, trying to intimidate him, suggest his marriage to Pam wasn't as happy as everyone said, implying he was somehow involved in eliminating his wife.

"You're barking up the wrong tree," he roared at them.

"Get this crap over with. Do whatever you need to do to eliminate me. Give me the lie detector test and get on with it. Quit wasting your resources on me. And go find the guy who took my wife."

On Tuesday morning, just before nine a.m., after a heavy rain the day before, a survey crew for the state Department of Transportation was testing for soil erosion underneath a raised section of Interstate 10 that crossed over the Atchafalaya Swamp, the largest stretch of undeveloped bayou in the nation that sits just west of Baton Rouge. As they walked along the banks of a Mississippi tributary known as the Whiskey Bay Pilot Channel, one of the workers spotted what he at first thought was a fish washed up on land about twenty-five feet from the water.

Brent Brevelle wasn't sure what he was looking at as he stepped off the dirt road used mostly by state workers, fishermen, and lovers looking for a secluded spot, and walked a few feet into the swampy woods. A pair of feet came into focus first, pointing straight up. He wasn't sure what he saw was real for a moment, but when he got within four feet, he was sure it was the nude body of a woman.

She was posed, placed in a little ravine lying perfectly straight with one arm behind her head and the other at her side, her feet together. Her skin was blinding white, her breasts bruised, and her face brown and discolored. Leaves had blown over the top of her head, which had no hair. Brevelle did not look long. The body had been there for at least three days and was partially decomposed, but he could still see she was murdered. A large mess of maggots were crawling in a deep slit across her throat.

The East Baton Rouge Parish Sheriff's Office sent Major Bud Connor to the Kinamore home with the news. Connor is chief of detectives with the department, a hardened, old-school cop who makes catching the bad guys personal. He sat on Pam's sofa in her living room, in the midst of her family photos, shots of her on a cruise with her family, hugging her son, and marrying Byron, and slowly, gruffly, he described what they had found. The woman was about five and a half feet tall, white, and was wearing a wedding ring and a medical bracelet. She had on no clothes, no other identifying markers except her toes—all but two were painted red. It appeared as if she was interrupted while cleaning off the polish.

He asked about the date on the inside of the ring. Pam and Byron's wedding day. That was enough. Investigators would have to confirm her identity with dental records, but her family already knew the truth. Pam was dead. Someone would have to tell Jacob his mother was never coming home.

From the autopsy, the coroner could tell she had been raped. Her throat was cut more than once, even though the first cut had been deep enough to kill her. No blood was found near her body. Although a rain had washed out the area the day before, detectives believed she was murdered elsewhere, then dumped.

At the swamp, state crime lab technicians collected a few beer cans and food wrappers and a phone cord found near Pam's body for testing, but no one was sure if the bagged items were clues or simply trash left in the brush long before she was killed.

The best piece of evidence came from Pam's body, left behind by the killer. She was outside for several days, but rape swabs picked up traces of semen deep within her vagina. The sample was sent to the state crime lab for DNA testing.

Speculation about the murder, however, would not wait for lab test results. Two days after Pam was found, the *Advocate* published a story that sent shock waves through the Baton Rouge community. Since 1990, nearly thirty murders of local women had gone unsolved. Many of the dead were black prostitutes, women caught up in drugs, running from the law, or putting themselves in dangerous positions with strangers. They were what police call easy-target victims: people without many friends or family to notice their absence.

But not all of the victims fit that profile. A number of the unsolved murders involved women who lived safe, stable, low-risk lives. Like the two most recent Baton Rouge murders, they were beautiful, energetic, independent women. And most were white. As the paper reported, some were abducted jogging in safe areas near the LSU campus. Others were killed in their homes in crime-free neighborhoods. Suddenly, the people of Baton Rouge were terrified. They feared a killer was preying on the best and the brightest, the very women who seemed the least likely to be victims. No one in the city felt safe anymore.

On July 29, 2002, the East Baton Rouge Parish Sheriff's Office faxed out a three-sentence statement, but its brevity did nothing to subdue the media firestorm the news would ignite.

Based on DNA evidence, the sheriff's office press release stated that Pam's killer was the same man linked to the two Baton Rouge murders.

The police had no other comments. They refused to discuss the case with reporters.

Lynne, however, always one to call things as she sees them, said what everyone in Baton Rouge feared.

"We have a serial killer in Baton Rouge," she told the nation during an interview on a network morning show a few days later. And she promised to devote every moment of her time, every ounce of energy, every thought in her head to hunting him down.

"I'm not going away," she told him through the lens of every TV camera she could attract. "When you killed Pam, you picked on the wrong family."

# CHAPTER 3

# The Capital City

Baton Rouge is Louisiana's capital city, home for half the year to the state's slickest politicians. The wiliest of them all, the late Governor Huey P. Long, was assassinated in the downtown capitol building; the bullet holes are still visible in the marble walls. His legacy of graft and corruption still lingers in its hallways, but the reigning superstar of this midsized Southern city is not politics.

Louisiana State University sits at the heart of town and occupies a central role in the life of the city. Nearly a quarter of the metro area's half million inhabitants call themselves students, former students, or employees of the state's largest and most beloved school.

The lush 2,000-acre campus of Italianate buildings, man-made lakes, and shady canopies of live oaks is a favorite spot for all the city's residents, who make use of the grounds for picnics, exercise, or just lounging in the green fields of grass. In the fall, the attention turns to touchdowns and fighting

Tiger songs because in Baton Rouge, football season is like a three-month religious festival.

The prayer robes flow with the school's colors of purple and gold and the house of worship is LSU's Tiger Stadium. Otherwise known as Death Valley, the stadium fills to capacity for most games, and the fans are notoriously committed to their home team.

The cheering and stomping of feet in the bleachers was so passionate one memorable fall evening, the university's geology department registered the earth shaking for twenty minutes. Nothing else seems to matter in Baton Rouge when it's game time.

Despite its size, Baton Rouge still acts like a small town. Glossy brochures and fawning Web sites about the city describe it as a friendly, fun place to live. At times, when the student population swells by tens of thousands, certain neighborhoods almost feel like a summer camp, where life is easy and fun, and no worries can ruin the day.

Perhaps it's the influence of young and naive students who don't know any better, but even in the central parts of the city, doors are left unlocked, and strangers still lend strangers a hand. The general attitude among the city's people—at least before the summer of 2002—is a sense that crime happens elsewhere, to other people, in bigger, meaner cities. And the politicians and business leaders hope to keep it that way.

When a forty-one-year-old woman was murdered at the start of the 2001 football season just down the street from the LSU lakes, Baton Rouge's daily paper, the *Advocate*, ran a 289-word story on the second page of the B section under the headline, "Death of Woman Found in Home Probed."

The word *murder* was not used in the story, and police were tight-lipped, if not evasive, about the cause of death.

Even a nearby neighbor seemed unperturbed by Gina Green's death, indicating her sense of safety remained unshaken—at least not yet.

"There's little petty crimes, like somebody stealing your garden utensils," she told the *Advocate*. "Other than that, not anything out of the ordinary. It's pretty quiet."

# CHAPTER 4

# GiGi Is Gone

On September 22, 2001, Gina Wilson Green spent the afternoon alone, riding her bike around the LSU lakes just a few blocks from her Baton Rouge home. The sun peeked in and out from behind the clouds as she pedaled along the paved pathways, past joggers and speed walkers and college students tethered to their dogs. She was trying to enjoy the day, not think about the September 11 attacks. She was a nurse; her twenty-five-year career was spent caring for others. She had recently spent time in New York City on business, making several friends in Manhattan. She was worried about them now and considered returning to the city to help, to offer her skills, to do something, but she knew she had responsibilities in Baton Rouge. She was the manager of a home heath care company. Her patients and employees needed her. So she stayed, focusing on what was good in her life, like enjoying the beauty of the LSU lakes.

Gina loved living so close to the university. At forty-four, she worked hard to keep her five-foot-five figure trim, and she felt safe exercising amid the clean, manicured grounds and friendly crowds on campus. No doubt, Gina turned a few heads that warm fall Saturday, but she was used to it by then. She rarely noticed how many men stared at her, their eyes lured by her looks. Maybe she didn't realize the power of her beauty. But everyone else noticed. Her face was a perfect heart shape of baby doll white skin framed by a full, wavy mane of espresso-brown hair and lit up by a big, blistering, bright smile. Her best feature, however, were her eyes, so blue they matched the deepest blue sea. When she smiled, they sparkled, too, like the sun on the ocean waves, reflecting an intense and bubbly passion Gina possessed in depth.

"Fabulous!" was the word Gina most often exclaimed. And it described best her own lust for life.

On that Saturday, Gina could have called untold numbers of suitors for a date, but late that afternoon, she picked up the phone and dialed the Baton Rouge number for her sister Amy. Gina was recently divorced and was longing for a dose of family time.

"What're y'all doing?" Gina asked.

"Nothing—" Amy, the youngest of three girls, was married with one daughter and another on the way.

"I'm going to come over . . ." Gina announced. She wanted to see Julia, Amy's two-year-old daughter.

Gina was the kind of aunt who could not get enough of her niece. Julia was like the daughter Gina could never have, and Julia seemed equally enamored with her GiGi, the flamboyant, gorgeous aunt who breezed in with armfuls of presents and unlimited hugs that lingered with the sweet smell of her perfume. Sometimes, Amy got the suspicion she was just the vessel used to bring Julia into the world for Gina. Watching the two of them together, Amy says, "taught me so much about motherhood and compassion."

Gina appreciated the little things in life, noticed the nuances that made a moment special. Her face glowed with a bright, joyful serenity when she simply held Julia and watched her drink from a bottle.

"God, I just love the noise she makes," she said.

Before divorcing, Gina wanted nothing more than a child of her own. She and her husband tried for years without success. The doctors blamed all the X-rays Gina had of her abdomen as a sick child.

Gina was born with defective kidneys that nearly left her dead before she was three. Surgery saved her life, but the procedure left her with only one half of one kidney. Not hopeful, the doctors said she would live in a constant battle for her health.

For the next ten years growing up in small-town Mississippi, Gina was in and out of the hospital, getting poked and prodded, needled, and X-rayed, but by high school, she was showing fewer and fewer signs of illness. She excelled in her classes, danced, played the flute, and twirled a flag in the marching band.

"The doctors were amazed at how she was doing," her mother, Margaret Wilson, recalled.

After high school, instead of avoiding hospitals and reminders of her own illness, Gina was determined to become a nurse. She graduated at the top of her nursing school class and easily landed a good job at a large hospital in Baton Rouge, where she became the go-to nurse for difficult patients and stubborn veins.

"She was exceptional with a needle," Margaret said. "If Gina couldn't hit it, it couldn't be done."

Gina knew instinctually how to calm the frightened and frustrated, sometimes with just a soothing touch or tender word. For others, she was the comic relief, quick with a joke or a goofy look that brought a little joy and laughter into somber hospital rooms.

But Gina's ambitions stretched beyond nursing. After several years working at the hospital, she was offered a job with a private home health care company, HCS Infusion Network, where she quickly climbed to a top position in management.

"It was a phenomenal rise," her ex-husband, Mark Green recalled.

Soon she was running the company's Baton Rouge and

Metairie, Louisiana, offices, and was in training to help open new branches throughout the United States, which is why she was in New York City that year.

By the time she turned forty, Gina had accomplished nearly everything she attempted—except motherhood. The one thing she wanted most eluded her, so she lavished her attentions on her niece Julia.

That Saturday night, after speaking with Amy on the phone, Gina took a quick shower and without putting on a lick of makeup, sped over to Amy's in her blue BMW convertible. After dinner, Gina and Julia dug into Julia's closet, pulled out all her prettiest outfits, and giggled through an evening of dress-up. When bedtime approached, Gina bathed Julia and settled into a rocking chair, where she sang and rocked the little girl to sleep.

Once Julia was tucked into bed, Gina and Amy started watching a movie, but Amy, five months pregnant at the time, fell asleep halfway through. Gina woke her up just after eleven p.m. to say good-bye.

"I walked her out," Amy said. "And watched her drive away."

Amy did not talk to Gina on Sunday, so she did not know Gina's burglar alarm was tripped at 3:42 a.m. that morning. Gina was at home sleeping. Her next-door neighbor had thrown a raucous party that night, but most everyone was gone by the time the alarm sounded, startling Gina from sleep. She was frightened. She lived alone with her black lab, Sweet Pea, who was too sweet to attack a stranger. Her phone rang almost immediately, and Gina sounded shaken when she answered. The security company's monitoring system wanted to know if she was OK. The operator told Gina the alarm was tripped by the dining room window, indicating a glass breakage. Gina did not hear anything in the house, but she stayed on the line as she walked from room to room.

In the dark morning hours, however, Gina did not find anything wrong with the window, nor did she see anyone outside her home. Gina knew alarms on windows sometimes trip simply from a loose pane or a strong wind. If she suspected someone was trying to break in, or had been peering through the window, she did not tell the operator.

She reported everything was OK, and the security company declared the event as a false alarm. The police were not notified, and Gina rearmed her system with the keypad. No other activity was recorded on her alarm system until 9:13 later that morning, probably when she first opened her door for the day.

None of Gina's friends or family saw or spoke with her on Sunday, which was not unusual. She usually used the weekend to catch up on laundry and housework. But on Monday, when Gina failed to show at work with no notice or phone call, her coworkers were immediately unnerved. She was usually the first one in the office before nine a.m. If she was running even fifteen minutes late, she would call them.

So when no one had heard from her by 9:30 a.m., Greg LeBlanc, one of Gina's staff nurses and a close confidant, began to worry. He called her home and her cell phone, reaching only her voice mail. He called the Infusion office in Metairie, a suburb of New Orleans, hoping she had gone there and simply forgotten to tell her Baton Rouge staff. The Metairie office had not seen or heard from Gina either.

For the next hour or so, Greg was swamped with work, but with every free moment, he called Gina again, leaving urgent, *"Please call me"* messages. As each hour passed with no word from Gina, Greg's coworkers urged him to go check on her at her home.

Greg finally got a break from his patients about half past noon and drove to Gina's home at 2151 Stanford Avenue. When he pulled into her driveway about one p.m., he saw her blue BMW parked in the carport at the back of the house. But he got no answer to his knocks on the front door. He pushed open the mail slot and called inside.

"Gina! It's Greg!"

Peering through the slot, he could see into the living room. The TV was on, but nothing appeared out of place. He guessed Gina might be in the bathroom. He tried to turn the knob, but the door was locked, deadbolted from the inside.

"Gina! Are you here?" he yelled through the mail slot again.

Greg walked down the driveway and around to the back of the house, which is surrounded on three sides by a tall wooden fence and the carport. On the back porch, Gina's black lab, Sweet Pea, was lying by the door. Greg knocked hard now, shouting Gina's name. He could see through the back door's glass panel into the kitchen area and all the way through to the front foyer and door. He saw Gina's jumbled set of keys hanging from the deadbolt inside. He turned the back door's knob and was surprised when the door opened.

"Gina!" He called out loudly, afraid he might startle her coming out of the shower. He walked straight through the kitchen and into the living room. A Diet Coke was on the coffee table. A towel was hanging over the back of a chair near the kitchen.

"Gina!"

Off the living room, a short hallway leads straight into the bathroom, where Gina's makeup, hair spray, hair brushes, and hair dryer were out, as if she was getting ready to go out. On either side of the hallway are bedrooms. The one to the right Gina used for storage, and it was piled high with boxes, furniture, and clothes. To the left was her bedroom. From where Greg stood in the hallway, he could see her bed. Several blankets and sheets were thrown on top of the mattress. Underneath, with a quilt pulled up to her neck, was Gina.

"Gina . . ."

As he walked closer to the bed, he could see her face. He thought she was asleep.

"Gina?"

She did not move.

"Gina . . ."

He walked up to her side. He could see she was nude. The right side of her body was exposed, and her right arm was hanging out from under the covers, draped off the side of the bed. Greg immediately noticed her hand was dark purple. His stomach turned. As a nurse, he recognized lividity when he saw it. Her blood had been pooling under the skin at the lowest points on her body for hours.

Stunned, horrified, heartbroken—Gina was a best friend—Greg retreated quickly out of her bedroom, resisting the urge to vomit. He called 911 on his cell phone.

"I believe my friend is dead," he told the operator. Unable to remember Gina's address, he walked out the front door to read the numbers on the side of the house. Then he realized he didn't know her street name. He shuffled through her mail to find it.

While he waited for the police to arrive, he returned to Gina's room. He needed an explanation. Gina was recently divorced. She wore a happy face. She seemed to enjoy her new freedom, but maybe . . . Greg looked for a bottle of pills or a note, thinking suicide, but found nothing. He steeled himself to look closer at her body. And there, he saw the answer. Around her throat was a necklace of bruises, several distinct purple finger impressions made while squeezing shut Gina's windpipe.

Baton Rouge Police Detective John Colter arrived at Gina's home about one thirty p.m. Right away, he noticed the killer had left no signs of a forced entry—no jimmied locks, no broken windows, no pried-open doors or splintered doorframes.

Either Gina had let him in—maybe she knew him—or he let himself in through an open door or window.

Inside the house, Gina's home looked like she was interrupted in the middle of doing her laundry. The ironing board was propped up in the kitchen, and a stack of clean clothes were neatly folded on the table. Nearby, an iron sat on the counter, unplugged.

The kitchen was freshly cleaned, spotless and uncluttered—except for a Miller Lite long neck beer bottle turned over in the sink and a bloodied striped blue shirt tossed over a chair.

Amy later identified the shirt as the same one Gina wore when she visited Saturday night.

As Colter walked through the house, he saw more pieces of

Gina's clothing in the living room. A black skirt was on the floor. A pair of stockings and silver chain-link belt were by the sofa. And a black thong was in the center of the room. He could not tell then, but lab tests later confirmed the panties were stained with feces—a likely result of strangulation, which causes the involuntary release of the bowels.

If the killer had come through the front door, his attack likely began in the living room, where he overpowered Gina, began strangling her and pulling off her clothes.

Stepping into the hallway off the living room, the evidence continued to tell an increasingly frightening story of Gina's struggle with the man. One heeled shoe was overturned on the floor. Nearby, a bracelet with a purple stone and Gina's hooped earrings were lying on the floor not far from a large clump of her long brown hair. Colter noticed dark stains on the carpet, which also tested positive for feces.

The killer probably had her nude and down on the floor at this spot. They struggled here, him pulling Gina's hair and ripping her earring from her lobe as he began raping her.

A few steps away, Gina's bedroom looked undisturbed other than the clutter of her possessions. A cowboy hat on an old fireplace mantel, clothes on the bed and dresser, knick-knacks and paperwork strewn about on every surface. On the floor, by the right side of the bed, a remote control and the handset of a cordless phone were found under the nightstand. The wooden four-poster bed, which was newly broken, was piled up with pillows and blankets, including a white quilted comforter that covered Gina's nude body.


Later that evening, Gina was taken to the Mobile Morgue, a glorified mobile home, which served as the temporary digs for the East Baton Rouge Parish Coroner's Office. The coroner's staff pathologist, Dr. Michael Cramer, performed the autopsy that evening.

From the external examination, Cramer could see the signs of strangulation: the broken blood vessels in the whites of her eyes and the necklace of bruising and scrapes around her throat. But under the skin, deep within the tissues of her neck, was severe hemorrhaging, the kind of damage that can only be caused by intense pressure, more than needed to suffocate her. More than likely, the killer squeezed tighter around Gina's throat as she struggled to escape. Bruises on the side of her left hand and right knuckles further suggest Gina was fighting violently against her attacker.

But he was stronger than she. He brutally raped her before she was dead. She was bruised all along the inner parts of her upper thighs and suffered severe injuries to her vaginal and anal areas that left her bleeding and deeply battered. She was not breathing by the time he was finished, at which time he cleaned her up and positioned her in bed as if she were sleeping.

The killer did not take anything of real value when he left. Only Gina's purse, which included her wallet, checkbook, and Nokia cell phone.

Ruling out robbery, investigators surmised Gina knew the man who attacked her. They suspected a possible date rape that turned deadly. Since her divorce in 2000, Gina had been dating a variety of men, many of them several years her junior. She was enjoying her life as a single, playful, independent, and sexy woman. She got her belly button pierced and bleached her hair blond. She was having fun after many years in an unhappy marriage. But police suspected that Gina might have let the wrong man into her home that weekend.

Detective Colter's theory offended and angered Gina's family. They knew Gina was sowing some wild oats, enjoying the attention from men, but she was smart about who she dated and always played it safe. Even her ex-husband, Mark Green, defended her savvy.

"Gina had taken self-defense classes," Green said. "She was very cautious and untrusting of strangers. She would never invite anyone in the house without knowing them very well."

She installed security lights around her house and never failed to use her burglar alarm. On her key chain, she carried a can of pepper spray, and Green says Gina also kept cans in the windowsills and near the doors. He insisted Gina would never leave her door open.

"It blows my mind that anyone could get anything over on Gina," he said. "She was that wary and that smart."

After Gina was killed, her mother, Margaret Wilson, re-called their last lunch together just a few days before she died. They met at a restaurant in New Orleans, and Gina seemed a little distracted. She said she sensed someone was watching her, possibly following her.

Detectives hit the pavement, interviewing Gina's neigh-bors, hoping someone saw something. They did not have much luck. Gina's neighbors to the right side of her home threw a loud, late-night party on Saturday, but they had not seen or heard anything unusual. One partygoer saw a white man, about five ten, heavy build, wearing a white T-shirt and khaki pants, walking down Gina's driveway into her carport sometime after midnight. But no one else came forward with any helpful witness information.

Gina's friends and family offered few other leads. She was not having problems with a boyfriend or spurned lover. She had no enraged enemies. She was not into drugs, didn't drink heavily, or live a high-risk lifestyle. She did not associate with the criminal elements of Baton Rouge, and she avoided dan-gerous predicaments. She lived a relatively normal life, work-ing hard at her job, enjoying her free time with friends, and looking forward to a bright future.

While some detectives sought answers by mining Gina's life, others hoped her missing phone might lead to the killer. Colter called Cingular Wireless on Tuesday and learned sev-eral voice mail messages were in her phone's mailbox. Colter knew one of those messages might provide the name or a clue that could lead straight to the killer. But when he asked to lis-ten to the messages, Cingular informed him the calls were privileged conversations, and that he would need a special wire tapping court order to obtain them.

Worried that whoever had the phone might erase the mes-sages and potentially destroy key evidence, Colter obtained a standard court order, which Cingular accepted, to change Gina's pass code needed to access and erase her voice mail messages. By Wednesday, Colter had the wire tapping court order, and Cingular allowed him to hear Gina's messages. She had three messages from Saturday night, one from a male friend who left his phone numbers, and two from her friend,

Molly, the last of which was at 10:25 p.m., when Gina was still at her sister's house. The next set of messages began on Monday at 11:06 a.m., when Greg began calling, wondering about her whereabouts. There were no messages on Sunday. There were no clues. Again, nothing suspicious, no leads for police.

The disappointment, however, was short-lived. Cingular informed Colter that Gina's phone was still on and receiving calls. Not only that, but Cingular had located Gina's phone in a general area of northwest Baton Rouge because the calls to her phone were pinging off a phone tower near Chippewa Avenue and Interstate 10.

Every call made to every wireless phone transmits an electronic serial number and bounces off the nearest towers. Wireless phone companies often use the technology to track down cloned and stolen phones, but in this case, they hoped the science would lead them to a killer.

Several investigators and police officers spread throughout the area of Chippewa near Interstate 10, a mostly deserted industrial section of the city, and began searching. They called Gina's phone several times, putting their ears to trash Dumpsters and stooping down near the ground brush. Nothing.

Colter called Cingular again and spoke with William Reed, who specializes in pinpointing wireless phones to within a few feet.

"We can't find it," Colter told him. "We keep calling it—"

"For God's sake, stop right now," Reed told him. "Don't call it anymore. You'll run the battery down. If the battery dies, I'll never be able to find it."

That Thursday, Reed got in his truck, geared up with loads of highly sophisticated equipment, and began a hunt for Gina's phone. He started with the help of a technician at the Cingular office, who was monitoring the signal strength of Gina's phone as it hit the Chippewa tower. At the same time, the technician monitored the signal strength from Reed's phone as they spoke through it.

The idea was to direct Reed's movements until his signal strength matched the signal strength of Gina's phone.

"Go toward your left, turn right, no, back left a little . . ." the technician told Reed.

When Reed turned onto Choctaw Drive, a gritty thoroughfare through Baton Rouge's industrial ghetto, the technician told him the two signals' strengths were almost identical.

"That's the closest I can get you," the techie said.

Reed next made use of another, more finely tuned piece of equipment, called the Trigger Fish. From another location, a call was made to Gina's phone, and Reed's equipment tapped into the call. By tapping in, the Trigger Fish's handheld monitor—a compasslike direction finder—points an arrow toward the location of the phone and indicates how strong the signal is based on the nearness of the phone.

As Gina's phone was ringing, the Trigger Fish pointed him west on Choctaw. Reed drove west, keeping an eye on the Trigger Fish arrow. The signal strength increased as he rolled toward an old meat packing business, and as he passed the vacant building, Reed saw the arrow swinging to his right, pointing toward the building and as he passed, the arrow continued swinging around until it was pointing to the building that was now behind him.

He turned his truck around and drove back to the building. Now the arrow pointed to Reed's left, again at the old Ready Portions Meat building. He turned onto a narrow gravel drive that took him behind the deserted cinder block warehouse and into an overgrown field.

The area was a lover's nest, a desolate hidden spot where men take prostitutes or illicit couples can meet and never be seen.

Reed's Trigger Fish monitor showed Gina's phone signal getting stronger once he turned behind the building. He stopped his truck and got out. He knew he must be nearly on top of the phone. He walked into the field, but could not see anything under the waist-high brush. Not knowing the details of Gina's murder, he was unsure if police had even found her body. Standing in this empty wasteland, the thought that she might be lying out there under the weeds sent shivers down his spine.

He turned back toward his truck. He needed to call the Baton Rouge Police out to search. Just a few steps away from his truck, he noticed a credit card on the ground. He bent down to pick it up. On its face read Gina Wilson Green.

Within twenty minutes, the overgrown field behind Ready Portions was crawling with crime scene investigators. Scattered throughout the property, they found several of Gina's credit cards, her wallet, bills in her name, receipts, makeup, and other contents of her purse. Someone had dumped it all out and strewn it wide throughout the field. Her phone was found several feet away from her other possessions. As they searched and bagged evidence, police came across other items that clearly did not belong in a purse: a pair of jean shorts and a kitchen towel with bloodstains.

At the State Police Crime Lab, analyst Angela Ross received more than fifty items of possible evidence in Gina's case from her home and the field off Choctaw.

First on her priority were vaginal and anal swabs taken from the autopsy as part of a sexual assault kit. Ross hoped to get a DNA profile of the killer from sperm or seminal fluid found on Gina's body. The crime lab had just begun conducting its own DNA tests, and Ross was one of its first analysts certified to perform the work. Unfortunately, she was unable to detect seminal fluid or sperm on any of the samples collected for the rape kit. Like a ghost, the killer had left nothing behind to test.

Ross looked at the other pieces of evidence submitted. Gina's shirt was spotted with blood, mostly around the collar, the chest area, and the front of the right sleeve. Ross figured the blood was likely Gina's, and a DNA test confirmed it. But Ross was more curious about the small spot of blood on the back of the shirt's right sleeve, up near the elbow area.

"I put myself in the situation," Ross testified later. "If I was attacked, where would I bleed? If I was hit in the face, I'd bleed in front."

But if her arms were flailing, or she tried to elbow someone grabbing her from behind, maybe popping him in the mouth, she might get her attacker's blood on the back of her shirt.

"I didn't see how I could get my own blood on the back of my arm," Ross said. "I thought it was suspicious."

Ross cut out a small piece of the back right sleeve, put half in a storage freezer, as is protocol, and tested the remaining half.

This time, she was successful. The spot on the elbow was not Gina's blood as Ross suspected. The DNA profile belonged to a man, most likely the man who killed Gina.

# CHAPTER 5

# The Red Stick and
# Plantation Properties

Baton Rouge dates back to 1699, when French explorer Pierre Le Moyne Sieur d'Iberville led a scouting mission up the Mississippi. About eighty miles north of New Orleans, Iberville and his party noticed the flatlands rising into the first high bluffs along the river. They rowed their longboats ashore where a small stream flowed inland.

Setting out on foot, the men came upon a tall cypress pole smeared in blood and adorned with fish and animal heads. The red stick—translated *baton rouge* in French—was the marker between the hunting grounds of two Native American tribes, the Houma and the Bayagoulas, or Bayou People.

The explorers marked the area on their maps, identifying it as Baton Rouge, and the name stuck as the settlement grew. Several attempts were made in the next two hundred years to change the city's gruesome moniker, but none succeeded.

In 1849, Baton Rouge was selected as the state's capital, flourishing under the cotton trade that came through its Mis-

sissippi port. The hub of river activity also helped the city re-
cover after the Civil War, but the region's biggest boom came
with the petrochemical plants that moved in on its river borders in the 1940s and '50s.

The roads north and south out of Baton Rouge are lined today with one of the nation's highest concentrations of oil
refineries and chemical plants, including facilities for Exxon-
Mobil, Conoco, and Dow. The drive up to Baton Rouge's ironically named Scenic Highway is a pass through belching
mazes of giant chemical pipelines constructed high up in the
plastic-singed air. The high rate of illness here has earned the
desolate stretch of land the name Cancer Alley.

Although the majority of Baton Rouge industry relies on
the petrochemical companies, a resident of the city with
enough means and money need not experience the foul-
smelling by-products of its economy.

Middle- and upper-middle-class suburbs have expanded
exponentially in the last several years to the metro area's
southern and eastern realms. New shopping centers that house
supersized Barnes & Noble stores, Starbucks Coffee stores,
and multiplex cinemas allow the residents to stay close to
home for all their needs.

The less well-off take a longer drive home to the suburban
subdivisions developing a dozen miles to the city's northeast,
expanding the once-stagnant population of the formerly rural
city of Zachary.

Town legend says Zachary got its name from a farmer,
Dearl Zachary, who in 1883 saw the Illinois Central Railroad
cut right through his 160 acres and build a stop not far from
his front door. The rattle and roar of the new steam engines,
carrying the goods and ambitions of the post–Civil War South,
might have promised new prosperity to the region, but for
Dearl Zachary, the trains mostly brought death.

His cows and horses never learned to stay off the tracks,
and after a number of expensive casualties, he decided to sell
his farm off for $900. Dearl then goes missing from history,
but he left his name for the town, which grew up on his land
around that old depot.

Today, the heart of Zachary sits at the junction of two
country highways, Louisiana 64, which turns into Church

Street as it passes through residential areas, and Louisiana 19, a bumpy thoroughfare that carries commuters north into town along a dozen desolate miles from Baton Rouge, past crumbling 1970s-era strip malls, brushy undeveloped fields, and the occasional precariously leaning mobile home, where the owners are content to sit on the porch and watch the world whiz by.

Zachary's population just topped 11,000 in recent years, but the small-town community maintains a distinct identity from its sprawling urban neighbor. The town is just six miles across and is surrounded by a barrier ring of vast open land, beyond which to the west are the industrial pipeways of the refineries.

To escape the smell and buzz of industrial life entirely, one need only travel a little farther north of Zachary on Scenic Highway, just beyond the reaches of Cancer Alley.

Tourists looking for the picture postcard of a small Southern town, a quaint and friendly little village with a storied history and antebellum roots, where the Spanish moss still drips off the oak trees in the lush yards of Victorian mansions and winding back roads lead to lily-white plantation homes, need only stop in Saint Francisville, Louisiana, located just thirty miles north of Baton Rouge.

In the mid-1700s, Spanish Capuchin monks brought the first European settlement here—although not for the living— to the highland bluffs overlooking a sweeping bend in the Mississippi River. The monks had established a mission church directly across the river on the low-lying western banks, but they soon learned the Mississippi's unpredictably rising waters made burials impermanent. When the monks looked across the river at the green, rolling hills ninety feet closer to the heavens, they began rowing their dead across the water.

The town of Saint Francisville grew up around the cemetery and took its name from the monks' patron, Saint Francis of Assisi. By 1790, the town was a busy trading post, attracting merchants, traders, and ambitious settlers from France, Spain, England, and the American colonies looking for fresh fertile land.

What they found was some of the richest soil and most beautiful landscapes in the South. Likened to a newfound paradise, the district surrounding Saint Francisville was named Feliciana, the Realm of Happiness, by its then-Spanish governors.

Within a few decades, the lucrative cotton crops saw Saint Francisville become the heart of one of the wealthiest districts in Louisiana, second only to New Orleans 160 miles south. Tens of thousands of its acres bloomed in white glory, enough to make dozens of millionaires. By the mid-1800s, Saint Francisville was the busiest stop on the Mississippi between Natchez and New Orleans, bringing goods and visitors from around the world to the backwoods of Louisiana. Soon, hotels and restaurants and stores of every variety crowded along the city's main drag. The town was a crown jewel in a time when cotton was king.

The new class of idle rich who populated Feliciana knew well why the *Encyclopedia Americana*, in 1831, called the region "the garden of Louisiana." The lush rolling landscape, unlike the flat and swampy lands common throughout the state, was blessed with varieties of plants and wildlife unseen elsewhere in Louisiana. Naturalist John James Audubon was so inspired by his visit to Saint Francisville that he stayed several years, painting many of his famous *Birds of America* pictures in the wild woods of the area.

"The aspect of the country was entirely new to me," Audubon wrote in his journal when he landed in town in June 1821. "The rich magnolias covered with fragrant blossoms, the holly, the beech, the tall yellow poplars, the hilly ground and even the red clay all excited my admiration."

During his stay, Audubon and his wife enjoyed the luxurious life enjoyed by their hosts, wealthy planters who erected ornate plantation homes among the hills, filling them with the best silk and lace, china and silver Europe had to offer. With each year, their lands grew more profitable and their mansions more elaborate.

But none of the burgeoning prosperity was possible without the sweat and labor of a rapidly expanding slave population. In the years before the first shots of the Civil War, Feliciana possessed more slaves per capita than any other region of Louisiana. A tax roll from 1853 lists 2,231 white residents and 10,298 slaves. If anyone was counting, they'd have seen the slaves outnumbered the whites by nearly five to one.

Everything in Feliciana changed, however, in 1863 with the Confederate defeat at the battle of Port Hudson ten miles to Saint Francisville's south. Although President Lincoln's Emancipation Proclamation came six months earlier, most slaves did not even attempt to obtain their freedom. But the sound of the marching drum and bugle of the victorious Union army beckoned them to the army camps at Port Hudson.

As John Evan, one of Saint Francisville's wealthiest planters and owner of Hazelwood Plantation, noted with a brief entry in his journal: "The Hazelwood Negroes all ran off to the Yankees on the ninth of June 1863."

The day essentially marked the end of the cotton era for Feliciana and Saint Francisville. During the next several decades, the area experienced a severe economic decline as the railroad system undermined the dominance of river traffic and Mississippi port cities.

Today, the wealthy planters are gone, many of their families having fled after the war, but their homes and legacies are offering a new kind of industry. In the last decade, town leaders have sought to revitalize Saint Francisville as a bed-and-breakfast tourist destination, a lovely, leafy spot to travel back in time to the antebellum South. Glossy brochures steer visitors to several local plantations, restored to their former glory, that offer tours of the home and grounds. In town, elected officials point to the old banks and hotels and mercantile shops newly renovated and now operating as antiques stores and art galleries and friendly gift boutiques.

The town's Web site, in a posted article by local writer Anne Butler, easily sells itself as a window into history:

> *Visitors are encouraged to take their time, stroll along the bricked sidewalks, peer past the picket fences through lace-curtained windows, savor the pocket gardens abloom with crepe myrtles in every imaginable color, marvel at the exuberant Victorian scrollwork and porch railings.*

Beyond the quaint historic town images, however, is a region with 8 percent unemployment and 25 percent of its people living in poverty. West Feliciana Parish, as the jurisdiction around Saint Francisville is now called, also remains mostly rural, with a population of less than 15,000 people.

For a century after the Civil War, the only job titles available to the thousands of freed slaves and their descendents who stayed among the hardwood forests and lush hills were sharecropper, manual laborer, and truck driver—or perhaps a laundress for the women.

The parish's largest employer is the Louisiana State Penitentiary at Angola, one of the nation's largest, most notoriously tough prisons. Situated on 18,000 acres of former plantation land—the first inmates arrived in the 1880s and were held in old slave quarters—the prison now houses more than 5,000 men, many of them serving life or sitting on death row.

More recently, the River Bend nuclear power station, a paper mill, and a sweet potato factory provided more steady-paying work. But good jobs remain scarce, especially for the lingering communities of poor, underemployed, undereducated blacks, many of whom have not forgotten the names of the plantations where their ancestors were born.

# CHAPTER 6

# A Child Is Born

On November 5, 1968, Florence Lee, a seventeen-year-old unmarried black girl from the backwoods of Louisiana, was rushed thirty miles from her ramshackle home outside Saint Francisville to the Earl K. Long charity hospital in Baton Rouge, where she gave birth to her second child, a son, who she named Derrick Todd Lee.

On the boy's birth certificate, Florence left the father's name blank. She knew Sammy Ruth, then twenty-nine, did not want to claim Derrick as his own. He already had a family—a wife and five children in Long Beach, California. He had left them the year before, and in June 1968, moved in with his young girlfriend, Florence Lee, at the home of her parents, Robert and Jane Mitchell Lee.

The living quarters were already crowded. Florence was one of thirteen children. She was born strong, thick-boned, and willful, with a spirit toughened further by early family responsibilities and an overworked mother's severe hand.

Jane Mitchell Lee did not have time to dote on her children. She had a hard life, and she did not expect it to improve. She grew up in the 1940s and '50s, before the civil rights movement hit rural Louisiana, and the landscape around Saint Francisville had not changed much since the Civil War.

Her own family's roots stretched back more than one hundred years in West Feliciana Parish. Her great grandmother, Charity Butler Hays, was born on Highland Plantation to two slaves, Hannah Hays and Jim Butler.

In a June 14, 1854, diary entry, Highland Plantation owner Bennett H. Barrow mentions three slaves in his accountings, placing monetary value on each one for inheritance procedures:

Jim Butler, 43, valued $1,000—one of the highest on Barrow's long list of slaves

Hannah, 33, valued at $700

Charity, 6, valued at $300

More than one hundred years later, their descendents were still working some of the same land.

The Lee family was near the bottom of the economic ladder. Florence's father, Robert Lee, labored at low-paying manual jobs—mostly farm work and truck driving—anything that did not require him to read or write. He signed his name with an X.

But that was enough to own land. In 1967, Jane Mitchell Lee heard about some property for sale just outside Saint Francisville. She spoke with her sisters-in-law, and the three women convinced their husbands—Robert and his brothers, Feltus and Sam Lee—to seize the opportunity and buy fifteen acres of land that once belonged to the nineteenth-century Hazelwood Plantation. The total cost was $7,500, which put Robert's monthly share of the mortgage at $25.

Although the property was ragged, weedy, mostly undeveloped land that was soon surrounded by trailers and tin can heaps and homes made of plywood, the Lees owned it, and that put them a class above many others in their poor community.

They were a proud family. Jane was a powerful matriarch, and Florence, learning from her mother, carried her head high.

In April 1970, still unmarried, she had another child with Sammy Ruth, a girl who she named Tharshia Demetra Lee. But Sammy made no plans to stick around to help raise her.

Instead, he gave Florence an ultimatum. He did not want to get married. He had not even filed for divorce. If Florence wanted him around, wanted him to help at all, she simply had to let him come and go as he pleased. Otherwise, he would stay gone for good.

Florence let him walk. She preferred to be the one in control. And finding a new man was not a problem for her. She was not gorgeous, but she was personable and made of spit and fire. She had a strong mind with her own ideas, and despite the oppressive poverty in her life, she knew how to kick up a good time.

Her oldest daughter, Tenieta Lynett Lee, was almost five when Florence came home one day in 1972 and announced she was marrying Coleman Barrow Jr.

Coleman was a lot like Florence's father: dark, pensive, and hardworking. He was also illiterate. Both men had grown up on the outskirts of Saint Francisville. Both came from a long line of people working the land. And both knew only hard times.

Barrow's father was a sharecropper on the same land his ancestors worked as slaves, Greenwood Plantation. The Barrow family took their name from the original owners of Greenwood, the prominent Barrow family.

The first Barrow to arrive in the hills around Saint Francisville was the wealthy widow Olivia Ruffin Barrow, who brought her family, slaves, and thirty wagon loads of possessions and gold from North Carolina in 1800.

They purchased thousands of acres of pristine land and named their new home Highland Plantation. Soon her pioneering family expanded its holdings and constructed bigger and more elaborate mansions, including Greenwood and Rosedown. By the early 1830s, the Barrow family and its descendents were some of the wealthiest landowners in the region.

Today, most of their descendents have moved on, but in their wake, an expanding web of Barrows descended from their slaves remain among the rolling back hills in an area aptly called Solitude, which surrounds the old Barrow plantations.

After Florence and Coleman married, the family moved to a trailer home in Bains, just north of Saint Francisville where Tenieta and Derrick learned quickly about their stepfather's disciplinary methods.

Coleman was a quiet man, but he was not an easy man. Florence let him know who was boss in the household. Tenieta remembers her mother as a domineering woman who believed men needed training to become good husbands. Tenieta also remembers her mother's belief in corporal punishment for her children, and how she did not interfere when Coleman inflicted it.

Tenieta recalled one instance when Coleman threatened her and Derrick with a fan belt ripped from the car engine. She can still hear Derrick crying.

Derrick was a hyperactive child, always fidgeting and moving and not necessarily paying attention to where he was going, which also made him accident prone. He once ran into a large metal wash pot used to cook cracklings and split open the bridge of his nose.

As he got older, his energy filled him with devilish mischief. He thought peeing on the walls was funny. He kicked the family dog just to see how the animal would react. Later, when the dog had puppies, Derrick picked one up by the neck and squeezed until the puppy yelped.

He was spanked for mistreating the animals, but his punishments never seemed to sink in. He was slow to develop. He wet his bed well into early adolescence, and no matter how much hot sauce Coleman poured on his fingers, Derrick continued to suck his thumb until high school.

His curiosity often led him into trouble. He was fascinated by the hogs that were kept in a pen a short walk from the family's home, but he was told repeatedly to stay away from them. He did not listen. Whenever he saw a chance, when his mother or older sister turned their heads, he ran out the back door and trotted over to the wire fence. One day he came scurrying back to the house screaming, his arm gushing blood. A hog had bitten his wrist.

Derrick needed constant attention and direction and bottomless patience, which Florence did not always have to give. She was short-tempered, and Derrick felt her anger in the frequent spankings, Tenieta remembers.

The job of watching after Derrick often fell to his older sister, who made sure he got breakfast in the morning, walked him into school every day, and held his hand until dropping him at his classroom inside Bains Elementary School.

But that did not mean he stayed put for the day. His first year, in kindergarten, he was labeled a teacher's handful.

"He couldn't be still," Tenieta recalled. "He couldn't sit at a desk. He would just disrupt or walk out of the classroom when the teacher wasn't looking. They just couldn't do anything with him."

Tenieta was called out of class a number of times to help find her brother. She was not surprised when she found him curled up on a hallway floor, sucking his thumb and refusing to go back to his room.

At other times, Derrick's teachers literally could not pry him away.

As a little boy, he liked to rub silky, smooth fabrics between his fingers. He often carried a worn piece of cloth with him. The softness and rhythmic rubbing calmed him. He was a tactile person, always touching and feeling things around him.

Women's stockings were a particular favorite. If he was sitting on the floor in class and his teacher was standing nearby, he was known to reach up and rub his hands along her legs. When he could, he climbed into her lap, stuck his thumb in his mouth, and eased to sleep rubbing her blouse. If the teacher was a white woman, he loved to play with her hair. One early year in elementary school, he became so attached to a teacher he began calling her Momma.

The teacher called Florence, who came up to the school to discuss it. When both women stood before Derrick and asked him who was his mother, he refused to speak. Later, he got a good lesson on who was his real mom from the sting in his behind, Tenieta recalled.

Derrick's teachers recognized early that he was not learning to read as fast as his classmates. But when they suggested he move into special education for children with learning disabilities, Florence disagreed.

She met with the principal, Jesse Perkins. She was adamant. She did not believe her child had a problem. Instead, she wondered if his teachers, many of whom were white, were not trying hard enough to work with Derrick.

During the next several years, Derrick habitually landed in the principal's office for disrupting class, not in a vicious or destructive way, but by talking out, refusing to listen, or bothering classmates.

"Of course, he was never wrong," said Jesse Perkins, who was principal at the time. "If he did something to somebody, there was always a reason, therefore it wasn't his fault. Rarely would he just accept responsibility for what he had done."

One afternoon, Perkins watched Derrick cut in line to get on his bus after school.

"Derrick!" Perkins called out to the boy, who turned around, wide-eyed, projecting innocence.

"Oh, Mr. Perkins," he said. "I was already here."

When Derrick was punished—with detention or restrictions on his freedoms in school—Perkins recalled, "He would try to convince you he didn't deserve it."

Perkins called Florence a number of times during Derrick's years at Bains. She always responded quickly, appearing at school with Coleman sitting tight-lipped at her side to discuss it. But she wasn't fast to believe the school's version of what happened. She liked to hear Derrick's version, too.

"Whenever she was in doubt about whether somebody had done something unjust to him, she spoke her mind," Perkins said. "She let people know how she felt—good or bad. She was very opinionated and confident she was right, even when she wasn't."

Around Florence, however, Derrick was different child.

"He shaped up," Perkins said.

The boy got quiet, subdued, and filled with yes ma'am and no ma'am. But he still worked his silver-tongued defense.

"He made himself heard," Perkins said.

Perkins could see Florence was a strict disciplinarian, but he never saw her do more than raise her voice at Derrick. Once they got home, however, Derrick was not spared punishment for undeniable bad behavior, like poor grades.

"He didn't understand that Ds and Fs were bad," Tenieta said. "He'd be happy with a report card filled with them. He'd take it home and show Mom, and she would whip him and tell him Ds and Fs were for Damn Fool."

Through their childhood, however, Tenieta remembers Coleman's punishments leaving the sharpest impression.

"He just got a thrill out of it," she says.

Coleman had little patience for Derrick. As Derrick grew, Coleman became increasingly frustrated with the boy's rambunctious behavior and inability to listen. Coleman regularly unleashed his anger on Derrick whenever he did not do as he was told.

"Derrick got the worst of it," Tenieta says. "Probably because he was a boy."

In the afternoon, in the few minutes before Coleman was due home, Tenieta often hurried to pick up Derrick's toys from the living room, knowing they would earn Derrick rough punishment. She tried to make sure he kept his room clean and went to bed when asked. But sometimes she could not protect him from their stepfather's volatile temper.

Coleman had little control over the rest of his life, particularly Florence. Coleman was *very* intensely suspicous of *her*. Tenieta remembers once when Derrick was not more than nine years old and Coleman asked the boy to keep an eye on Florence while he was away at work—basically spy on his mother, even if that required him to walk around the house and peek in at her through the bedroom window.

When Derrick's reports on his mother did not satisfy Coleman, Coleman might punish Derrick anyway because he did not believe the boy. When the punishments came, Derrick often ran, slipping away, as fast as he could, looking for a place to hide. One night, in a panic, Derrick threw himself into a metal bed frame while trying to scramble underneath. He came up bloodied and bruised from busting open his lip.

* * *

Outside his immediate family, Derrick grew up with countless uncles, aunts, and cousins, some of whom were near his age. They all lived in or near St. Francisville.

Even his relationship with Coleman had its bright spots. Coleman took Derrick on as his son, and Derrick always referred to him as Dad. And like a father, Coleman taught Derrick the skills of manhood: how to fix cars, how to drive a truck, and how to hunt.

Derrick loved the outdoors and took well to the sport of creeping through the woods in wait of a kill. When he was too little to fire a gun, he shook squirrels out of the trees for Coleman to shoot. As he got older, he learned to down and skin raccoons, rabbits, and deer.

They found the best hunting fields, driving deep into the undeveloped lands of East and West Feliciana parishes. Derrick would hunt those areas for years to come, never losing his taste for catching his prey. He liked to fish, too. And with so much water in Louisiana, he discovered many favorite out-of-the-way spots to drop his line and spend several uninterrupted hours alone.

As a young teenager, however, he was less adept at pursuing women. At West Feliciana High School, a school with an even mix of black and white, middle-class and poor, Derrick was a skinny, awkward kid who suffered intense embarrassment from his reputation as a special education student.

He never forgot his classmates' taunts of "Retard" and "Stupid." He did not participate in sports, although he spent one year playing the snare in the marching band, and he did not date—at least not until he met the girl who would become his wife.

Instead, he was developing an insatiable habit of peeping at women in their homes.

Everyone in the neighborhood knew about it. He began when he was still a boy, peering through the bedroom windows of his young female cousins. When he advanced to grown women, the complaints began to come in.

Tenieta remembers one neighbor, Darlene Swallow, came knocking at her grandfather, Robert Lee's, door. The woman said she caught Derrick watching her through the window.

"If you don't believe me," she told Robert Lee, "check his hands. He cut them on the window."

Derrick's hands were cut. He was literally caught red-handed. His grandfather scolded the boy and told him to stop peeping in women's windows.

"You could get shot," Robert Lee warned him. He thought of Derrick's peeping as a prank, more of the boy's mischief, something a child might do to satisfy his curiosity about the opposite sex. Like others in the family, he figured Derrick would grow out of it.

# CHAPTER 7

# A Bloody Fight

On Friday, May 31, 2002, just before noon, Charlotte Murray Pace ducked out early from her job at the LSU business school and hurried to her car. An old roommate was getting married the next day in Alexandria, a central Louisiana town about one hundred miles northwest of Baton Rouge, and Murray needed to leave town by midday to make the rehearsal dinner that night.

She planned to drive up in her new black BMW, her dream car that she recently leased after learning she had landed a $50,000-a-year job in Atlanta with the international accounting firm of Deloitte & Touche. The job, which would begin in late August, was payoff for years of hard work and determination. Just a week earlier, the honor roll student graduated from LSU's business school, where she became the youngest person—at twenty-two—to earn an master's degree in business administration from the program.

Her mother, Ann Pace, was so proud to watch Murray, as

everyone called the dark-haired spitfire from Jackson, Mississippi, accept her degree. At a celebratory dinner the night before, Ann could see Murray looked more beautiful than ever at the center of attention, her big blue eyes flashing with delight, a smile spread across her face as she basked in the glow of her success.

Ann could remember when Murray was born during the Jackson floods of 1979, the last child of three children for her and her then husband, Casey Pace, a lawyer.

"She seemed to be born very independent," Ann recalls. And from the start, Murray seemed to know what she wanted and didn't want from life. Some of her earliest sentences were, "I will not. You cannot make me."

Ann quickly learned she could not hold her daughter back. The little girl wanted to be on the swim team at five. Her first-year, she set the under-six record for the backstroke, a time that still stands today in Jackson. At six, she joined her first soccer team, the Mosquitoes, which solidified a lifelong love of the sport. She started elementary school early, and joined the gifted classes with her older brother John, then seven. Unlike John, however, who was a quiet, soft-spoken kid, Murray never showed a streak of shyness. She was outspoken and tough, even as a toddler.

When an overgrown bully on the special education bus—shared by the gifted and the remedial students—began taunting John, he stoically withstood the abuse. But the day the bully started in on Murray, he got a painful shock.

She was quiet until all the students were off the bus. Then she walked up behind the boy, tapped him on the arm, and as he turned around, she pulled back her fist and landed it square in his face, knocking him down the hill.

She wasn't sorry, either, when she was gathered with her parents in the principal's office. She was sure she was justified.

"He picked on me, and he picked on my brother," she said. To the little girl who was taught to stand up for what's right, how could she be wrong?

"She was always convinced that if she chose to do something, it must be OK," Ann says.

And usually, it was. Murray seemed to have the power to make the waters of life part for her. Life was working out as she planned it, with perfect precision. She graduated high school a year early as she wished, finished her undergraduate degree at twenty, and was on her way to a lucrative career by twenty-two. Murray could not have been happier with how things were working out.

After the business school graduation dinner, Ann and her daughter shared a long hug before parting. The evening had gone by so fast.

"I hardly got to talk to you, Murray," Ann said.

"I'll be here all summer, Mom," Murray smiled back in that reassuring way. "We'll have plenty of time to talk."

Just a few weeks earlier, Murray had planned to move home to Jackson for the summer before embarking on a new life in Atlanta, but at the last minute she and a roommate, Rebekah Yeager, decided to rent a town home in the Baton Rouge university area for a few months.

On May 31, the two young women, both smart, savvy, and soon to be working professionals, were still in the process of moving from their rental home, which they shared with two other students, on Stanford Avenue to the three-bedroom at 1211 Sharlo. Neither had slept at the new place yet, but they were scheduled to meet there at one p.m. that Friday for the drive up to Alexandria.

After leaving campus, Murray stopped at Benny's Car Wash on Perkins Road at Stanford Avenue. She loved her new car—the BMW was a gift to herself, a treat for all her hard work—and she liked to keep it sparkling, just like herself. Murray was hyperaware of her appearance, not in a self-conscious, vain way, but because she enjoyed looking good. She was a tomboy growing up, a rough-and-tumble athlete with big bones, bigger muscles, and a wide, square face. But when she reached high school, she transformed herself into a glamour queen after discovering a love of clothes and makeup.

When she went outside, her face was on and her clothes were pressed. Even for soccer practice she did her hair and makeup. At night, for parties and barhopping, she flashed herself up more. She liked her skirts short, her shirts tight, and her boots high, all of them preferably accented with animal prints. But she never looked gaudy or slutty or cheap. She wore it with moxie and style. No one could doubt this girl had class. Her looks lit up a dark bar, and her fiery charm enlivened a dull party.

She spent thirty minutes at Benny's Car Wash. She drove through the automatic wash, then spent a few minutes vacuuming before heading to the Sharlo town home less than ten minutes away.

The place Murray and Rebekah rented was much nicer, cleaner, and seemingly safer than the run-down rental property they shared on Stanford. The Sharlo neighborhood was popular with students and young families, located just two miles north of the LSU campus.

From Brightside Boulevard, a busy thoroughfare that cuts across the city, Murray turned down Alvin Dark Avenue, the main entrance road that winds back into the neighborhood's apartment and town home complexes. One block in, she turned left onto Sharlo and parked in her carport sometime after twelve thirty that afternoon.

Her unit was the first one on the street, at the beginning of a whole block of units that are connected by shared walls. From the carport, Murray walked through a tall gate that leads into her backyard, a grassy area surrounded by an eight-foot-high wood fence.

The back door opens onto the dinette area, which leads into a galley kitchen and then opens up into the living room. Rebekah was due home any minute. While she waited, Murray fixed herself a sandwich, took off her shoes, and sat down on the couch with a Diet Dr Pepper and her favorite magazine, *Cosmopolitan*, to eat in front of the TV.

Just before two p.m., Rebekah pulled her car in next to Murray's and hurried toward the house. She was running late. She had squeezed in a last-minute hair appointment, and now she was behind schedule an hour. If she was going to make the rehearsal dinner, she and Murray had to leave for Alexandria immediately.

She turned her key in the back door deadbolt, but when she tried the knob, the door was still locked. She turned the key in the deadbolt the other way. Still locked. That's when she realized the doorknob, not the deadbolt, was locked. That was strange. She and Murray usually locked only the deadbolt.

Rebekah thought little of it, though, as she unlocked the door-knob and hurried inside.

"Hi, Murray!" She called out as she rushed into the kitchen. She did not notice the bloody footprints on the linoleum floor as she passed into the living room. "I'm late!"

In the living room, the TV was on, a blue plate with the half-eaten sandwich was on the arm of the sofa, and a Diet Dr Pepper was on the table nearby, still cool. Rebekah did not see the blood splattered on the wall as she hurried toward her bedroom.

"You ready to go?"

Rebekah did not even notice the smears on the doorframe as she stepped into the room. What she did see was far worse, and the images were so horrific, so shocking and unbeliev-able, that they only flashed in her mind in pieces. She could not take it all in at once.

Murray was lying on the floor between her dresser and the bathroom door. She was covered in blood. Other than her shirt, which was pushed up above her breasts, she was nude. Now Rebekah noticed the blood on the walls, everywhere, splattered in places that she could not understand how it got there. She looked back at Murray and noticed small holes all over her chest.

In shock, Rebekah ran outside to her car for her wireless phone and called 911. As the phone rang, she screamed for help.

"Someone hurt my friend," she told the 911 operator when he answered.

He needed the address, which Rebekah did not yet know. She went back into the home and out the front door to look at the address numbers.

"1221 Sharlo. Hurry!"

The 911 operated asked if Murray was still alive.

Rebekah went back inside, back into her room with Murray.

"Touch her," the operator instructed Rebekah. "Is she cold?"

Rebekah knelt down by Murray's side and touched her arm. She was still warm.

"Can you give her CPR?" the operator asked.

Kneeling next to Murray, Rebekah reached to turn her best friend's head toward her. She recoiled in horror. Murray's throat was cut wide open. The slash wound was so deep the knife cut into the vertebrae of her spine.

Rebekah fled the home again, running outside into the bright, beautiful Friday afternoon just as a police car was passing. She flagged him down and followed him back inside, so hysterical that he could not understand her words.

As soon as he saw the blood in the living room, he drew his gun and ordered Rebekah outside, where she collapsed onto the front porch.

Minutes later, the patrol officer called in the homicide. Baton Rouge Police Detective Chris Johnson was next on the rotation list to get the case. By the time he arrived at 1211 Sharlo, crime scene tape was already unfurled around the home, and a crowd was gathering in the afternoon sun.

Johnson was familiar with the neighborhood. He knew it as a safe, low-crime area with well-maintained properties and a large population of students. Murray's row of town homes was one of the nicest complexes around, with carports, fenced-in backyards, and swings on the front porches.

The way the town homes were situated also cut down on traffic noise. The front doors opened up to a courtyard, not a road, requiring visitors to walk into the complex area using a sidewalk from Alvin Dark Avenue.

As Johnson approached Murray's front door, he noticed nothing looked disturbed on the porch, nor could he see any signs of forced entry. The blinds on the living room window were open, allowing him a clear view inside and, for anyone inside, a clear view outside of someone standing on the porch.

Johnson did not need to take too many steps inside to know he had a bad murder to solve: a good-looking, young LSU student slaughtered in her home. The media would be all over it. For good reason.

This was one of the worst murder scenes Johnson had ever seen. Blood was everywhere: on the carpet, the walls, the doors, the kitchen floor, and bathroom sink. The victim, Murray, was brutalized, almost mutilated. From one look at her body, Johnson could see the wild rage unleashed on her. Police call it *overkill*—when more than enough wounds are inflicted to cause death. That kind of violence comes with intense emotion and is usually done by someone who knew the victim, someone with motive to kill.

Johnson needed to inquire about Murray's ex-boyfriends or spurned suitors. He hoped Murray's family and friends could quickly offer up a good suspect; otherwise, the city would have a frighteningly dangerous murderer on the loose.

While Johnson went to work with interviews, the Louisiana State Police Crime Lab began collecting evidence from the crime scene. Piecing together a murder from what's left afterward is sometimes difficult, but in this case, the trail of blood told a horrifyingly clear picture.

The blood spatters on the wall began in the living room, near the couch where Murray was sitting eating her sandwich. The sandwich was only half-eaten; the rest was still sitting on the arm of the sofa. Clearly, she was attacked here. Crime scene investigators could not find the handset of her cordless phone, leading them to believe the killer hit her first with the phone.

The blow to her head probably was as shocking as it was painful. She would have been dazed, stunned, terrified at the sudden realization she was under attack. She must have known she was in a fight for her life. She ran toward the hallway, for the bedrooms, but he caught her, lashing again at her, this time splaying blood across the walls.

She struggled as he got her to the ground, slammed her head against the wall, leaving red brush marks from her hair now sopping from the blood oozing from wounds. He was trying to rape her, trying to pull off her clothes. She managed to get inside the bathroom, her bloody bare footprints revealing her path past the sink, which was also spotted with drops of her blood.

But if she had a moment's freedom from him in the bathroom, it was not to last. Her final moments were spent in Rebekah's bedroom, where the killer unleashed the worst of his rage on her. As her blood drained, so did Murray's strength from her body. He had her pinned to the bed. She probably knew she was going to die now. She was too weak to fight anymore. He pried off her gray Banana Republic pants, the legs turning inside out as he peeled them from her body. He continued to beat her, splattering blood on the walls and headboard. He smacked her with a clothing iron, breaking it into pieces. He grabbed a flathead screwdriver, and plunged it again and again and again into her face and eyes and chest and stomach. He dropped her to the floor with a final slash to her neck and watched the last seconds of her life slip away.

Crime lab analyst Julia Naylor, specialist in blood and other biological evidence collection and testing, focused on Murray's body, which might still be able to point a finger at her killer.

Murray was lying on her back in a large, sticky pool of blood with her left arm under the bed and her legs spread apart slightly. Her striped halter top was pulled up above her breasts, and she had nothing on below her waist. Her torso was covered in blood and small, round puncture holes. Her face was bruised and bloody, much of it coming from a large cut on the left side. Her hair was so soaked with her blood investigators were unsure of the color.

Naylor cautiously squatted down next to her.

Right away, she saw that the blood coating Murray's bare torso had a lighter colored streak in it, as if a drop of clear liquid had dripped onto her body and rolled down the side of her rib cage. Naylor smeared a cotton swab along the streak, hoping the fluid might be the killer's seminal fluid or sweat.

Using ALS, or alternative light source, a blue light that makes biological material—blood, saliva, semen, skin cells—glow in the dark, Naylor spotted several splotches on Murray's body. She collected thirteen swabs, including one from a spot deep inside Murray's upper left thigh area, near her buttocks—a likely place for seminal fluid.

In the kitchen, Naylor's colleagues lifted bloody shoe prints that went from the front of the house toward the back door, indicating the killer exited through the back and locked the door on his way out.

The only other obvious and significant piece of evidence—or lack thereof—was a bloody gold band found near Murray's body. Then there were the missing things: Murray's keys, the handset of her telephone, and a broken piece of the clothes iron used to smash in her skull.

Outside the house, detectives took out their notebooks and

began questioning neighbors. They quickly learned Murray was new to the neighborhood, so few people had even met her. They knew nothing about her life or her friends, and no one saw or heard anyone coming out of the house between twelve thirty and two—no one except Rebekah, whose blood-chilling screams still lingered in the air.

Even Murray's next-door neighbor, who shared a wall with Murray and was at home while she fought bravely for her life, heard nothing, although he remembered his dog scratching wildly at the wall at one point during the day.

Although they had not been home at the time of the attack, several of Murray's neighbors were anxious to tell detectives about a stranger they had seen hanging around the complex that morning and the day before, right near Murray's town home, almost as if he was watching it.

He looked suspicious, like he didn't belong in the neighborhood or had no purpose for being there. He wasn't walking to a bus stop. He wasn't doing yard work or delivering a package. He wasn't at a doorstep waiting for friends. He was just standing there, leaning against a tree, looking in the direction of Murray's row of town homes.

Separately, four neighbors told police about the man. In general terms, they described the same person. He was dressed in blue laborer's work pants and a long-sleeved green shirt. He was tall, maybe six feet. He was not white. His skin was light brown. They guessed perhaps he was Hispanic or a light-skinned black man. He wore a goatee and a mustache, a thin one, and he had a wide, flat nose.

One neighbor, Chris Villemarette, thought the man was acting so suspicious, he circled back around the block in his truck to get another look at him—but the man was gone. Even a police officer saw the man the night before the murder.

Working as a private security guard for the neighborhood while off-duty, a Baton Rouge police officer saw a man matching the same description hanging around the area. Just as the neighbors said, the man looked out of place, suspicious, and the officer stopped him, questioned him, and told him to get on his way.

Detective Ike Vavasseur, assisting Johnson, scribbled the

descriptions of this suspicious-looking man into his notebook. Several of the neighbors offered to help a sketch artist draw the man's face, and then they waited for police to call for their assistance. The call never came.

# CHAPTER 8

# A Mother's Nightmare

Nearly 200 miles away in Jackson, Mississippi, Ann Pace was working late on Friday, May 31. She managed a doctor's office at the University of Mississippi hospital, and there was always more work—thankless, underpaid work—to be done. Ann enjoyed her job, but she was glad her daughter had done it right, gotten a master's degree, prepared for a high-paying professional career. Murray's starting salary was more than Ann ever hoped to earn.

Just before six, Ann went home with plans to stay in for the evening. She was looking forward to a quiet weekend. She was just settling in when her son, John, called from Alexandria. Like Murray, he had been invited to the wedding, but by six p.m. his sister had yet to show up. He did not know why.

"Momma, I think there's something the matter," he said. "I feel worried."

Ann sat up and listened. John was not the worrying type, and his concern unnerved her. She told John she would try to call Murray.

"Don't worry," she told him, although she was trying to reassure herself. "You know Murray; she's always late."

Ann dialed Murray's cell phone number but got no answer. She left a message. The last time she had heard from Murray was earlier that day, when she called Ann's cell phone. Ann missed the call and planned to call her daughter later.

Ann knew Murray would call her as soon as she got the message. About seven p.m., Ann got another call from John.

"Don't worry, Mom, Rebekah's grandmother is sick. Murray went with them to the hospital."

Ann was relieved to hear Murray was fine, a simple explanation for her absence.

A few minutes later, however, the phone rang again. This time, the voice on the line was Murray's good friend Jessica. She was calling from Baton Rouge, and she could barely speak.

"Miss Ann, Miss Ann . . ." was all she could say through her sobs.

Ann's stomach seized. She immediately thought Murray had wrecked her car again. Just a few months earlier, Murray had totaled her old, beat-up Nissan, but she walked away with barely a scratch. Maybe this time she wasn't so lucky.

"Jessica, what in the world is wrong?"

"Oh, Miss Ann, something terrible has happened, something really terrible has happened . . ."

"Jessica, tell me . . ."

"Oh, Miss Ann, Murray was killed . . . She was murdered . . ."

Words like that, a concept like that, just don't register quickly in a mother's head.

"You can't take it," Ann says. "Murray seemed so immortal, even to me. I never worried about Murray because she was so in control of herself and so capable. I couldn't imagine something like that happening to Murray."

Ann's mind could not accept the thought. None of it made sense. *Why hadn't the police called?* she thought.

"No, Jessica, you must be wrong . . ."

"I'm not wrong," Jessica cried. "I'm not wrong. I'm so sorry, Miss Ann."

The kitchen walls around Ann began to spin. She forced herself to breathe, but her body went numb as if she were no longer in it. She felt like she was floating above herself. *Is this real? Am I really living this? Please let this be a mistake, a horrible mistake.* She dialed her ex-husband's phone number.

Casey Pace couldn't believe it either. He was a lawyer; he knew legal procedures. He assumed police were supposed to notify the victim's families.

"They would have called us," he told Ann when she called.

"You didn't hear Jessica," Ann said. "She's hysterical."

"I'm going to call the police."

He called Ann back just a few minutes later. He had reached the Baton Rouge Police Department. They couldn't tell him anything. They were checking into it and would have an officer call him back.

"I'll call you when I hear something," he told her.

Ann waited in her kitchen for his call. She didn't cry, or at least she can't remember if she cried. She just shut down. Her mind went blank. She sat still, paralyzed, barely breathing, barely alive, until the phone rang.

"Annie . . ." he said. "It's true."

"No . . ."

"What Jessica said is true. Murray's dead. She's been murdered."

"I'm going there . . ."

"Wait," he said. "Don't drive. I'm coming over."

The next call Ann made was to her son, John. He didn't recognize her traumatized voice.

"Are you my mother?" he kept asking as he began crying. "Is this my mother? You don't sound like my mother. This can't be true."

Ann's daughter, Sam, was living in Texas, where she was working on her Ph.D. She just screamed and screamed and screamed, "No! No! No!" The noise coming from Ann's oldest daughter sounded as if she, too, was being killed.

* * *

Suddenly, it seemed, Ann's house was filling up with people. Unable to speak or even think, Ann crawled into a closet and sat in the darkness.

"I didn't want anybody to talk to me or touch me," she said.

Just before nine, Ann and Casey and several other family members set off for the nearly three-hour drive from Jackson to Baton Rouge. During the drive, Ann stared out the window and tried to comprehend the hurricane of destruction roaring into her life. She wrote a poem:

> *Sometime between the last day of May and the first*
> *   day of June*
> *The sun forgot to rise and so did the moon.*
> *The earth fell from the sky, lost the track it should*
> *   take*
> *And left us in darkness with heartache*

They would stay with a friend, who lived in Baton Rouge. At two a.m., the Baton Rouge police came to the door. They needed to ask the family a few questions. The most obvious ones: Did anyone want to harm Murray? Had she received any threats?

"Everyone loved Murray," Ann said. "Who could want to hurt her?"

The police would not tell Murray's family much, just that she was murdered. They did not reveal how, or any other details of the case. They said they needed to protect the integrity of the investigation, and they would be in touch.

The next several hours passed in a blur. The friend offered food, but no one wanted to eat. Casey went by himself to a guest bedroom and shut the door. Ann sat in a chair by the door. She didn't know what she was waiting for. She just wanted time to rewind. No matter what she did, she could not get her legs to stop shaking.

"I didn't feel like me," she says. "It was like a body was standing in for me, but I was gone somewhere else."

Sam arrived in the twilight hours. She was dead calm, but her face looked ravaged. Her eyes were squinted shut, swollen, and red and streaks of tears were running down her cheeks.

As she walked through the door, she hugged her mom tight and looked at her hard. Sam was now the caretaker.

"Mother, are you all right?"

They decided to drive over to Murray's town home as soon as the sun came up. Ann immediately noticed the windows were wide open. She tried to peer inside but could not see anything. No police were present, guarding the crime scene, which Ann thought was strange.

"I couldn't figure out why they left the window open," she says. "And if they left the window open, why wasn't somebody there to keep people out?"

Ann wanted to walk inside, see what had happened in there. She needed to know more about her daughter's last moments. Just a week before, Ann was imagining her daughter's bright future. Murray was going to conquer the world. She had so much to look forward to. She was safe and healthy and fine. No, she was perfect. How could she be gone?

From interviews with Murray's friends and family, detectives Johnson and Vavasseur pieced together a map of Murray's life during her last days, which gave them several leads to pursue.

After her graduation May 24, she and her roommates threw a crowded keg party at their home at 2107 Stanford Avenue. The crowd was mostly friends and people the women knew from school, but a few people attended who the roommates did not recognize, people with tattoos and grubby clothes.

After the party, Murray and a few friends continued the night at a nearby bar on Perkins called the Caterie, a popular hangout for both students and the older locals. As usual, a man approached the good-looking group of women and began flirting with them. He claimed to be a cop and then flashed a set of handcuffs. He even snapped them around one of Murray's friends' wrists before admitting he was not an officer of the law. He was a little weird, but he did not seem dangerous—at least not at the time.

The next day, while the women finished moving out, Murray went shopping for cleaning supplies at the Wal-Mart a few blocks away, also on Perkins. A few hours after she returned, she realized her purse was gone, possibly stolen, but she was not sure if it was taken from her basket at Wal-Mart or from her home.

Later that week, when she pulled into her new carport, a stranger approached her while she was still in her car and on the phone with one of her roommates.

The man said he was looking for his friend at Murray's town home, but Murray did not recognize the name he gave.

"No one by that name lives here," she told him and returned to her conversation with Jessica.

But the man was not satisfied. He did not leave.

"Do you need anything else?" Murray asked the man, this time with a little edge in her voice.

Again, the man said he was looking for his friend.

"He doesn't live here," Murray repeated. "I just moved in, but he did not live here before, either, because I knew the people who did."

Murray went inside, and the man went away, but his presence in her carport upset the normally cool and confident young woman. When she spoke with her father that night, she mentioned it, telling him the encounter gave her the creeps.

Two days later, she was dead.

A party with strangers. A man pretending to be a cop handcuffing women at bars. Murray's stolen purse. A bizarre encounter in her carport. To cops, the incidents are all suspicious but difficult to track down. Rather than focus on unpromising trails, Police Investigation 101 says follow the closest lines from the victim first—namely people who knew Murray.

From Murray's friends, detectives also learned about a few men she had either dated or recently spurned. One had written Murray a nasty letter after they parted ways. Another had attempted to kiss her several times against Murray's wishes. And there were others who had suffered unrequited infatuation with Murray's vivacious spirit.


In the early days after Murray's murder, Ann barely functioned. Her oldest child, Sam, needed to remind her to take a shower and change clothes, to get up and eat. Ann was dazed.

She did not want to go forward in time. "I felt like every second that passed was taking me farther away from Murray," she
says. "I just wanted to grab her and hold onto her."

Ann wanted to see Murray's body at the morgue, touch her
one last time. Her family was against the idea, they did not
want to see Murray dead, and Ann did not have the strength to
go alone.

The only thing left for her to do as a mother was figure out
what to do with her daughter's inanimate body. The funeral
home director recommended against an open casket.

"I can't fix this," he told the family. "There's not a way to
fix this."

Knowing that Murray "never, ever, ever wanted anybody
to see her not at her best," Ann knew her beautiful baby would
have to be cremated. Her ashes would be spread in some of
her favorite places. The ceremonies gave Ann some peace, but
she still felt she needed to better understand Murray's last
moments.

Ignoring friends and family, law enforcement officials and
counselors, Ann insisted on looking at the crime scene photos
and autopsy shots of Murray. She told herself she wanted to
prepare for what would inevitably come out in court. But really, she was compelled to feel closer to Murray at the time of
her passing.

"It was absolutely essential," Ann says. "It's the alpha and
the omega. I'm her mother. I was there at the beginning and it
was as near to the end I could get. She endured it. I felt like,
*Oh, God, I can endure seeing it.* It was a way to be with her
through it. It was the only way to do it."

The images of Murray's death now haunt Ann when she
tries to go to sleep at night, especially the ones showing
Murray's eyes. In a frenzy, her murderer stabbed Murray
dozens of times in the chest and face with a screwdriver. In
several jabs, he stuck her through the eyes, the screwdriver's
metal rod cracking through the skull at the back of her eye
sockets.

To ward off the images, Ann keeps a favorite picture of
Murray at her bedside. Snapped not long before her death, the
photo is a close-up of Murray and a friend. Murray, in a play-

ful pose, is sticking her tongue out. And her big blue eyes are shining playfully. They are open wide and sparkle like a reflection of the sun.

"You see how pretty her eyes were . . ." Ann says. "That's one of the things I remember from her injuries. He destroyed her eyes."

# CHAPTER 9

# Rumors

Murray Pace's murder sent shudders through a normally placid Baton Rouge public. The city sees more than forty homicides a year, but most are the typical fare of urban life and poor neighborhoods: fatal robberies, drug disputes, turf wars, domestic violence. The murders are tragic, avoidable deaths, but they make some sense. The killers had a motive. The victims were in harm's way. Understandable. Not necessarily acceptable, but cynically expected. The media covers the cases, but the headlines usually fade within a few days, and the murder is forgotten.

Murray's case was different. Her murder was the type of crime that shocks a community and gets the whole town talking. Young, beautiful MBA grads don't usually come under attack inside their homes while eating lunch on a sunny Friday afternoon. Particularly in a neighborhood like Sharlo.

For decades, the area one mile south of the LSU campus was trusted as a safe place for students to live and play. Most days, the neighborhood is abuzz with people walking their dogs, friends hanging out on their balconies and porches, and landlords mowing the lawns. Police don't usually go to Sharlo or nearby Tigerland, a maze of rentals named after the LSU mascot, except to take reports of occasional bike thefts or to break up a loud party. So when Murray's murder hit the news, the neighborhood's sense of safety was suddenly shattered.

Baton Rouge police did not release many details about the killing, except to say Murray died from multiple stab wounds during a struggle, but word spread quickly that her body was brutally slaughtered. In the absence of information, rumors fueled the fervor, speculating that she was dismembered with a machete, that her organs were removed, that her heart was left on the kitchen counter.

The fear was contagious. In the days after Murray's murder, the neighborhood went ghostly quiet. Young women left their apartments to stay with friends. Families kept their children closer and checked the locks on their doors more often. Sales for security alarms doubled, leases were broken, and For Rent signs—a rarity in a neighborhood where friends usually take over friends' leases—blossomed around Murray's town home.

Like the detectives, Sharlo residents who stuck around hoped Murray's killer would be someone she knew, someone police could quickly and easily track down. But after a week passed without an arrest, the idea that a madman might be on the loose took hold in the neighborhood and began to spread through the city.

People talked about other unsolved murders and the disappearance of single women in Baton Rouge. In May, another LSU graduate student, Christine Moore, disappeared while jogging along the Mississippi River. No one imagined the cases were connected until they realized she lived just around the corner from Murray.

Then the news broke that Murray, just days before she was killed, had moved from Stanford Avenue, where she lived three houses down from Gina Green at the time of her murder eight months earlier.

Questioned about Murray's link to Gina, police spokeswoman Corporal Mary Ann Godawa said investigators were aware the two women had been neighbors, but they did not believe the slayings were connected.

Other than their addresses, the women and their murders had little in common. Murray was stabbed to death, and her throat was slit. Gina was strangled. Murray was in her twenties and in graduate school. Gina was forty-one and working full-time as a nurse. The two women did not socialize in the same circles, they did not know each other's names, and other than their addresses seemed to have no similarities except the BMWs they both drove.

When Gina was killed, Ann remembers Murray and her roommates were frightened. Ann bought Murray a gun to protect herself, but the weapon never got to Baton Rouge. Ann had insisted Murray learn to shoot it first, and Murray never found the time. Besides, Murray told her mother several weeks after Gina's murder, police had found the killer, a man Gina knew.

Ann was shocked, just like many other people in Baton Rouge who assumed the case was solved, when she learned in early June that no one had ever been arrested for Gina's murder. The case had not been closed. Only its story, like so many other unsolved murders in the city, had disappeared from the public eye.

On Friday, June 7, an army of police investigators returned to Murray's neighborhood and, in a rare gesture, invited the media to tag along. News satellite trucks parked along the road as officers stopped pedestrians and cars, not just to ask questions about Murray's case but to inform residents of a community meeting with the Baton Rouge police that Chief Pat Englade planned for the following Wednesday night.

A crowd of about three hundred people—including a number of LSU students' parents who drove in from out of town—showed up for the meeting at the Louisiana School for the Deaf just around the corner from the Sharlo neighborhood.

Packed into a room teeming with frustration and fear, the audience grilled the police officers and Chief Englade about the case.

Do you have any suspects? Did Murray know her killer? How did he get inside her home? What did he do?

The police, who numbered about a dozen, remained tight-lipped about the investigation, but they confessed they had no good suspects, and they did not know yet if she knew her killer.

Scant new information was released, most notably that the killer left no signs that he forced his way inside.

When confronted with the rumors, investigators refuted tales that Murray was dismembered or disemboweled, revealing only that she was stabbed multiple times and her throat was cut.

Englade assured everyone that police were working hard on the case, tracking down dozens of leads, but they could not discuss it.

"I know that sounds unfair," he told the audience. "But the most valuable thing to you is that we get this person off the streets."

Police did not speak of the ring found at Murray's head or the missing phone or her missing keys and wallet. They did not share information about the shoe print or the broken iron. Those pieces of evidence they kept to themselves in an effort to preserve the integrity of the case. They did not want to reveal their hand to the killer or to anyone who inexplicably might want to take credit for the murder.

One woman stood up and asked Englade how he would feel if his daughter was living in the Sharlo neighborhood. And with stunning candor, Englade said parents might want to convince their young daughters to move from the neighborhood. Telling parents their children were completely safe in Sharlo, he said, "would be an absolute lie."

Yet when residents questioned him about the city's other unsolved murders, like Gina Green and Christine Moore, Englade tried to dispel their fears. Faced with a city on the verge of mass panic, he calmly, persuasively insisted no evidence existed that the cases were connected.

# CHAPTER 10

# Derrick's Dance with the Law

Derrick first felt the cool metal of cuffs slapped around his wrists when he was just thirteen. It was the beginning of a long cat and mouse game he played with Louisiana law enforcement.

On November 8, 1981, Derrick was out messing around the Blackmore neighborhood as usual late that night, looking for something to get into. The Blackmore Sweetshop was a neighborhood store where the kids gathered for soda pop and candy. Derrick broke into its storehouse, broke up some bottles, and ransacked the place just for fun.

His arrest was for simple burglary. At the time, he was still a juvenile. The arrest, the judge hoped, was enough to scare him. Derrick was placed on probation and stayed off police radar for awhile. But only because his neighbors did not call the police to report his continued peeping.

Derrick was getting worse, not better.

"He was obsessed," his sister, Tenieta said. "That's all he cared about."

But his victims, who included several of his relatives, did not want to call in the police. Mistrust of cops is rampant in the poor black community where Derrick lived. But in Derrick's case, neighbors did not want bad blood with Florence and her family. The word on Blackmore Road said she practiced voodoo. And Florence did not like to hear accusations about her beloved and only son.

Tenieta remembers the day when a woman came by to talk with Florence about Derrick's peeping.

"Before she could get the words out, Derrick jumped on her," Tenieta said. "He shook her and knocked her down and told her she was lying."

Florence pulled Derrick off the woman, but she was not excessively apologetic. Florence threatened the woman, too. She twisted the conversation around, accusing the woman of trespassing and making false allegations. By the time the woman left, she feared for her own arrest.

Florence, however, could not protect Derrick while he was out on the street. On August 8, 1985, at the age of sixteen, he was arrested again, this time in downtown Saint Francisville for attempted second-degree murder.

Derrick and his cousin, Jadi Marshall, were hanging out at the Green Door Café, when another teen began harassing them. It's unclear what happened next, but the other teen ended up with his belly cut open and nearly bleeding to death on the sidewalk.

The way Derrick told it to his family, the teenager pinned Jadi to the ground, punching his face. As Derrick tried to pry the guy off his cousin, the young man only wrapped his hands around Jadi's throat and squeezed. Jadi struggled to speak, telling Derrick, "Get the knife. Get the knife." Derrick says he handed his knife to Jadi, who then stabbed the teen in the stomach.

Derrick claimed innocence. And apparently law enforcement authorities were unable to sort out what happened because the charges disappeared.

By the time he was seventeen, Derrick's peeping no longer

seemed like a young boy's curiosity. Fathers and husbands in the neighborhood were beginning to consider it threatening. And they did not like the response they were getting from Florence. Derrick was becoming more aggressive, spending more time, not less, creeping around windows at night.

In February 1986, Derrick's uncle Al was fed up. Derrick had been peeping at his aunt Janet for two weeks. Al complained to Florence about it, but Derrick continued. On February 3, Al called the West Feliciana Sheriff's Office to report a Peeping Tom. He did not name Derrick, but it was a warning shot. He wanted the family to know he was not going to ignore Derrick's behavior anymore.

In June 1986, Derrick finished high school, earning a vocational degree, and soon got a job as a pipe fitter at Brown & Root, a labor contractor in Baton Rouge. He continued to date his high school girlfriend, Jackie Sims, a quiet, gentle girl who was over the moon in love with him. They seemed happy and were headed toward marriage and creating their own family together. On the surface, Derrick's life seemed to be treading on a good track.

But Derrick had another life that was developing just as fast and traveling in a different direction. His mischief was spiraling into a life of crime. Before he graduated from high school, he set his own car on fire for the insurance money.

His cousin, Carl Lee, was driving north on Highway 61 to Saint Francisville, when he saw Derrick walking away from the flaming Oldsmobile. When Carl stopped to pick him up, Derrick was laughing when he told Carl what he had done.

At night, Derrick was still peeping. He was expanding his territory, sneaking around Saint Francisville's new subdivisions, where the white folks lived.

Just before midnight on July 2, 1988, Derrick parked his truck on Highway 10 a quarter mile outside the Saint Francisville city limits and walked onto the wooded grounds of Rosedown Apartments. He knew exactly where he was going. He climbed up to a second-floor porch, took his shoes off, and crouched down on his knees to spy on the woman inside.

A neighbor in the complex saw him and called in the complaint at 12:03 a.m. As the officer drove into the complex, he shined the patrol car's spotlight up to the balcony and saw a black male in a red shirt kneeling by the railing. Derrick moved quickly.

He jumped off the balcony and ran into the woods behind the apartments. The officer called for backup and chased after the shadowy figure, but by the time he got behind the buildings, Derrick was gone. He was hightailing it through the woods toward his parents' house.

He left behind two important things, however: his shoes, placed side by side on the balcony, and his car, which was registered to Derrick Todd Lee.

When he heard the call come in, West Feliciana Parish Sheriff Bill Daniel rang his buddy, Angola Warden Burl Cain, and got the prison's bloodhounds out to the apartment complex within a few minutes.

The dogs followed Derrick's scent from the balcony through the woods, across a small creek, and straight to his parents' home.

Derrick was soaking wet, from sweat and crossing the creek, when he got home, so he hid his dripping clothes before police arrived. But when the police showed up with the shoes from the balcony, Florence and Coleman admitted they belonged to Coleman and that Derrick often wore them.

Derrick was booked for attempted burglary of an inhabited dwelling, a felony. Two months later, however, the West Feliciana Parish District Attorney's Office allowed him a bargain, a lowered charge of unauthorized entry in exchange for a guilty plea. Derrick agreed and was sentenced to one year, but the jail term was waived in lieu of probation for two years.

A few months later, on September 17, Derrick married Jacqueline Sims at a little Baptist church in Solitude. The couple had been dating since high school. And Jackie was the only real girlfriend Derrick had ever had. She was nuts for him despite her father's disapproval. Henry Lee Sims did not think Derrick was good enough for his daughter.

Henry worked in an oil refinery plant. He made decent money, enough to afford a comfortable, albeit small, home for his family and expected better things in life for his children.

Lee was from the wrong part of town. His family was poor, troubled, and Derrick was barely making it through special education classes at high school. Henry feared Derrick was only after the money Jackie inherited from her dead mother. He urged her not to marry Derrick, but Jackie was nineteen and pregnant with the couple's first child. The train was already on the tracks.

The new couple moved into a trailer park on Highway 965 near Derrick's family and tried to play house. Derrick continued to work off and on as a pipe fitter and laborer at the ExxonMobil Chemical Plant just outside Baton Rouge. When the plants had no work for him, he caught jobs at the local Saint Francisville Grocery Depot, stocking shelves.

When night rolled in and the job was done, Derrick was not the type to sit at home and watch TV with his wife. He was a roamer, and the world of southern Louisiana had just opened up to him.

Derrick explained years later that he first learned how to live as a single man after he got married. He began barhopping at night, but not just the familiar haunts of Saint Francisville and Solitude. He traveled the rural two-lane highways that crisscross the Louisiana backcountry, stopping at roadside bars in little towns like Jackson, Zachary, Alsen, and Baker, and earning a reputation as a flirt and womanizer.

His teenage shyness with women had transformed into an insatiable pursuit of sex. He hit on every woman within ten feet of him. He bought them drinks, lavished them with attention, told them they were beautiful, and hung on their every word. He asked them to dance, told them he knew how to treat a woman, then, before the night was through, he propositioned them, promising they would fall in love with him if they had sex.

At heart, though, Derrick was a mama's boy. For years, he remained intensely attached to his mother, stopping by her trailer home almost every day after work, after an evening out, or sometimes in the middle of the day. But his visits were not always pleasant. His relationship with his mother was contentious.

Derrick acted like he still lived at the home, helping himself to beer, plopping down on the couch, and expecting to be fed. When she protested, he turned the tables on her, picking at her, pushing her buttons, hoping to see her squirm.

"You got nothing in here cooked for your son," he'd say, peering in at an empty refrigerator. "What kind of mom are you?"

If he had a few beers in him, he dug deeper, harassing her about the way she raised him: "You weren't the kind of mom we could talk to."

He was angry with her about Coleman's punishments. She had not protected him. She had sat back and watched. "You didn't do us right," Derrick told her.

Florence did not want to hear it. She did not like him disrespecting her in her own home. But Derrick kept at her, pick, pick, pick. He was no longer a scrawny kid. She could not pick him up by the arm and slap his butt. And Derrick was no longer afraid of Coleman's fan belts.

Derrick was bigger now and the master of his own household, earning his own money, making his own rules, living as his own man. He had learned not to back down. Sometimes the only way Florence could escape his taunts was by fleeing into her bedroom and locking the door.

On February 17, 1989, Derrick's sister, Tharshia, then eighteen and still living with their mother, tried to lock him out of the family's trailer. He was in a rage, banging on the door, demanding that she let him inside.

"I'm gonna give you an ass whopping like nobody ever had," he yelled.

She yelled back, telling him to go away, that it wasn't his house. Derrick didn't care. He took out the glass in the door and reached in to unlock the doorknob.

"This ain't your home, and I'll go into any place I feel like," he said. "And no one can stop me."

He was cursing and yelling while Tharshia called the police. She filed a complaint with the West Feliciana Parish Sheriff's Office, and Derrick was arrested for unauthorized entry. He was taken to jail, and his probation officer, Don Phares, was notified.

Phares spoke to Judge William Kline, who presides in West Feliciana Parish court. Kline told Phares to keep Derrick in jail on possible probation violation until he made the $75 bail.

A few weeks later, at Florence's request, the West Feliciana Parish District Attorney's Office lowered the charges to trespassing, a misdemeanor. On April 13, Derrick pleaded guilty. Judge William Kline sentenced him to thirty days in jail, but the time behind bars was again waived in lieu of a special condition Kline made for Derrick's probation. He was to begin seeing a psychologist, Robert Snyder, for anger management sessions.

But Derrick did not keep up with his therapy sessions. In August 1989, Phares wrote to Judge Kline advising that Derrick was not seeking treatment. Phares did not receive a response. Nor was Phares notified when West Feliciana Parish sheriff's deputies were called out to Derrick's house on February 2, 1990.

Derrick was in a rage, cursing at Jackie and banging around their home. He grabbed his wife's arm, twisted it behind her back, and forced her outside. As she stumbled to catch her balance, he slammed the door and locked her out.

She called police about eleven thirty that night for help. She needed an officer's assistance to get inside her trailer and collect some of her clothes. She told the police she planned to file charges and request a restraining order against Derrick the next day. But overnight, something changed her mind. Instead of pressing charges, she moved back in.

Three months later, on May 23, he started slapping her around again. This time she called her father. Henry had been urging his daughter to leave Derrick, and when he arrived, he told Derrick what he thought of him. Derrick refused to let Jackie leave, blocking her way and punching at Henry as he tried to intervene. After Jackie and her father managed to get outside, Derrick ran in the trailer and came out threatening them with a gun. Fearful of what Derrick might do, Henry left alone, and Jackie called the police.

Deputy Randall Holden arrived just after eleven p.m. He parked in front of the trailer, and just a moment later, Henry pulled in behind him and got out of his truck. As Holden walked to the front door of the house, Derrick stormed out and walked right past him, not even exchanging a glance, and rushed straight toward Henry.

"Whoa!" Holden called to him. "You need to stop. Derrick! Stop!"

Derrick ignored the officer and continued like a flung arrow toward Henry, cursing and threatening the older man. Fearing Derrick was about to hit his father-in-law, Holden grabbed Derrick's arms, cuffed him, and placed him in the patrol car.

After speaking with Jackie and her father, Holden took Derrick, then twenty-one, to jail, where he was booked with disturbing the peace. Holden had told Jackie and Henry to come to the station to make a statement.

Derrick pleaded guilty to the charge two months later and paid a $100 fine, but he got no jail time, nor was his probation yanked. He was learning he could do what he wanted with little consequence. And on August 31, 1990, he was released from his probation for successful completion.

He didn't take long to get into trouble again. On October 29, he was arrested for instigating a fistfight at Price's Bar in Saint Francisville. The Saint Francisville Police charged him with disturbing the peace, a misdemeanor that carried yet another minor sentence: one day of public service, a $20 fine, and three months of probation.

He paid the fine, but not before filing his own complaint with the police. He alleged his mother, instead of him, collected from the city the $100 bond Derrick paid to get out of jail on October 29, and he wanted it back, even if he had to charge his mother with theft.

At the time, Florence was having her own troubles. She and Coleman, who was earning $5.50 an hour driving cement trucks, were struggling to pay their bills. The creditors were circling, winning several judgments against them for nonpayment of loans. The courts garnished 25 percent of Coleman's wages and began seizing their few possessions: a stereo, a TV, a radio, tools, a lawn mower, and a dozen shotguns.

Then in November 1991, Florence's father died. As the oldest child, the responsibility of caring for their mother fell to her. Soon, Jane Mitchell Lee was living with the Barrows in a home built on a piece of Robert Lee's original tract of land.

The house was an old Acadian-style cottage with a steep roofline and a wide front porch stretching across the front of the house. Derrick continued to stop in for daily visits, taking not a small amount of pleasure from the shrunken role Coleman was playing in the household.

Not even his stepfather had any power over him now. Nobody could tell Derrick what to do anymore. Those days were over. He was going to do as he pleased, when he pleased.

# CHAPTER 11

# The Rumors Are True

In the first weeks of June 2002, while city residents grilled Baton Rouge police about possible links between the city's recent spate of unsolved murders of women, the Louisiana State Police Crime Lab was busy processing evidence from Murray's crime scene.

On June 13, Julia Naylor began testing for DNA on the swabs she collected from Murray's body, focusing on the one she took from inside Murray's thigh, near her buttocks. The swab tested positive for semen, and soon Naylor had a DNA profile. A few days later, Naylor also found the same DNA profile from a swab taken off Murray's cervix. Whoever he was, he clearly had sexual intercourse with Murray near her time of death.

At the time, the Louisiana State Police Crime Lab was still new at DNA testing, having just begun doing its own DNA analysis in the fall of 2001. Previously, its analysts would only test evidence for the existence of blood and semen and other biological material. If the investigating agency wanted further DNA testing of the evidence or analysis of a suspect's DNA, they had to hire a private lab to do the work.

Consequently, the lab had not yet set up a state database of forensic DNA profiles. That meant crime lab analysts could not quickly and electronically compare the DNA of Murray's killer to the DNA of known criminals. Nor could they compare it against other unknown DNA profiles collected from crime scenes that remained unsolved.

If analysts needed to compare the DNA of Murray's killer to a suspect's DNA, or compare the killer's DNA to DNA collected at other unsolved murders, they would have do so manually, or more precisely, by eye in a side-by-side examination looking for a match.

The O. J. Simpson trial and more recently television shows like *CSI* have made *DNA* a familiar household term. Most people are aware that with the exception of identical twins, everyone's DNA is unique, and we all carry it around in our cells. Used in criminal investigations, DNA can act like a genetic fingerprint, allowing police to make a damning match between DNA found at a crime scene and a suspect's DNA.

The valuable qualities of DNA for investigators is its abundance—DNA is in the cells of our blood, our skin, our saliva, all our biological material. And its pesky habit of staying behind after the crime is committed is also helpful. Speaking can transfer invisible drops of saliva. A drop of sweat transfers skin cells. So can a simple touch.

In fact, humans shed about 40,000 skin cells a day, leaving them in the clothes they wear, on the bed they sleep in, and on the people and objects they touch. Generally, the rule of thumb says ten seconds of contact is required to leave DNA behind, but in some cases it only takes a moment, particularly for people who are called *good shedders*.

A forensic DNA match, however, is not a comparison of a person's entire genetic code. The technique of DNA fingerprinting involves looking at a small section of DNA, thirteen particular spots—or loci—on the long strands of genes.

At each loci are two genetic markers, one inherited from

Mom and one from Dad. The markers are a combination of the four chemical bases that make up DNA: adenine, thymine, cytosine, and guanine. But in forensic DNA analysis, the markers are identified by numbers and in graphic form, by various shades of gray lines on the DNA strand or ladder.

The thirteen loci used in forensic investigations were specifically picked for identification purposes because they are at spots on the genetic code known to vary between individuals. At least 99.9 percent of human DNA is exactly the same for all people. The remaining 0.1 percent makes individuals unique. The thirteen loci are a part of the 0.1 percent.

The thirteen loci were also selected for identification purposes because the markers at those spots do not have any known purpose. They don't determine eye color or skin tone or propensity to develop diabetes. In fact, scientists refer to the genes at those spots as "junk DNA."

When comparing sets of thirteen loci, two individuals might share the same markers at some of the thirteen spots, but scientists believe no two individuals—living or dead since the beginning of humankind—share the same markers at all thirteen loci.

They base this not on hard evidence from comparing every person's DNA but on statistical models derived from databases comparing thousands of DNA profiles. So a DNA match of a suspect's DNA to biological evidence at a crime scene is not so much an absolute identification but rather an astronomical probability—usually about one in 50 to 100 billion—that the DNA could belong to someone else.


By early July 2002, detectives working Murray's and Gina's murders were striking out with their suspects. They had asked the crime lab to compare several men's DNA to the DNA found in their separate cases, but so far none matched.

Around that time, during a coffee break at the State Police Crime Lab, several analysts were sitting around a break room table chatting about their various cases, when Naylor and Angela Ross, who was working Gina Green's murder, spoke of the unknown DNA profiles they each obtained from their crime scene evidence.

As the two women discussed the details of Gina's and Murray's murders, their boss, Jim Churchman, commented, "You ought to compare those two profiles."

It was not an order or an urgent request, just simple curiosity.

The Baton Rouge police had not suggested the cases were linked, nor had they requested the lab do a comparison of the DNA from the two murders, so no attempt had been made to do so. But nothing prevented the lab analysts from doing it on their own.

When the results came back, Churchman was just as surprised as Ross and Naylor by the exact match at all thirteen loci. They immediately called detectives working the two cases.

Detectives Johnson and Coulter got the news on Monday, July 8, and they, too, were surprised by the link. They had discussed their cases, but they did not suspect the same man was responsible. Both were home invasions, but other than that, the two cases seemed different. Murray's murder scene was so bloody and brutal. The killer was filled with rage. Gina's murder was also violent, but the killer seemed to be calmer, collected. He had not lost control. And he did not use a knife; he strangled Gina. Coulter did not believe her murder was random. He suspected Gina knew her killer.

Focusing on the differences in the murders, including the wide gap in the victims' ages, the investigators had been thrown off the idea of a connection. Detectives are taught that repeat killers usually use the same methods of killing and pick out similar victims. Detectives figured that the only thing linking Gina and Murray—their Stanford Avenue addresses— was more of a coincidence than a sign their murders were connected.

They were wrong. On July 9, 2002, the Baton Rouge police called a press conference to break the news. What the city had feared, and the police had tried to dispel, was true. The unsolved murders of two Baton Rouge women were committed by the same man.

Chief Englade told the public that several suspects in both cases had already been eliminated, including a black man arrested a week earlier for kidnapping and rape. But they had several more suspects they planned to pursue. He promised the cases would take top priority until the killer was behind bars.

Meanwhile, investigators hoped police might find the killer simply by uploading his DNA match to the FBI's national Combined DNA Index System or CODIS, a database of more than 2 million DNA profiles of convicted criminals and unknown profiles from unsolved crime scenes.

"We need a break," Englade said. "One piece of evidence or information could obviously turn this whole case around."

In both cases, the killer left no signs he forced his way in the house, meaning he likely convinced these smart, savvy women to open their doors. So in his parting statements, Englade urged women, particularly single women living alone in Baton Rouge, to be cautious. He did not say it, but everyone got the message: the killer could strike again anytime.

# CHAPTER 12

# A Surviving Witness

By 8 a.m. on most days, Diane Alexander was deep into her nursing rounds at Lafayette General Hospital. But at the last minute on July 9, she got the morning off.

At forty-five, she was a busy mom and wife, and she savored the extra time to sleep in and catch up on a few errands. For ten years, she had worked as a nurse to help support her family. And that summer, she was also attending school to earn an advanced nursing degree to boost her salary. Graduation was just two weeks away.

At 8:30 that morning, she left her trailer home in Breaux Bridge, a rural cajun town about twenty miles west of Baton Rouge, and drove to Lafayette for a quick shop at Sam's Club and the Wal-Mart next door. On her way back, she made several stops—the grocery, a gas station, and then the bank—squeezing in as much as possible before she had to get dressed for her afternoon shift.

She pulled into her gravel driveway about eleven and carried her packages inside.

For years, Diane, a short, sassy, light-skinned black woman, had lived along Jeffrey Broussard Road, just on the outskirts of town, with her husband and teenage son. The front of her home faced the sparsely traveled two-lane highway. Behind it, way across a large, overgrown field, is a street of small homes occupied by people who keep to themselves. To the left is an even larger, more overgrown abandoned farmer's field. To the right, nothing but trees. And across the highway, more than one hundred yards away, is a well-tended ranch home.

Despite the isolation, Diane was comfortable in her home. She never had any problems with the neighbors or crime. She felt safe, safe enough that she never feared staying in the home alone when her husband was away overnight for his job as a truck driver. But Diane was not naive, either. She did not like opening the door to strangers, and she was not afraid to be rude if someone was treading on her property. So when a man came knocking on her front door about noon that Tuesday, Diane had her guard up.

"Hi, my name is Anthony," the well-groomed young man said. "I'm from Monroe, and I'm looking for the Montgomerys. I'm supposed to do some construction work for them, but I don't know where they live. Do you know them?"

The man kept a polite distance from Diane, standing back from the door a bit when she opened it, and he didn't seem nervous. He appeared as if he honestly needed help, like he was legitimately lost. He seemed sincere, friendly even. He extended his hand as he introduced himself and smiled warmly. He was clean-shaven, with freshly cropped hair and wore a crisply pressed white golf shirt with blue stripes and jean shorts.

"No, I don't know them," Diane told him. "I don't know any Montgomerys."

Although he appeared harmless, she kept the glass storm door closed between them as she spoke.

"What about your husband? Does he know them?"

"No, my husband doesn't know them either." Honestly, Diane's husband wasn't home. He was away until later that evening. But she did not volunteer that information.

"Well, can I borrow your phone book to look them up?"

"Hold on." Diane went into her kitchen and got the phone book. She cracked the storm door open, handed it to the man on her porch, then closed and locked the door again. She had already started cooking her lunch, and she went back into her kitchen to check on the food. The man knocked again.

"Can I use your phone?"

Diane reached for her cordless phone in the kitchen and handed it to the man on the porch, cracking the storm door just enough to pass it through. He seemed to dial a number, but Diane was paying little attention to him now. She was busy inside getting ready for work, ironing her uniform, enjoying the gospel music she was playing on the stereo, and anticipating eating her lunch.

"Excuse me, ma'am?"

Diane went to the door again, opening it a crack to get her phone. "Yes?"

"I can't seem to find them . . ." he said. From the stereo inside, the sound of gospel music spilled out onto the porch. "I like gospel music, too," the man volunteered. "I used to sing in a gospel choir. You want to hear me sing?"

Diane did not have the time for small talk. She was ready for this man to leave. Her patience was about to end, and his presence on her porch was starting to make her feel uncomfortable.

"Can I help you with anything else?"

He smiled. "You sure you don't know the Montgomerys?"

"Yes, I told you. I don't know anyone around here with that name."

"And your husband, you sure he doesn't know them?"

"No, he doesn't know them either."

"Can you ask him?"

"Look," she snapped back. "My husband's not here . . ."

As soon as the words fell out of her mouth, the man lunged. Like a cobra, he struck fast, quickly getting inside the door. He grabbed her by the neck with one hand and shoved her against the open door.

"I'm going to rape you, bitch," he told her. "Take me to your bedroom."

Diane began praying. She couldn't believe what was happening. She tried to stay calm and think her way through it. She decided not to resist, fearing her resistance would make it worse.

"We don't have to go to the bedroom," she said. "We can stay right here."

"I have a knife," he warned. "If you try anything, I'll poke you in the eye."

He laid her down on the living room carpet near the sofa and told her to take her panties off.

"I can't move," she told him. "You have me by the throat."

He let go of her neck, and Diane did as he told her. He pulled her denim ankle-length dress above her waist, took his own clothes off, and lay on top of her. His face was pressed against her left ear as he began to thrust against her.

"I've been watching you," he whispered in her ear.

"Where did you see me?"

"Shut up! Shut up!"

He was sweating now, profusely. Salty droplets fell on Diane's face and neck. But he was having trouble obtaining an erection. While he thrust against her, she remembered her leg fell from where he propped it up on the sofa. "Ah-ah," he said, and placed her leg back up on the sofa.

At one point, she saw him place the knife at her side. She felt around for it with her fingertips, and after finding it, she lifted it up over his back. He was still trying to rape her, but he could not get an erection. She looked at the knife as he struggled to penetrate her and could see now that the blade was small, probably a paring knife.

*Oh, Lord,* she thought. *If I stick this man, that may only anger him more. He may kill me.*

"Ah-ah, bitch," he said, suddenly realizing what she was doing. He grabbed the knife from her hands. He stood up and looked around the room. He put his clothes back on, having failed to get an erection. Diane tried to keep her eyes focused on his face. She noticed he didn't have such a bad face. He looked like he was a nice guy, perhaps could even have a family somewhere or at least a girlfriend. She couldn't understand why he needed or even wanted to rape her.

"You're not such a bad-looking guy," she told him.

"No, I'm not," he said, showing no emotion. His eyes were still scanning the room. "Stay right there. I'm not going to do anything to you."

He seemed to leave her sight for a few moments, but then he returned and straddled her at the chest. He pulled off his white knit shirt, leaving a T-shirt underneath. Then he leaned over her and wrapped a cord around her throat.

He twisted it tight and began pulling hard against her windpipe, but Diane had managed to stick her fingers underneath the cord before he cinched it. She rolled over on her right side, away from his view, and as he pulled the cord from behind, she pushed out on the cord around the front of her neck.

The next thing she remembers is a painful smashing blow to her head. She does not know what he hit her with, but her vision began to blur and spin. She slipped in and out of consciousness, remembering only flashes of time.

She's not sure how many times, but she knows he continued to hit her in the face and head with something hard, fracturing her skull in several places and leaving a six-centimeter-deep gash on the left side of her forehead.

Suddenly, he was startled, as if he heard something. He stood up, as if to check a window, then he came back to where she was lying on the floor. Looking down on her, he lifted his left knee up high and stomped his foot down hard, using all of his weight, onto her stomach before running out the back door.

Outside the home, Diane's son, Herman, was returning from his classes at the University of Lafayette. In the driveway, he saw a gold-colored car, which he thought was a Mitsubishi Mirage, parked facing toward the road. He pulled in beside it and parked behind his mom's car. On his way to the house, he noticed the gold car's hood was dented between the headlights, and a front plate with a car dealership ad "Hampton Has It" was damaged. He was unfamiliar with the car, but figured his mom had a friend from church visiting.

He went in the front door with one thing on his mind, calling his girlfriend, so he did not consider why the door was partially open. He pushed it in and walked straight for the kitchen counter, where the phone usually sat. But the handset was not there.

"Mom," he called out. "Where's the phone?"

"Help . . ." Herman heard his mother's voice, so weak, coming from the living room. That's when he noticed her lying in a pool of blood on the floor leading into the hallway. Her dress was pulled up above her waist, and her face, her neck, and her chest area were covered in blood. "Herman, get a knife," she said. "He's still in the house."

"Where?" his mind was trying to catch up with the rage exploding inside him. "Where is he?"

Herman noticed the back door slightly ajar, and he bolted outside just in time to see the gold car turning right, squealing away onto Louisiana 31. He ran to his car, then realized he didn't have his keys. He raced inside, grabbed his keys, and as fast as he could, backed out of the driveway and tried to catch up with the gold car. He followed Highway 31 almost into Breaux Bridge, but he was unable to spot the gold car again.

Back at the house, when Diane realized her son had left to chase her attacker, she knew she needed to call an ambulance for herself. She managed to pull herself off the floor and staggered back to her bedroom, where she used another phone to dial 911. She could barely see through her eyes, which were swollen shut from the beating.

When the ambulance arrived, the paramedics determined her condition needed an emergency air evacuation. A medical helicopter landed in her backyard, and while Diane was airlifted to Lafayette General, the detectives called to the scene were unsure if she would survive.

Saint Martin Parish Sheriff's Office Detective Sergeant Evans Williams was assigned as lead detective on the case, but he was assisted by a young detective, Lieutenant Arthur Boyd, who had known Diane for years because he went to high school with her oldest son. He was disturbed by the reports of Diane's condition, and he vowed to find the man who did it. This kind of attack was rare in Saint Martin Parish and even less common in Breaux Bridge.

Unable to speak with Diane directly, Boyd interviewed Herman for whatever details he could provide. Herman described what he saw in the house, the man driving away, the car, and he added one last detail. When he walked past the car before going inside the house, Herman saw a phone cord hanging out of the driver's side window. He didn't know if it was important.

Inside the house, Sergeant Samuel Inzerella, who was processing the scene for evidence, discovered a long piece of phone cord, which once stretched from the kitchen wall, down the hallway and into a back bedroom to a computer, had been cut and a twelve-foot piece was missing. Diane's attacker had used a knife or some other cutting tool to slice through the cord in the kitchen, and then again at the start of the hallway. He took the piece he had cut out and used it to try to strangle Diane.

After bagging a piece of the cut cord as evidence, Inzerella also determined Diane's panties, her purse, and the handset to her phone were missing from the home. Clearly, the attacker was trying to cover his tracks, removing any evidence that he might have touched. Inzerella dusted the house for prints, focusing on the front door, the back door knob and a broken vase on the living room floor, but he was unable to lift any identifiable prints. Whoever had committed the crime was either wearing gloves or he was very good—or very lucky—at not leaving prints. He left no trace of himself.

When Boyd and Williams arrived at Lafayette General to interview Diane later that day, her eyelids were swollen shut— a puffy purple mass surrounding both sockets—and she was still bleeding from two deep cuts in her head. Ligature marks and severe bruises were also evident around her neck. She had difficulty talking about the attack, but she was able to tell the detectives how the man got into her home and a little about his looks: a black male, light brown complexion, clean-shaven, and somewhere between five eight and five eleven, with a style of speaking that was more city than country.

Before the end of the day, the investigators compiled what they knew of the suspect's description, his car, and the mode of attack, then disseminated it to all police agencies and the news media. After Diane was released from the hospital five days later, she was ready to do a sketch of her attacker. She couldn't get his face out of her mind. And she remembered more about his looks. She met Boyd at the sheriff's office July

15, 2002. They used computer software called FACES, which is designed to help police and victims develop composite sketches of suspects.

When she finished, Diane was satisfied that the computer sketch showed a close resemblance to the "Anthony" who knocked on her door six days earlier. The only quibble she had with the image was the hair. The software could not get the placement of the hairline quite right, although everything else looked right.

The sheriff's office sent another bulletin out on police communication networks and updated the news media, this time including the sketch of the unknown man, new details about the clothes he was wearing, and a picture of a gold Mitsubishi Mirage like the one Herman described. That week, the sketch and updated information about the case ran in the local papers in Saint Martin, Lafayette, and the other parishes immediately north of Baton Rouge. But no link was made with the city murders.

The news reports of Diane's attack sparked several phone calls from other Saint Martin women who had also received a frightening visit from a suspicious man asking to use the phone.

Rachel, a forty-one-year-old black woman, told police a similar-looking black male forced his way into her home a few days before Diane was attacked.

She, too, was off work that day, a weekday, and she planned to spend the morning cleaning her mobile home. She had just let her dog out when she heard the animal barking aggressively, more aggressively than he ever had.

She went to her front door and looked out the window. In the driveway, a burgundy truck was parked facing the roadway—not how visitors would normally park by pulling in next to her car. She looked around but did not see anyone, not just yet. Then a black male was suddenly on her porch steps, walking quickly up toward her. Before she could say anything, he began telling her, "Ma'am, ma'am, I need to use ya phone! I need to use your phone!"

She was startled. She thought there must be a problem in the neighborhood. His insistence knocked her off guard. She opened her screen door to him a crack.

"What's the problem?" she asked as he continued his rush toward her.

"I need to use your phone!" he said as he got to the door, not stopping to wait for her permission to enter. Before Rachel could ask another question, he was walking inside. He did not hesitate. Rachel backed up into the living room, suddenly realizing a stranger had just pushed his way inside her home.

She got some distance from the man and stood with a chair between them. She tried to remain calm. Instinctually, she knew not to turn her back on him. But she needed to get him out. Quickly.

"I didn't say you could come in here," she told him, gathering her nerve. "Who are you?"

"Uh, I'm, uh . . ." he tried to walk around her into the kitchen.

Rachel pushed him. "Wait. Where are you from?"

"I'm, I'm not from here," he said. Rachel noticed he looked nervous, jittery. "I'm from New Orleans."

Rachel did not take her eyes off him. She wanted to make sure she could remember his features if he tried something. But the man kept turning his head from side to side, as if he didn't want her to look him directly in the face.

"Well, who are you trying to reach?" she asked.

"I'm looking for a John Schmith," he said.

"Who?"

"John Schmith."

Rachel sensed he was lying. She had never heard of such a name and got the feeling he was making it up. But she did not want to let him see she was afraid. She kept her composure, giving him a stern warning.

"Sir, you're in my house without permission," she told him again. "I work for the state police. If you try anything stupid, I swear to God, I will kill you right here in my house."

Her threat did little to scare the man off. He seemed almost emboldened. And his nerves calmed, like he was more amused than bothered by her words.

"No, ma'am," he assured her. "I'd never do anything like that. No, Ma'am . . ."

But his words did not ease Rachel. Since he had walked inside, he had been looking around the home, down the hallway, as if casing the place to see if anyone else was home. His gaze stopped on several photos on the walls.

"You married? Have any children?" he asked her. "Who's that? Those pictures on the wall?"

Rachel didn't want to answer his questions. She was unmarried and lived alone. Rachel looked backward over her shoulder, pretending that someone was in the back.

"I can call someone who might be able to help you find him," Rachel said. She had no intention of giving him the phone. She would make the call. That's when she noticed the man had an erection. She knew then that he was not there to use her phone. She dialed the number for the Breaux Bridge police, ringing the line of a friend, Sergeant Aliene Dardar.

"Miss Aliene?"

"Hi, Rachel . . ." Dardar recognized Rachel's voice. "What is it?"

"Do you know a John Schmith?"

"No, Rach, who needs to know?"

"Well, um, someone's here, um, you know, at my house looking for a John Schmith . . ."

"No, Rach, I don't know who that is. I've never heard of him."

Rachel did not know how to reveal how terrified she was that an intruder was in her home, so she asked, "Well, do you have a unit around the area?"

The words jolted the man standing in her living room.

"Ma'am, ma'am . . . Never mind . . . That's OK . . . No problem . . . I'll find him . . ." And he dashed out of the house.

Rachel dropped the phone and bolted to the door in hopes of getting a license plate number, anything, but he was already speeding away. All she could see was the burgundy truck and possibly an extra tag, like a temporary tag, in the back window on the driver's side. She went back inside and told Aliene what had happened, and she asked for an officer to look for the truck.

A number of patrol cars responded, stopping every burgundy truck in Breaux Bridge for the next hour, but they did not find the man she described.

\*   \*   \*

While Diane's assault was a major case for Saint Martin, the crime got little attention in Baton Rouge, just a short drive east on Interstate 10 from Breaux Bridge. Her attempted rape and brutal beating did not light up on the big city police radar, which was overwhelmed at the time with the first throes of the serial killer investigation.

Then on July 29, Pam Kinamore's murder was linked, and the city was in full panic mode.

Saint Martin Parish Sheriff's investigators called Baton Rouge police about Diane's attack, but the Baton Rouge investigators were not interested in the case. Diane's attack, which she obviously survived, did not fit the Baton Rouge serial killer's style.

His victims were white and lived in Baton Rouge. Diane is black and lived fifty miles outside the city.

But more important was the color of his skin. A black man attacked Diane, and at the time, Baton Rouge police were receiving information that the serial killer was a white man.

# CHAPTER 13

# A Task Force Forms

According to the FBI, which defines such terms, a murderer officially becomes a serial killer when his victim count reaches three. With Pam's death, Baton Rouge officially joined the unfortunate ranks of Seattle, Gainesville, New York, and every other city inflicted with the terror of a faceless, merciless, unpredictable human hunter roaming its streets. And with a serial killer comes another serial killer requisite: a serial killer task force.

In late July 2002, the Baton Rouge public was clamoring for local authorities to bring in outside assistance for the case.

Lynne Marino was particularly vocal about the need to bring in experts with experience solving serial killer investigations. On August 1, she called Governor Foster's weekly radio show and urged greater cooperation between state and federal law enforcement agencies.

"I am asking you to call in all the agencies in the state to assist in searching for the killer," Marino said to the governor.

"We have a serial killer. We need to call in the FBI not just to do profiles but to aid us in this investigation."

As she pointed out, "Not many towns know how to deal with a serial killer."

A few days later, the Baton Rouge police chief announced the formation of the Multi-Agency Homicide Task Force. As its name indicates, the task force was made up of several law enforcement agencies.

The group, however, included all of the agencies already working together on the case, namely the Baton Rouge City Police, the East Baton Rouge Parish Sheriff's Office, the State Police and its crime lab, the FBI, the U.S. Attorney's Office, and the Baton Rouge District Attorney's Office.

But the coordinated effort was quickly expanded into one of the largest murder investigations in the state's history. A tip line was opened, daily press briefings were held—even if no new information was available—and the task force spokeswoman, Mary Ann Godawa, soon became a household name.

Almost every day, Godawa asked the public to look among their friends and acquaintances, their coworkers and neighbors, even their loved ones and relatives for signs of involvement in the murders—something they said, an unusual absence during the time of the murders, nervous behavior when the conversation turned to the serial killer.

"We feel there is someone out there who does know something and just hasn't called it in yet," she told the public at a late August briefing.

•

Finding a serial killer is one of the most difficult types of investigations for police because the victims are murdered randomly. Usually the killer does not know them nor does he have any connections to them.

Most murders have motives—financial gain, jealousy, anger—something that connects the victim to the killer. And in the majority of cases, the victim has personal ties with the murderer.

These motives and personal relationships help police link the crime to the criminal. If those connections do not exist, police lose an essential tool in their investigative basket. They have no good leads to whittle down a list of suspects.

In a serial killer case, every male in the region begins as a suspect. Nearly a quarter million males live in the Baton Rouge metropolitan area. Half of them are adults under sixty-five. Even if police slashed another 50 percent—an excessive number—as too old or infirm to commit murder, that still leaves an initial pool of 75,000 potential suspects around the city.

But what if the killer did not live in Baton Rouge? What if he was just passing through Baton Rouge occasionally? If that was the case, the number of potential suspects seemed limitless.

Investigators needed ways to narrow their suspect list. And at the onset, the task force found reason to eliminate nearly half the region's suspect pool based on an eyewitness account of a man who believed he saw the killer on the night Pam Kinamore disappeared.


At about three a.m. on July 13, a few hours after Pam was abducted from her home, a truck driver on Interstate 10 thought he was imagining things when he passed a white truck going westbound. They were cruising along at nearly eighty miles per hour while crossing through the Atchafalaya Swamp.

The trucker had not heard about the search for Pam—the story had yet to hit the news—but after a moment or two, the trucker was sure he was looking at a nude woman slumped in the truck's passenger seat.

The trucker had little time to make note of the truck and its driver through the darkness. Moments after he saw the strange image in the night, the white truck slowed down and exited at Whiskey Bay.

The trucker immediately dialed 911. Since he had crossed over into Iberville Parish, his call was patched through to that district's sheriff's office. He was then shuffled around to different police agencies, but his call never got to East Baton Rouge Parish, where they were searching for Pam.

The trucker was out of town for several days, but when he returned and heard about Pam's murder investigation, including where her body was dumped, he called Baton Rouge investigators.

It was their first big lead in the case. They had been hungry for it. After hearing his story, investigators were convinced he had seen Pam Kinamore and her killer. But he could not provide many details.

In an attempt to tap into his subconscious memory, police put the trucker under hypnosis, during which time he provided more information.

In a subsequent press release, police announced:

*On Saturday, July 13, 2002, at 3:00 AM, the night of Pam Kinamore's abduction, a motorist observed a pickup truck on I-10 that is now believed to have contained the victim. The motorist observed a white female in the cab of a pickup truck that was westbound on I-10 and exited at Whiskey Bay.*

*The driver of the pickup was a white male, thin to medium build.*

*The following is a description of the truck: 1996–1997 Chevrolet, bearing a Louisiana license plate. It had aging white surface paint, long wheel base, single cab, black rear bumper with bad paint job, fleet side body style, no tool box, smooth tailgate, tinted rear window, 2 headlights side by side, on each side of the truck, inside cab light located at top and center of rear window. Attached are photos of a similar truck as described above.*

The reaction was instantaneous. The public and police were relieved to know something about the killer, something to latch on to, a small bit of knowledge.

Then on September 3, the task force provided another requisite of serial killer investigations: the killer's psychological profile.[1] The task force had been promising the public for

---

[1] FBI Serial Killer Behavioral Profile, see Appendix A.

weeks that FBI agents were doing their magic, studying the case, examining the kill sites, the crime scene photos, the autopsy reports, and would soon provide that most intriguing and allegedly insightful part of a serial killer investigation: the predictions of the killer's behavior.

Anticipation was like that of a summer blockbuster release. When the task force released the FBI's report to the public, many in Baton Rouge rushed to get their own copies. Much of the profile information, however, was kept secret for police eyes only, but the released information was deemed important enough for the public to hear because it "will help the public help us," Englade said at a news conference.

Police especially urged people to look closely at a loved one, good friend, or family member they might already suspect, and ask themselves, *Does he fit the profile?* The FBI was confident the killer did not live in isolation. He had coworkers and possibly even a wife and family. Someone was close to him, someone had information that could help break the case.

"We realize how hard it would be to make that call on a loved one," spokeswoman Mary Ann Godawa said at a press conference. But that call might be the one to end the killer's reign.

In the report, FBI profilers said the killer was probably between twenty-five and thirty-five years old, but they stressed no suspect should be eliminated simply based on his age. They wanted the public to focus on his personality as they described it:

He is strong, capable of lifting at least 155 to 175 pounds. His power would be useful on his job, probably manual work that does not pay well. His finances would be tight, keeping him at an average to below-average level of the socioeconomic hierarchy of the Baton Rouge area.

Yet this man wants others to see him as attractive and appealing to women, particularly attractive, wealthy women from a higher class than him. His interactions with such women, however, would reveal his lack of sophistication, and he would appear awkward. If the women he approaches are nice to him out of sympathy or politeness, he likely misperceives it as mutual attraction. He might perceive more of a "relationship" with the women than what is there and brag about it to his male friends and coworkers.

In his free time, whether he's driving around or at a bar, he watches women, sometimes following them, perhaps even casually running into them in an attempt to get close to them or learn more about their habits and where they live. His watching and his need to watch take up so much of his time, those closest to him could not miss it. But he would rationalize his obsession by saying, "I just like women."

His low-key style, however, would not raise suspicion.

"He may come across to some women as a 'nice guy' who might have tried to get a little too close too soon, but otherwise is a non-threatening person," the profile says. "He may go out of his way to be helpful to women in an effort to get closer to them. This veneer of harmlessness is his shield of protection from suspicion."

He blends in, and even if he had an awkward encounter with a woman, she might not think to report him to police. If rejected, however, his temper could flare, and he would be determined to retaliate.

Before killing Gina, Murray, and Pam, he likely developed limited information about them, perhaps learning their routines and determining their living situation. The final decision to attack them, though, might have been impulsive.

Invading the victim's homes at times when people were in the vicinity or might return to the house to find him was high-risk behavior for the killer, indicating he probably enjoyed the heightened adrenaline rush of possibly being caught.

He is cool under pressure and has a propensity in other aspects of his life to engage in high-risk behavior. This makes him impulsive but not necessarily reckless. If determined to do something, however, he would pay no heed to the consequences. When he wanted something, he did not care what or who was trying to stop him. He would complete his mission.

One noticeable omission from the FBI's profile is an opinion on whether the killer was believed to be a white or black man. Yet when task force spokeswoman Mary Ann Godawa released the report, she told the media that the killer was white, and the FBI did not publically disagree. It was a mistake that would come back to haunt everyone.

# CHAPTER 14

# Murder One in Oak Shadows

With each ring of the phone, Tracy expected her mother to answer. It was Sunday night, August 23, 1992, and Connie Warner always stayed home on Sunday nights. Tracy imagined her mother sitting in the purple recliner, cross-stitch in hand, ready to watch her favorite television show, *Star Trek: The Next Generation*. Her mother never missed that show. But the rings at the house continued unanswered.

*Darn it.* Tracy thought as she hung up the phone. *Where is she?*

Tracy was at her freshman orientation for Louisiana State University in Baton Rouge. She wasn't ready to make the fifteen-minute drive home to Zachary. She knew her mother was expecting her, waiting anxiously to hear every detail of the weekend, but Tracy was reluctant to go home; she had a nagging sense to stay away from the little ranch house she shared with her mom.

"Mom's not answering," Tracy told her boyfriend, Andre Burgos, who attended the orientation with her. "I should probably go home."

Tracy and her mother were close. For five years, they lived at 1716 Job Avenue. Connie bought the three-bedroom home after twelve years of hoping and saving and surviving cohabitation with her parents. The house was perfect for the two of them—just a quick drive from Connie's parents and close to Tracy's high school.

Oak Shadows was a new subdivision on the outskirts of Zachary. The homes were modest but well built, attracting working families and single moms who could not afford the bigger houses in town. Connie, a dedicated Baptist, especially liked how the neighborhood streets were named after biblical characters, like Job and Saul and Leviticus.

Tracy remembered the day they got the keys to their new home. She had never seen her mother more thrilled or more eager to spend money. Connie couldn't start buying fast enough. She was like a new woman. They moved in on New Year's Eve, and by the first few days of 1988, the house was filled with a new refrigerator, washer, dryer, love seat, bedroom furniture, tables, curtains, and Connie's favorite accessory, a silk dogwood tree that she propped up behind the living room couch.

A lifetime of dreaming poured out into that 1,500 square feet. Until then, Connie's life had been little more than one disappointment after another. She had long ago settled into a dull routine of work, sleep, cooking, and cross-stitching.

Early on, Connie learned not to ask too much of life. She seemed to accept a place among the plain and overlooked, a background person, someone who never sought the spotlight. Even as a baby, she was so quiet, her parents sometimes forgot she was in the house. They could put her down for hours and not even hear a whimper. Through her school years, rather than playing outside with friends, she preferred to spend her afternoons alone reading in her room with the door closed.

Unlike her sisters and, later, her daughter, Connie never blossomed into her beauty. At five-foot-three and 130 pounds, she had a boxy figure, with big bones and fleshy limbs, which was not flattered by the simple, inexpensive clothes she wore.

She never fussed much with her hair either. For years, she kept it in the same unremarkable helmet of dishwater brown curls, a low-maintenance style that did nothing to slim her rounding face. Makeup might have brightened her green eyes or brought color to her fair skin, but Connie rarely bothered with the stuff.

Instead, she remained hidden behind her big round glasses with lenses as thick as ice sheets. Without them, she was nearly blind, able to see only vague, fuzzy shapes before her in a fog of gray.

Connie's attentions were more easily and happily focused on her daughter.

They had a rough start together. Tracy was born with severe allergies and a weakened immune system. She was hospitalized for three months and needed another eight of isolation. During the chaos of hospitals and doctors' visits, Connie's husband, Tracy's father, simply stepped out of the picture. Connie was broke and buried under mounting medical bills. Without a job or friends in an unfamiliar Virginia city, Connie had nowhere to go until her parents, Jack and Betty Brooks, called.

"Come home," they said. "Stay with us."

Connie did not like the idea of returning to her parents' home. She left Zachary after high school to attend a Baptist college in northern Louisiana and had never returned. She had fallen in love with another student, who impressed her with talk of preaching and commitment to family. She married before she finished her second year of school, and for the next several years, she went along with him as he skipped from one preaching program to the next, one big idea to the next, in towns throughout the South.

Soon she was praying for him to go back to school or settle down into a steady job. She was receiving money from her parents to help make ends meet, but moving home was something else. That hurt her pride.

"She was the kind of person who didn't like to ask a friend for the time of day," Betty Brooks said.

Connie agreed, reluctantly, but only for Tracy's sake. The little girl needed constant attention and medical help. Connie would be unable to work and support them without her parents' help. But she promised herself: *I will buy a home for us someday. As soon as I can afford it, Tracy and I will have a place of our own.*

Twelve years later, with savings from a meager state salary as an accounting assistant, Connie fulfilled her promise, and the next five years were the happiest in her life. She and Tracy bonded. Connie attended all of Tracy's sporting and after-school events. She was the mom who showed up first to set things up and stayed late to clean up. She had no social life of her own. She had given up dating years before. If she wasn't with Tracy or at work, she was usually at home, reading the latest science fiction novel or cross-stitching her Christmas presents in front of the TV. To Connie, however, it was a good life.

The drive toward Zachary did not erase Tracy's unease that waning August night. As she and Andre sped north on Louisiana Highway 19, through the long, dark stretches of the abandoned farmland separating Baton Rouge from Zachary, Tracy's thoughts flittered around a nightmarish scenario, an unwelcome idea that had been haunting her for months and rushed back in strength that night: *What would happen if Mom isn't there when I get home? What if she is just gone, forever?*

Tracy did not think of it as a premonition, not at the time anyway. All that summer, since her graduation from high school, Tracy was often visited, usually while she was driving home, by the same rude and frightening image: She walks into an empty home, her mother's presence erased from the world.

*That's ridiculous,* she'd laugh to herself, pushing the idea out of her mind. *That would never happen.*

Tracy blamed her nerves, some subconscious fears she might have about all the changes in her life, particularly leaving high school in small-town Zachary behind and starting college in the city. But she had been worried about her mother lately. She seemed so sad, even Tracy's friends noticed.

"You need to spend as much time as possible with your mom," they told Tracy. "She's afraid she's losing you."

Tracy planned to live at home while attending school, but

she and Connie both knew their lives were changing. Tracy was home less and less. She was busy with her friends and spending a lot more time with her boyfriend in Baton Rouge.

Even though school had not yet started, Connie was already missing her little girl. She missed cooking her dinner and laughing about Tracy's disastrous dates. She missed the shopping together and visits to McDonald's. She missed their nights in front of the TV, just the two of them, Tracy sitting at Connie's feet, trying to cross-stitch like her mom.

It's not that Connie wanted to hold her daughter down or keep her at home. Connie was thrilled when Tracy got a full academic scholarship to LSU. She strictly encouraged her daughter's education. Connie hadn't earned her degree until late in life and she was painfully aware of how that had held her back. She didn't want Tracy to face the same fate.

Connie wanted nothing more than to give Tracy the freedom to explore all opportunities. She refused to let Tracy work during high school not only to make sure she stayed focused on her studies, but also so the teenager could enjoy her free time and youth.

"You'll be working the rest of your life," Connie told her daughter. "Have fun now."

But the idea of Tracy growing up and moving on, as much as she wanted her daughter to become independent and self-sufficient, was also difficult for Connie. She had lived for Tracy for so many years. She scheduled her days and life around her daughter. Everything she worked for, her reason for getting up in the morning was Tracy, and soon, she knew, Tracy would no longer need her. She would be gone.

Maybe that's why she picked the picture she was cross-stitching that night: A woman staring at herself in the mirror. Maybe she was trying to look at herself, too, find new meaning in her life, discover who she would become in the near future.

The lights were on at the house when Tracy parked in the carport next to her mom's maroon Chevrolet. She took her time gathering things out of the car: her overnight bag, all the pamphlets and flyers she picked up during orientation, her purse.

She was in no hurry to go inside. She wished she didn't have to. She wanted to go anywhere but there.

She remembered what her mom had said about taking her high school parking sticker off her car before parking at the LSU lot. Local rivalries. Someone from another high school might see it and scratch her car. Unlikely, but it could happen, so Tracy spent several minutes scraping her Zachary High sticker off her back window. When that was done, she loaded herself up with her things, locked her doors, and headed toward the house. As she walked around her mom's car, she saw the other Zachary High sticker. *I should get that one, too,* she thought. Anything to not go inside yet. She walked toward her mother's car door, but then changed her mind. *I'll do it later . . .*

The first thing Tracy noticed when she went inside was the television. The volume was at full blast. She walked into the living room and turned it down.

"Mom," she called out. "I'm home."

No answer.

"Mom?" Tracy walked into the living room. Her mom's cross-stitch was on the floor in front of her purple recliner, the same place she always placed it if she was just getting up for a glass of water or to answer the phone or see who was at the door. Connie never left it out if she planned to leave the house.

Tracy walked toward her mom's bedroom, expecting her mother to be in the bathroom.

"Mom . . ."

Tracy saw the bathroom door was open, but the room was empty. Connie was not in the house.

Tracy knew it was strange. Connie always let Tracy know if she was not going to be home. Tracy thought perhaps her mother had gone to visit a neighbor, even though Tracy knew she was not the visiting type. The clock was about to strike nine, though, and Tracy was sure her mom would walk through the front door any minute for *Star Trek*.

But when nine o'clock came and went without her mother's appearance, Tracy began to worry. She called her grandparents' house but got no answer. Maybe her mom had gone with them to visit Connie's sister, Carolyn.

Carolyn and her husband own Greenwood Plantation, the towering white Greek revivalist plantation home in Saint Francisville. Connie often worked at the home giving tours.

"Is Connie with y'all?" Tracy asked Carolyn over the phone.

"No, isn't she at home?"

Jack and Betty Brooks had just left Carolyn's house, so Tracy waited a few minutes before trying them at home again. The drive from Saint Francisville takes about fifteen minutes.

"Do you know where Mom is?" Tracy tried not to sound concerned when she reached her grandfather. "She's not home."

Jack Brooks didn't need to hear any more. His daughter was too predictable, her habits were too routine for her to be gone this late without telling someone. He was already in his pajamas when Tracy called, but he was dressed and out the door in seconds.


When Jack Brooks arrived at his daughter's house, he walked through, looking for any sign, a note, anything of where Connie might have gone. What he saw as soon as he walked into her bedroom, however, terrified him.

In Connie's bedroom, on her bed that she never left unmade, the sheets were tangled up as if she had rolled and thrashed frantically on top of them. The mattress had slid off the box springs' base. A pair of pink pants were on the floor, stained with blood. Connie's thick eyeglasses, the ones she couldn't see without, had fallen to the carpet. Her second pair of glasses, which she kept by the bed, were still on the nightstand. He knew she could not have gone far, and certainly not on her own, without them.

He walked over to the nightstand. The drawer was pulled open. Inside was Connie's can of mace. *Oh God, she must have been trying to reach it,* he thought.

Jack called his wife.

"Betty, you need to come over here as quick as you can," he said. "Something's not right. I'm calling the police."

* * *

Zachary Police Officer Lawrence "Butch" Kling was one of the first officers to arrive at Connie's house. His colleague, Officer David Courtney, was already there talking with Jack.

Jack led the officers inside, through the carport door and into the utility room off Connie's kitchen. Kling noticed the washer and dryer were shoved against the wall and on the floor were three drops of blood. Nearby, a section of a belt Connie liked to wear was just inside the door. It looked like it had been cut.

The officers searched the house, looking in closets and under the beds. When they went back outside to the carport, they found three lavender buttons from Connie's shirt on the cement floor and noticed that the dust on the passenger side of Connie's car looked as if it was brushed off as if someone had slid against the side of the car.

When they opened the car door, they were hit by a raw smell. A pile of vomit was found on the backseat floorboards. Kling knew that a blow to the head, a concussion, can provoke vomiting. He looked at Courtney. They needed to look in the trunk.

But Connie's keys were missing. After a few minutes of searching, Jack returned with an extra set. He handed them to Courtney, who went to the back of Connie's car. Courtney hesitated a moment after he stuck the key into the trunk's lock. Kling could feel his chest tighten while he stood nearby and watched Courtney turn the key.

The trunk was empty.


The idea that a forty-one-year-old single mother was abducted violently from her home in one of Zachary's safest neighborhoods was mind boggling to the police. That didn't happen in their little town. People got killed in Zachary, but usually on the outskirts in the roadside bars or trailer parks during an argument or drunken brawl. The person responsible was usually still on the scene when police arrived, or was not hard to find because of the number of witnesses. Such cases usually fell under manslaughter charges and often ended with a guilty plea.

The police force in Zachary did not see many murders in

the first degree. They did not have experience in complicated crime scene investigations. In fact, the force only had two detectives at the time, and neither had any homicide training. Connie's case was a learning experience, and unfortunately the investigators were starting at the bottom of the learning curve.

Kling and Courtney knew enough to send Connie's car to the state crime lab, but little else was done to collect evidence that night. When they handed the scene over to the detectives, they simply went back to the police station to file a missing person report about Connie.

Meanwhile, a swarm of other police officers and fire department officials and Connie's family members and friends gathered inside her home. Tracy made coffee in the kitchen for the crowd, some of whom were lounging on the furniture and walking throughout the house.

Little effort was made to search the neighborhood and surrounding fields for Connie that night. Unable to sit still, Jack led his own walk-through of the empty lots near Connie's house. He urged police to go with him to look inside a vacant home that was a block over. The house was locked, and police did not get a warrant to go inside, so Jack peered in through the windows. He called out for Connie. But he saw only a still and quiet darkness inside.

Jack's mind was racing. *Where could she be? Who could have done this? How did it happen?*

Her attacker had left no signs of a forced entry, nor was anything of value stolen. The only things missing were her keys and a kitchen knife from a set of four. Jack knew Connie usually kept her doors locked. She was mistrusting of strangers. She wasn't the type to open her door to someone she didn't know.

*Maybe she knew him,* Jack thought. *But who could possibly want to hurt Connie?* She didn't have any enemies, not that he knew. She barely had any friends.

As the night passed into the early morning hours without Connie's return, any doubts about the circumstances of her disappearance faded. She was not at the store or at a friend's house and forgot to tell anyone. She was gone. Snatched from the home she loved so dearly. Her family was waking up to a nightmare. They returned to the Brooks home a few miles away and waited for the phone to ring. No one slept.

As the days wore on with few new leads and no obvious motives for her disappearance, the focus of the investigation intensified on Connie's family, particularly Tracy and her boyfriend, Andre.

The two teenagers' stories did not match up when they were questioned separately. Although Tracy told her mother and then the police that she was staying with a girlfriend in Baton Rouge that weekend, Andre admitted Tracy had stayed with him at his mother's home. Further questioning of Connie's family members revealed ongoing and heated conflicts between Tracy and her mother. Police quickly learned Connie was not fond of Andre, who had dropped out of high school and possessed a quick and furious temper. Connie had tried to convince Tracy to attend college out of state so she would not live near Andre. But the teenagers were determined to stay together.

Without another good explanation for Connie's disappearance, police theorized the young, passionate couple had done away with Connie for insurance money. The idea was laughable. Tracy and Andre were unaware that Connie even had a life insurance policy. What's more, Connie had named her parents as the beneficiaries, not Tracy.

But the police were stuck on Andre. They didn't like his attitude. The first night Connie disappeared, he was at her house talking tough with town officials. They didn't like his accusatory tone.

"Are all these extra sightseers necessary?" Andre asked, wondering why so many volunteer firefighters were in the house sipping coffee. "There's no fire here."

A few days later, when police called Andre in to the department for questioning, he was arrogant and argumentative. He was impatient with their interrogation, frustrated by the line of their questioning: Where were you on Saturday night? Who were you with? What time?

To Andre, the questions were pointless. He had more important information he wanted to discuss.

"Y'all need to look for this black guy I saw watching her house . . ." Andre told the police. "I can give you a description . . ."

The interrogators were not interested, at least not enough

to get a sketch and investigate Andre's account. They wanted Andre to answer questions, not deflect the focus onto another suspect. Whatever notes were taken about the black man Andre told police he saw before Connie's disappearance simply fell through the cracks of the investigation. But Andre never forgot him.

Less than two weeks before Connie disappeared, Andre was on his way to pick Tracy up at her home sometime in the afternoon. He turned onto Job Avenue, a street of only a few blocks, and noticed a black man standing at the end of the street across from Tracy and Connie's house.

Andre could not see the man well, only enough to know the man was looking in his direction as he pulled in front of Connie's house. Andre, who grew up in a tough neighborhood, always looking over his shoulder, had learned to read people as friend or foe from a distance, and this guy didn't look right. He looked out of place. He was sort of pacing, with his hands in his pockets. He wasn't walking through the neighborhood or waiting on a porch for someone. He was not near a car or a bike. He was just standing on the sidewalk, in between two houses, and seemed to be staring toward Connie's house.

When Andre got out of his car to go inside, the man appeared to be looking in his direction but quickly looked away when Andre looked up at him. He was gone when Andre and Tracy came out of the house a few minutes later.

A day or two later, Andre saw the man again, around the same time, between three p.m. and five p.m., in the same spot, sort of catty-corner from Connie's house. As before, the man was dressed in jeans and a T-shirt and staring in the direction of Connie's house.

*That's odd,* Andre thought, wondering what to make of this man. He did not recognize him as one of Connie's neighbors.

While Andre was looking down the street at him, a small kid, a white child, leaning precariously off a toy scooter, pedaled in front of the man. As the boy got close, the man reached down as if he was playing with the boy, straightened him on the toy, and gave him a little push on his way down the road.

Andre did not see any other adults around and still thought the man's presence seemed strange, but he shrugged it off.

He was not so calm when he saw the same man again a few days later, just a week before Connie disappeared. Again, he was across from Connie's home, looking as if he had no reason to be there.

Instead of pulling into the driveway, Andre stopped near the man to get a good look.

"He kind of gave me a dirty look," Andre recalls. "He was kind of staring me down."

Andre's quick temper flared. He put his car in Park and got out.

"Hey!" Andre called to the man, ready for a confrontation. "What's the deal? You got a problem?"

The man seemed startled, surprised almost that Andre had stepped out of his car. He looked down and, mumbling what sounded like a few choice curse words, quickly walked off.

Andre was furious from the encounter. He was bothered that the man had simply walked off without explaining himself. Andre went inside Connie's house still fuming.

"Did you see that black guy standing outside?" Andre demanded of Connie and Tracy. "Do you know that guy?"

Connie and Tracy had not seen the man, at least not that they could remember.

"I don't know who this guy is or what he's up to," Andre told them, "but be careful. He could be scoping out the house."

Andre's worst thought was that the man wanted to burglarize the place. After Connie disappeared, Andre began to believe the man was planning something far more sinister.


In the days after Connie disappeared, police were having little luck on finding clues to her whereabouts. The only phone calls the Brooks family got at their house that first week were offers of help. Strangers brought by casseroles. Minor acquaintances posted fliers around town. The mayor promised all of the city's resources would be used to solve the case.

Jack, however, quickly tired of sitting by the phone for news. He had just retired in 1991, and he needed to do more than wait for police to find Connie. Every day, he took long drives, sometimes with his sons-in-law, through the back-country surrounding Zachary, conducting a morbid search, his eyes scanning the roadside ditches and grassy fields. At bridges, he pulled the car over, got out, and peered under-neath. He stopped at culverts and alongside creeks. He wasn't sure if he really wanted to be the one who found her, but he had to do something.

The news of Connie's abduction was on the television every night, but her story began to lose prominence after a few days. Hurricane Andrew had just destroyed parts of Miami and was on its way to Louisiana.

By August 29, the storm was bearing down on southern Louisiana, and the Baton Rouge region was swamped under two days of heavy rain. If Connie was dead, Jack wondered if police would ever find her body after the waters receded.

But on September 2, a truck driver in Baton Rouge made a gruesome discovery when he pulled over to the side of the road to check his wheels. He was parked in front of the JE Merit property on Sorrell Street, a mostly deserted industrial area in northern Baton Rouge.

When he stepped out of his cab, he noticed the stench. Then he saw the body. She was so badly decomposed, she looked like a mummy, curled up in a grassy area several feet from to the road. Her blouse was up around her neck, expos-ing her panties. She did not have on a bra, which was consis-tent with Connie's habits. When at home, she often puttered around in nothing but a large shirt and her underpants.

The autopsy revealed she suffered three powerful blows to the top of her head, possibly from a hammer. One of the frac-tures cracked her skull across the top almost from ear to ear. Another blow left a half-dollar-sized hole in the right side of her skull.

Near her body police found a pair of pants, which were taken into evidence by the Baton Rouge Police Department. Since Connie was found within the Baton Rouge city limits, her murder became a shared case between the city department and Zachary.

Detectives focused on Andre for months, but after he passed a polygraph, the investigation shifted to a man Connie had tutored for years. When he was questioned, he stammered and sweated, and finally clammed up and hired a lawyer.

Without quality evidence—the crime scene was contaminated and poorly worked—the case seemed to be going nowhere. The only good information police discerned was a neighbor's sighting of a shadowy figure walking out of Connie's carport on the night she disappeared.

Under hypnosis, the neighbor described seeing a man carrying something large in the crook of his arms and putting it into a dark-colored sedan. The man then covered up the object with a blanket and drove away. The woman did not get a good look at the man, however, because the streetlight overhead was flickering on and off as he disappeared into the night.

# CHAPTER 15

# On the Books in Zachary

The Zachary police first learned Derrick Todd Lee's name just after midnight on November 21, 1992.

In the town's quiet country club subdivision of Fenwood Hills, Ron Benge pulled into the driveway of his home at 1434 Eagle Drive. He planned to drop his teenage daughter off and go back out, but as the lights of his car swept across his yard, he saw an unfamiliar ten-speed bicycle on the ground and the home's side door ajar.

He was not expecting his son home from college that weekend, but that was the only explanation he could come up with for the open door. Crime was almost nonexistent in Fenwood Hills. People left their cars unlocked and belongings unattended in their yards. What's more, Ron was certain he had locked the house before he left earlier that evening.

He put his car in Park and went inside ahead of his daughter, calling out to his son. He walked into the kitchen and through the living room, where he noticed the back door was also open. He moved into the hallway but stopped short. A stranger, a tall black man in a blue police-style jacket, was walking out of his son's room, as cool as the dew, acting as if he belonged in the house.

"What are you doing in here?" Ron demanded, ready to run. Ron had never seen the man before.

"I'm looking for Monroe," the man said, his voice calm, almost friendly as he walked toward Ron with an out-stretched hand.

Ron was not interested in shaking the stranger's hand.

"No Monroe lives here," he said, backing up.

"Oh, I'm sorry . . ." The stranger tried to act as if he had done nothing wrong, like his presence in the home was an in-nocent mistake.

Ron was not buying it. "Call 911," he yelled to his daugh-ter, who was still in the kitchen.

"I'm not trying to break into your house or anything . . ." the man said, his tone turning defensive as he hurried toward the door.

Ron was not going to stop him. He just wanted the guy to leave, which he did, quickly.

The man hopped on the bike and, pedaling fast across the grassy lawns toward Highway 964, he disappeared into the night.

Zachary police got the report as a burglary in progress. Sev-eral patrol cars sped toward Fenwood Hills. Benge's home was just a few blocks in from the subdivision entrance off Highway 964.

En route, two officers spotted a black man wearing a blue jacket standing in the Azalea Cemetery across the highway from the Fenwood Hills subdivision. As they watched, the man jumped in a maroon Buick Electra 225 and sped off, leaving the same light blue girl's ten-speed on the ground that Ron had seen just minutes ago on his front lawn.

The Buick headed north on Highway 964, accelerating up to ninety-five miles per hour and ignoring the police sirens and lights chasing behind. As they raced up the two-lane rural highway, farm fields flying by in the pitch-black of night, the officers saw the blue jacket come flying out of the driver's side window.

Another officer waiting for him two miles up the road pulled into the roadway as he heard the sirens coming, forcing the Buick to slow down.

With his police lights and sirens blaring, Officer Darryl Lawrence pulled close behind the Buick, which then came to a stop.

"Step out of the vehicle!" Lawrence shouted at the driver. "With your hands up."

The man complied.

"License and registration . . ."

The man said he did not have it on him, but he identified himself as Derrick Lee.

Lawrence advised Derrick of his rights, then slapped cuffs on him and placed him in the backseat of the patrol car. The next stop was Ron Benge's house.

"That's him," Benge told police.

Derrick was charged with simple burglary and resisting arrest, not a major crime in the big scheme of things. To Zachary police, Derrick was just another small-time criminal.

No one suspected the petty burglar might have been involved in Connie Warner's murder just three months earlier in Oak Shadows, which is a short walk across Highway 964 from Fenwood Hills.

Even the fact that Derrick was caught driving a similar car—a maroon Buick—as the one seen outside Connie's home the night of her abduction did not spark a second look at him as a murder suspect.

The Benge burglary case was open and shut, no more investigation needed. An easy night's work for police. Derrick Todd Lee was caught almost red-handed. He was identified by the victim. No further questions required. Process him through the court system. End of story.

It was the kind of criminal case that most defense lawyers would recommend taking whatever plea bargain the district attorney might offer.

Derrick, however, was not a typical defendant. Even with irrefutable evidence of his crime, Derrick wanted his day in court. He wanted a chance to convince a jury he was innocent.

His trial took place on May 11, 1993, and against his lawyer's recommendation, Derrick took the stand in his own defense. He insisted he was only looking for a friend inside the Benge home, that his presence was an honest mistake.

He was charming. Well-dressed. Sitting in court, he looked like a nice, clean-cut, honest guy. He was far from a rough-edged criminal type. He seemed personable and polite. Behind him in the courtroom audience, sat his wife and two small children. He had a son and daughter now. They appeared to be a decent, law-abiding young family.

When Derrick testified, detailing an elaborate story about looking for his friend Monroe, he looked straight at the jurors, projecting a sincere face—something he'd been practicing his whole life.

Mary Durusau was the foreperson on the jury. She had spent years as a court reporter for a Shreveport, Louisiana, newspaper, and she had seen dozens of defendants testify, but none this good. He was an ace con man.

"He told us an elaborate story," Durusau recalled. "He was looking for this guy, Monroe, that he supposedly met earlier in the day, he wasn't sure where he lived, couldn't tell us his last name. It was just layer on layer on layer of lies."

Then Derrick launched into the story of his life, how he was a father and a family man and held down a difficult job.

"He told some wild cockamamie tale about being the operator of machinery that heated up to a bazillion degrees," Durusau said. "He was just rambling. He was trying to say, 'I'm a good person, why would I be out doing this?' He really wanted us to like him."

When the jury began deliberations, Derrick's charm nearly won over a few softhearted jurors. One woman felt they should not convict Derrick simply because he would be taken from his family.

In the end, however, more rational heads prevailed, and Derrick was convicted as charged. Derrick was angry. Behind him, Jackie started to cry. They knew he could not get out of this one without jail time. He was sentenced to four years.

For so many years, Derrick's crimes were met with forgiveness and plea bargains in West Feliciana Parish. Just that January, while he awaited trial for the Zachary charge, he had been arrested in Saint Francisville for breaking into an elderly man's trailer near his mother's house. He and a friend barged in through the front door and threatened the seventy-four-year-old man, Melvin Foster, who told them to take his few measly bucks. They could have just run away afterward, but Derrick decided to beat the old man bloody with a stick. Yet the charges were not pursued by prosecutors. By luck, ignorance, or apathy, Derrick continued to escape punishment and repercussions for his increasingly violent crimes.

# CHAPTER 16

# Like Something Out of a Horror Movie

At the crossroads of two rural highways on the outskirts of Zachary, five cemeteries sit side by side under a canopy of ancient oaks. At night, the curtains of Spanish moss dripping from the trees' gnarled branches block out all but the thinnest slivers of moonlight. Among the crumbling tombstones is one for Alice Taylor, a beautiful young bride who died young and broke her husband's heart, inspiring a long-lived ghost story.

As town legend goes, Alice was a witch, and she still haunts the grounds every Halloween night. For years, local teens dared each other to sleep on her grave, and one year, they broke into her tomb, pulled out her crumbling skeleton, and made off with one of her pinky finger bones.

Mostly, though, Alice's grave became the gathering spot for late-night teenage rites of underage drinking, marijuana smoking, and awkward first-time sexual encounters in the backseats of their parents' cars.

On Saturday night, just before midnight, April 3, 1993,

eighteen-year-old Ricky Davis and his fifteen-year-old girl-friend Michele Chapman braved the dark and a booming thunderstorm to park deep inside Buhler Plains Cemetery, just yards away from Alice's grave.

The rain beat down on Ricky's 1992 Toyota Corolla as they climbed into the backseat. As the lightning flashed between the rolls of thunder, their kissing progressed to disrobing. They had but one or two garments left to unload when the left rear door of the car suddenly jerked open.

Michele looked up as a black man, his dark clothes dripping from the rain and his eyes wild with fury, leaned into the backseat, clutching a six-foot-long cane knife. Without a word, the man began hacking at them with the rusted metal blade, swinging it up and down, hitting the car ceiling, then slicing into Ricky's head and arms and torso as the teenager struggled to move between the knife and Michele.

Each blow struck deep. Ricky's skull was cracked open, and bone fragments shattered into his brain. An artery was sliced in his neck. When he tried to grab the ax, his hands wrapped around the blade, severing tendons in his hands and nearly slicing off his thumb. Michele, too, was sliced along her arms and legs.

Their screams echoed through the empty cemetery. Then, just as suddenly as he appeared, he was gone.

A set of headlights shined into the back window of their car.


Officer Troy Eubanks had been out patrolling that night, just riding the streets. He was traveling north on Old Scenic Highway, along the perimeter of the cemeteries when he happened to see a light at the back of the Buhler Plains Cemetery.

Through the rain, he could not tell what it was, but he guessed it was the dome light of a car.

"Kids," he thought. He had busted teenagers having sex near Alice's grave before.

Eubanks turned his patrol car through the wrought-iron entrance gate and, seeing that it was a car parked at the back of the grounds, he rolled slowly toward it. As he pulled in behind the car, he pointed his spotlight at the Toyota's rear window.

He saw two teenagers, half naked, huddled together. But

when he noticed their bodies were smeared with red liquid, he immediately assumed they were pulling a prank, fooling around with fake blood or ketchup.

He got out of his car and walked toward the Toyota. He tried the back door, but it was locked.

Come on . . . he thought. Game's over. He knocked hard on the window.

The girl recoiled from the door, screaming, "It's him! It's him! He's back!"

From the terror on Michele's face, Eubanks quickly realized this was no joke.

"What the hell?" he shouted. He shined his flashlight on his uniform, so the couple could see his badge. "It's OK. I'm a police officer. Open the door."

Ricky reached across Michele and unlocked the door. When Eubanks opened it, he saw blood everywhere. The teens were drenched in blood, and the backseat was soaking wet with it. Eubanks felt as if he had stumbled onto the set of a horror film. He immediately called for ambulances. He had never seen anything like this in Zachary.

He was even more stunned when Michele told him what had happened, how a black man had suddenly attacked them unprovoked with a six-foot bladed harvesting tool.

Eubanks had seen no one on foot when he drove into the cemetery, but he and another officer searched the area. With the rain and the drenched, muddy grounds, they were unable to find footprints. The man had vanished.

Additional emergency crews were unable to help further the search that night because just about the time Eubanks found the couple at 12:05 a.m., lightning struck the steeple at the church across Old Scenic Highway from the cemetery igniting a five-alarm fire that decimated the old building.

If the man who attacked Ricky and Michele was still in the area, he would have had hours to escape town unnoticed.

"He picked a damn good night to do it," Eubanks said.


Detective Bruce Chaisson was assigned the case, and the next morning he and several other officers returned to the cemetery to look for evidence. They found nothing but old beer cans and liquor bottles where the teens were parked. But as they walked in the direction of where the suspect ran, investigators could see someone had cleared the chest-high weeds in a path toward a pond beyond the cemetery borders. In the path was a six-foot-long, wooden-handled bush ax. On its end was a thick, eighteen-inch machete blade. They had found their weapon. A few more feet down the path, at the pond's edge, were two fishing poles and a lambskin car seat.

When Chaisson spoke with the property's owner, he said he did not allow anyone to fish at the pond. Whoever had done so was quiet about it.

Chaisson took the items back to the station as evidence, but he hoped to get more information from Michele and Ricky, who had suffered severe injuries.

Ricky was in surgery for eight hours, as the doctors tried to stop the bleeding from his arteries and sew together his wounds. He was in the hospital for several months. For weeks, he was covered in bandages and casts and required several subsequent surgeries. When he was coherent enough for police to interview him, he was unable to provide a description of his attacker.

He did not get a good look at the man's face, only the back of his head as he ran away. But detectives thought he was hiding something. They suspected the attack might be drug-related because no one had ever seen such a random attack in friendly little Zachary.

Detectives did not push Ricky for more answers. They could see the teen was traumatized. Years later, he still sleeps with the lights on and obsessively checks the locks on his doors.

When detectives visited with Michele, she agreed to look at a photo lineup. She had already provided the description of a black male, in his mid-twenties, medium build, and wearing dark clothing. Officers thought her description was uncomfortably close to a description of Troy Eubanks. In the hysteria from the attack, she could be confused about the looks of the man who attacked her.

To check their concerns, investigators put a picture of Eubanks in the lineup. Michele selected him, unaware that she was pointing out a police officer. With such a problematic identification, the detectives knew the case would be hard to prosecute.

For the next several years, the investigation languished and got cold. The detectives assigned to it were transferred to different jobs, and the case got passed off to new officers.

In the first weeks after the attack, police assured Michele and Ricky and their families that the man would be caught, but as time passed, everyone began to lose hope. By the end of the year, the case fell into the purgatory of criminal investigations, another unsolved mystery for the tiny town of Zachary.

# CHAPTER 17

# A Task Force Treadmill

In the summer of 2002, few men in the city of Baton Rouge escaped at least a moment of suspicion—from their neighbors, coworkers, workout partners, wives and girlfriends, or strangers. When the task force set up its tip line, the phones rarely stopped ringing. No one realized how many weird, dangerous, and threatening men lived in southern Louisiana. And suddenly, they were all suspects. The first few weeks of the investigation, the tip line fielded more than 3,500 calls.

The volume of tips was so overwhelming, the task force subcontracted the job out to a local answering service, Answer Quick. The Baton Rouge firm's employees were not police officers, but they were trained to collect as much information as possible about the tip: a name, car make and model, license plate, suspicious activity, criminal record, etc. The tips were then typed and e-mailed to the task force command center at the city's Office of Emergency Preparedness, which received the information almost instantly.

Right away, authorities realized they needed a system to keep the information organized and prioritized and ensure work was not duplicated, so the task force set up a conveyor belt for data processing.

At the beginning was the tip. When the e-mail from the tip line arrived at the command center, one of several police officers assigned as screeners reviewed the information and determined if it was worth further investigation.     •

Unfortunately, a large number of tips were useless because the caller did not provide information that could facilitate a follow-up. The tip would describe a vague story of a white male with a scruffy beard and a creepy stare following a woman around a Wal-Mart without additional information, nothing about the car he drove, the color of his hair, or anything identifiable about the suspicious man.

For obvious reasons these types of tips garnered low priority, and most were simply entered into a task force database of tips and possible suspects.

The tips with names and traceable information, however, were taken more seriously.

After the screener made a recommendation whether or not to pass on a tip to a detective, the report was reviewed by a supervisor, who could agree or disagree. Regardless of the supervisor's decision, the tip then proceeded to data entry, where the information was typed into the database. If a follow-up was approved, the tip was then assigned to one of three teams of detectives covering different areas of the metropolitan area. The team leader would then assign the lead to a detective, who was responsible for tracking down the suspect and trying to either clear him or bust him and then report back to the team leader about the disposition of the lead.

The detectives never got to the bottom of their suspect piles. They carried dozens of leads at a time, and the work was nonstop. Investigators put in sixty, seventy, or more hours a week tracking down the city's most bizarre people as well as a large number of seemingly harmless types. Their goal was to eliminate suspects as quickly as possible and move on to the next potential suspect.

A suspect could clear himself in several ways: documenting that at the time of one of the murders he was in jail, out of town, or at work. Black men were also instantly cleared. As a policy, the task force had decided to narrow their suspects to white men. They did so based on a witness who reported—under hypnosis—that he saw a white man driving a white truck near Whiskey Bay with a nude woman slumped in the front seat the night of Pam's disappearance. But most definitively, an innocent suspect could rid himself of the cops if he opened his mouth for a twirl of the cotton swab and a DNA test.

Investigators collected hundreds of DNA swabs in the first few months.

The State Police Crime Lab tried to handle all the testing, but the cost for each analysis was $900, and with only four analysts on staff, a long backlog gridlocked the process. Hundreds of swabs from suspects sat on the crime lab shelves for months waiting to be tested.

What's more, hundreds of rape kits from past crimes dating back decades also sat on the shelves untested, many of them pushed to the end of the line because the serial killer case took priority. One of those kits, however, perhaps one with a living victim who could describe her attacker's face or other useful details, might contain the serial killer's DNA.

Ultimately, several months into the investigation, the crime lab began outsourcing tests of the swabs, making the job cheaper and faster, so cheap and fast that it became more efficient for investigators to simply ask a suspect for his DNA rather than spend the time trying to track down his alibi.

This is a new shortcut in police investigative work that has been ushered in by the forensic use of DNA—and not always for the good. Overworked and underpaid, a detective's goal in the job is to get solid, court-proof evidence linking his suspect to the crime in the fastest, least labor-intensive way possible. DNA is about as solid as it gets. If DNA evidence from a bloody knife found at the scene of a murder will identify the killer, why waste precious investigative hours rooting around in the possible suspect's garbage? This shortcut can create a tendency in some detectives to neglect old-fashioned legwork that is often needed to solve crimes. And sometimes that neglect leads to important missed clues and investigative opportunities.

In Baton Rouge and environs that summer and fall of 2002,

police asked more than 1,200 white males for a cotton swab of their mouths, a procedure that collects both saliva and skin cells containing DNA. Most men cooperated to clear their names, requiring little additional police work. But a few men refused, sending red flags up for investigators and rallying the police troops.

"When we had a refusal, we took that very seriously," task force investigator Detective David Smith testified later. "We would stop whatever we were doing. That entire team [of detectives] would be dedicated to resolving that lead in one way or the other."

Police watched the suspect until they could learn more about his whereabouts during the murders. Sometimes, they simply followed the suspect around until he dropped a cigarette butt or threw away a coffee cup or soda can he had been sipping, anything that might carry his DNA.

There were also strong-arm tactics and, on rare occasions, the police obtained a court order.

One Baton Rouge man, Floyd Wagster, was handcuffed— but not arrested—by East Baton Rouge sheriff's officers and hauled into the police station after refusing to give his DNA. Investigators ignored Wagster's repeated requests for an attorney and threatened to put him in jail if he did not submit to the swab.

Secretly, Wagster, who was on probation for marijuana possession, recorded the conversation with one of the investigators, Major Bud Connor.

"You gonna give DNA," Connor said. "We're gonna go get a court order to get it from you. How you want to handle that? You want the court order? Fine with me. I'll light your ass up on the fucking news."

Connor was not bluffing. When another Baton Rouge man refused to provide his DNA, police filed a warrant to obtain it by court order.

Investigators had received two tips suggesting police check out Shannon F. Kohler, a forty-four-year-old welder with a twenty-year-old burglary conviction. Kohler denied involvement in the serial killings, but he refused to provide his DNA on principle.

He believed investigators were conducting an irresponsible dragnet, bullying and harassing innocent people along the way.

"The threats weren't direct, they were just implicit," Kohler told the *Advocate*. "They mentioned that, well, these aren't public records, but if we have to get a court order, that's going to be public record, and who knows what could happen then."

Faced with Kohler's continued refusal to give up his DNA, investigators did request the court order. Instead of filing the warrant under seal, however, as they had been doing with other documents in the case, investigators filed Kohler's warrant without a seal.

Within days, his name was all over the papers and television news. Kohler's public outing made refusing a DNA swab a potentially humiliating and damaging decision even for the innocent.

The task force came under intense criticism for what skirted the edge of coercion. Granted, why should an innocent man impede the serial killer investigation by refusing to cooperate and submit to a swab? But the problem was not the innocent making trouble for police, it was the possibility that police were making trouble for themselves.

Lawyers and law enforcement officials worried about the legal ramifications at trial if police coerced the serial killer to submit to the swab that cinched his arrest. Evidence or information given by a suspect under coercion or duress can be thrown out of court as illegally obtained. Theoretically, if the serial killer gave up his DNA under police threats, defense lawyers would have a strong argument to declare the DNA evidence—the best evidence in the case—inadmissible.

But investigators were willing to take that risk. And everyone knew no judge in Louisiana, where the judiciary is elected and politics often wiggle around the law, would let a serial killer out of jail based on a technicality.

So the swabbing continued unabated.

Still the case garnered more detectives than any other investigation in state history.

More than 24,000 white trucks were registered in Louisiana, and detectives were ordered to track down all of the owners and drivers. Officers from all divisions of the task force agencies were pulled into the case. The East Baton Rouge Parish Sheriff's Office dedicated fifteen detectives from the narcotics division alone.

No matter how many officers they put on the case, no matter how much time they invested, all the leads led to dead ends. Even the ones that lookcd so good detectives could feel it in their bones that they had the killer. Then his DNA would clear his name.

Eventually, the database of tips and suspects grew so large—more than 10,000 leads—the task force had to upgrade to a more powerful computer system.

With all the legwork and man-hours, however, investigators remained confident they needed to catch just one lucky break, hear from that one person who could lead them to the serial killer.

But a tip does no good when police are looking in the wrong direction.

On September 4, one of the tips about a white truck led to Derrick Todd Lee. When the detective learned Derrick was black, however, the officer cleared him as a suspect and closed out the lead two days later.

# CHAPTER 18

# Derrick Starts Again in Lake Charles

On July 6, 1995, the doors to Dixon Correctional Institute in Jackson, Louisiana, flung open for Derrick, releasing him early on good behavior after he served two of his four years on the 1993 Zachary burglary conviction. The stint was the longest he had ever served, and he came out with Bible verses and teachings of the Koran on his tongue.

"I'm gonna get my life straight with God," he told his friends. "Can't go back inside. A terrible place. Wouldn't wish it on nobody."

Toward the end of his term, he spent several months on work release at a halfway house in Lake Charles, Louisiana. Located at the far southwestern corner of Louisiana, Lake Charles is a spirited old Cajun town about 130 miles from Baton Rouge that sprang up on the shores of a sparkling freshwater lake. Town legend claims the infamous pirate Jean Lafitte frequently passed through "Charley's Lake" in the early 1800s and buried some of Napoleon's stolen treasures along its white, sandy shores.

Each year in May, in fact, the city holds a two-week festival—Contraband Days—to pay homage to Lafitte and his swashbuckling ways. The celebration begins when locals, dressed up as buccaneers, storm the banks of the city, capturing the mayor and declaring Pirate Rule over Lake Charles for a fortnight of raucous rollicking.

Whatever the draw was, within days of Derrick's release, he loaded his family in the car and moved them out of Saint Francisville into a small rental home at 2224 Tulip Street in a working-class neighborhood of Lake Charles. They arrived without furniture, jobs, or enough money to properly feed themselves. For the first few days, Derrick, his wife, and their two children slept on the floor. They literally did not have a pot to cook in.

But his luck changed when his neighbor, Robert Welcome, a man aptly named, stopped by the first day they arrived to introduce himself.

Derrick was instantly chummy, and Robert didn't ask questions about the family's obvious dire straits. Robert was just glad to have a new friend next door, someone who seemed like a good-time man, someone he could drink beers and trade tales with as the sun set every day.

A few days after the Lee family moved in, Derrick asked Robert to help pick up some furniture at his mother's house in Saint Francisville, three hours away. Robert knew Derrick and his family were sleeping on the floor, and he did not want to disappoint his new buddy, so he agreed to go. He was glad to be able to help a man down on his luck.

Not long after they returned, Robert noticed Derrick's situation was getting no better. Derrick's children, ages seven and five, often came by Robert's house to play with his eight-year-old son and never wanted to go home.

"Y'all got something to eat here?" Derrick Jr. asked Robert one day.

"Why?" Robert said, laughing at what sounded almost like a demand more than a question.

"We haven't had anything to eat, me and my sister," he said. "We're hungry."

"Go tell your mother, then . . ." Robert said.

But Robert's wife, Barbara, quietly fixed the kids sand-wiches. She had done it before. In the days since the Lees moved in, she had befriended Jackie, and she knew they were in trouble financially.

For the next several weeks, Robert and his wife invited the Lee family over for dinner several nights a week. They cooked food enough for ten people. Big meals of red beans and rice with mustard greens or smothered steaks or liver. On Fridays, they ate fried catfish or shrimp with rolls or toast.

Derrick was always polite when he was inside the Wel-comes' home. Barbara liked to make the place comfortable with neatly arranged furniture, family pictures on the walls, and plants and knickknacks placed lovingly throughout the home. When she was there, the air usually smelled of her cooking, thick scents of onions and garlic or sweet rising cornbread. All her guests felt instantly at home.

Derrick admired Barbara's decorating and cooking and of-ten complimented the landscaping Robert had done around the house. "One day, my house is going to be like this, too," he told them. "Real nice."

Others soon appreciated Derrick's pleasantries in the neighborhood.

Judy Malvo, a divorced mother, was in her late thirties when Derrick moved in across the street. She spent a lot of time working outside in her yard, and Derrick took notice.

"Your yard looks real nice, ma'am . . ." he told her one day.

"Oh, thanks, but it needs mowing," she said.

"I'll mow your lawn," Derrick offered with a grin.

Judy didn't know if he was hitting on her or not, but she ac-cepted the favor.

In the weeks that followed, Derrick often stopped by to chat with her.

One day he asked, "You got anybody?"

"No, I just got divorced, and I'm not looking for anybody," she told him, laughing. "Besides, you're married."

Derrick gave her a big grin. Judy figured he must be play-ing with her, harmless flirting. He seemed so respectful and polite. He was all *ma'ams* and *thank yous*, and talking about

Jesus and God and the Bible. She can still hear him saying, "The Lord is always there . . . He's looking after us."

"Derrick really knew the words in the Bible," Judy recalled. "Lots of people talk about the Lord, but he would quote scripture, saying verses out of the Bible."

If God was looking out for Derrick, He was not helping him find a job. Weeks passed, and Derrick remained unemployed. But that didn't seem to bother him.

"The Lord will provide for me," he'd tell his neighbors. And they believed him. He acted as if he had the whole world under control and felt not a care in the world.

But it wasn't God that provided for him. Whenever Derrick ran short on money or food, his neighbors were the ones who offered to help him out.

"People did for him," Robert said. "Everyone liked him."

To them, Derrick was like an exciting addition to their humdrum lives.

He was not like most people in the neighborhood. He was engaging, always on, playful, friendly, the guy who liked to man the barbecue grill at neighborhood gatherings and keep the conversation popping and laughter rolling.

In a neighborhood of struggling families and high school dropouts, Derrick stood out like a valedictorian using "big college words" that few understood, Robert said. When the ladies were not around, Derrick launched into tales of his escapades with women, bragging about how many he'd had, how easy they were to bed.

"You ever been with a white woman?" he asked his new black friends.

He had also returned to peeping on women, both black and white, in their homes. And he was about to be caught again.

On September 6, the two-month anniversary of his release from custody, Derrick was watching a young woman through her bedroom window just past ten p.m.

The woman's sister, who lived next door, thought he was a prowler when she happened to see him snooping around the house.

When Lake Charles police responded to the ensuing 911 call, Derrick was gone, but the woman's sister was able to provide a description of his clothes: a blue T-shirt and red ball cap.

Several patrol cars were sent to the neighborhood, and a few minutes later Derrick was spotted in the backyard of a home two blocks away. He bolted. For fifteen minutes, officers and a few men from the neighborhood chased him on foot through backyards and over fences, including a five-foot-high chain-link fence that was knocked to the ground as Derrick rushed to climb over it.

Police finally caught up with Derrick in another backyard a few blocks away, where he surrendered and claimed innocence.

"My car broke down," he told authorities. "I was just looking for help."

He was running, he said, because he was being chased by four white men.

Derrick laughed about it when he told the guys in his neighborhood a few days later, after he was released on bail.

"They could have shot you!" Robert said.

Derrick didn't seem to care. "She was naked . . ." he said, giggling.

From the way Derrick talked about women, no one was surprised that his wife Jackie was so submissive.

Ida Stevens, an elderly neighbor who babysat the Lee children when Jackie was working, remembers a quiet, shy young woman.

"She was friendly," Ida said years later. "But she wasn't a big talker."

She sometimes opened up to Ida about her dreams, about how she hoped to get a better job and maybe, someday, return to school for a nursing degree. But she never revealed any troubles with Derrick. She gave Ida the impression he was a hardworking, responsible family man.

"Thank God things are going well," Jackie told her one day. "When Derrick was in jail, his mom and family did not really help me."

Jackie, whose own mother was dead, was stoic about it. She could accept that Derrick's family would not take care of her. But neglecting their own grandchildren? Their own flesh and blood? Ida could tell that Jackie was hurt by that.

"I was doing for those kids what probably their own grandmother wouldn't do," Ida said.

Ida figured that's why Jackie seemed so grateful, telling Ida, "Thank you so much!" even for the smallest favors.

On the rare evenings that Jackie joined Derrick at neighborhood gatherings, however, she spoke hardly a word unless spoken to. She appeared tentative around her husband. Her reasons for the fear became obvious to Robert one Saturday night, a few weeks after they moved in.

Derrick and Robert and some of the neighborhood guys had been drinking earlier that day, and Derrick mentioned he had just bought a car for himself. He seemed proud, but to Robert, the purchase seemed selfish. Derrick was still unemployed and still unable to feed and clothe his children.

A few hours later, as Robert watched from his front yard, just ten feet away from Derrick's driveway, the couple began to argue as they stood near the car. Derrick's voice rose above Jackie's, cussing and hollering, echoing down the street where the neighborhood children were still out playing.

Robert hated seeing Derrick yelling at Jackie. She was such a gentle lady when she came over to visit Barbara. He felt helpless when he saw Derrick pushing Jackie backward, shoving her away from him as he yelled at her.

"Cut that shit out . . ." Jackie protested.

Robert thought Derrick was trying to show off for the guys in the neighborhood, who were still outside and in earshot of the fight. But then Robert saw Derrick's body tense into a coil of anger. Then he let loose. He swung hard at Jackie and hit her in the face. She nearly went down to the ground. Covering her swelling face, she ran inside and called the children to her.

Robert did not like to pry in another man's business, but this time, he had to say something.

"Hey, man, you don't need to be hitting your wife . . ." Robert called out to Derrick. "There's kids out here."

Derrick ignored him. He stepped into his car and sped off.

After six weeks, Robert finally got tired of the still unemployed Derrick coming over for dinner almost every night.

"Look, I've got a family of my own to feed and support," he told Derrick. "You've got to get a job . . ."

He suggested Derrick speak with their neighbor, who

managed to get Derrick a union position at a paint blasting company.

But in the next few weeks, Derrick's troubles only got worse.

His violent outbursts became almost routine in the neighborhood, and he seemed not to care who witnessed them. He swatted at Jackie at barbecues and beat his children for the slightest infractions.

One afternoon, Robert saw Derrick Jr. running down the middle of the street, his young legs pumping as fast as they could with Derrick right on his tail.

"Goddamn son of a bitch, mother fucker!" Derrick was yelling as he swept the boy up off the road. "I told you, don't leave the yard!"

Holding his son three feet off the ground by his flailing arm, Derrick tore a branch off a tree and began whipping the boy, who was screaming and crying, drawing several neighbors out of their homes. Snot ran down the boy's face, and he sobbed louder with each snap of the branch against his back.

"Quit beating him!" Jackie yelled as she ran toward them.

"Get your fat ass back in the house," Derrick shouted back, "or I'll beat you like this, too!"

Watching from across the street, Judy Malvo overcame her reluctance to meddle in her neighbors' lives.

"Stop whipping that child!" she yelled at Derrick. "You whipping him too hard!"

Derrick ignored her until she came to his side.

"That's enough," she said. "You're going to hurt him . . ."

She got the stick away from Derrick, who was lost in a rage. Pulling the boy's arm, Derrick marched inside his home and slammed the door.

Neighbors started to grow wary of Derrick, but his charm was hard to resist for some. Despite himself, Robert still liked Derrick. He was fun to be around, entertaining, and always lively.

"The guy was down to earth," said Sean Simpson, another of Derrick's new neighborhood friends. "Real cordial."

Sean enjoyed the long discussions, "good debates," he called them, with Derrick about God and faith and life.

Derrick not only could quote the Bible, he was also well-versed in the Koran. He told Sean that God was protecting him, providing for him as he tried to make a fresh start in life.

"Going to prison tore my family apart," he said. "I didn't want my kids to see me in there."

He told Sean about his Peeping Tom arrests, but insisted that his trouble with the law was in the past. He swore, and Sean remembers his intensity, that he never wanted to go back behind bars.

"Man, you don't never ever want to experience prison," Derrick said. "You've got to fight to eat dinner, fight to keep your clothes. People trying to gang rape you. Nobody should have to experience that."

From all Derrick's talk of reform, Sean thought Derrick was a good guy who just ran into a little bad luck. He never witnessed Derrick get rough with his family or yell or lose his temper. Derrick said he was planning to buy the house on Tulip he and his family were renting. He never mentioned his money problems. He only talked about how much his life had improved since the first weeks out of prison, when he was living with his family in a $100-a-week hotel room.

"You don't know how it is," he told Sean, "not knowing how you're gonna support your family. Cooking on a hot plate, using an iron to make grilled cheese for your kids. But if you have faith in God, He will provide. That's why I follow Muhammad. I've been provided for. I got a job, a house, a car."

September 24, 1995, was Sean's birthday. He was celebrating with a series of beers, getting drunk and having a good time with the guys, including Derrick. As the night wore on, and the beer and cigarettes ran low, Derrick suggested they make a run to the store.

"Let's go, man," Derrick nudged Sean. But Sean wasn't gonna get pulled over for drunk driving. He wanted no trouble with the law. He was trying to stay straight.

But Derrick was insistent. He hounded the others until Robert relented. Sean and Derrick and Robert piled into Robert's white Dodge Dynasty for the beer and smoke run.

On the way back, Derrick told Robert to pull over.

"I need to take a leak . . ."

Robert drove into the parking lot of the Salvation Army thrift store. Derrick hopped out and disappeared behind some Dumpsters.

When he returned to the car, he was carrying an armful of clothing.

"Pop the trunk," he said to Robert.

"What are you doing?" Robert said.

"I need clothes for my kids," Derrick said. "Pop the trunk." He had raided the clothing donation bin for the Salvation Army store.

"Ah, man . . ." Robert was reluctant, but it seemed almost harmless to take giveaways, stuff other people consider trash. So he joined Derrick, and the two men loaded the car up with clothes and suitcases and bags of shoes.

"That's enough . . ." Robert finally called to Derrick. "Let's go." He was getting nervous, sweating in the still night air.

Derrick got back in the car, unruffled, and Robert sped out of the parking lot.

Robert turned onto the main road, feeling a rush of adrenaline through his veins. He wasn't used to breaking the law so blatantly. He was glad they were done. Then the blue lights lit up in his rearview mirror. A Lake Charles police car was on their bumper. The cops had been parked across the street from the Salvation Army and had watched their every move.

Robert's wife Barbara pawned their furniture to bail out her husband and, after a few days, in response to Jackie's pleadings, they reluctantly did the same for Derrick.

But since that night, Robert says, "I broke loose from him."

Sean did, too. When he saw Derrick a few days later, Derrick tried to apologize in a not so direct way.

He walked up to Sean and extended his hand. "Man, you shouldn't have been there," he said. "I don't know what to tell you right now . . ."

"I don't want to hear it," Sean shot back.

"Look, it just happened, it wasn't planned," Derrick said. "It ain't no big deal. You're gonna get out of it. You'll be able to beat it."

"You screwed me," Sean said. "I've got nothing else to say to you." He walked away from Derrick's continued attempts at excuses, and he never spoke with him again.

But Derrick was gone soon anyway. The Lee family abruptly left their home in mid-November. A few days before, Judy Malvo remembers Jackie banging on her door, asking to come inside. She needed to use Judy's phone to call someone in Saint Francisville. Judy noticed immediately that Jackie looked upset.

Her hair was out of place, and her blouse looked stretched or torn.

"What's wrong?" Judy asked her.

Jackie wouldn't say. She never revealed what went on behind the closed doors of her house.

But Judy could hear the desperation in Jackie's voice when she made the call to Saint Francisville.

"Can someone come pick me up?" she whispered.

Judy never saw Jackie again after that day, and by the end of the week, Derrick was gone, too. He quit his job on Friday and was gone by that night. No one in the neighborhood recalls even seeing him pack up to leave. They figured he must be running from something.

# CHAPTER 19

# God Giveth,
# God Taketh Away

On their return to Saint Francisville in November 1995, the Lees moved into a run-down trailer park off Blackmore Road within walking distance of Derrick's mother. Although conditions of Derrick's parole for the Zachary burglary required he remain employed, Derrick had trouble finding work. The family was struggling, the bills were piling, and their marriage was deteriorating.

Then in February 1996, Jackie's father, Henry Lee Sims, was killed in an explosion at the plant where he worked in Port Allen, Louisiana.

Derrick was not sorry to see him go. The two men had never gotten along. Henry never stopped trying to convince his daughter to leave Derrick. And his death meant Jackie would receive a large settlement, at least $250,000, from the plant where he was killed.

Meanwhile, Derrick needed to find a job to satisfy his parole officer, Don Phares. Derrick was skirting the edge, walking very close to blowing his parole and landing back behind bars.

Phares was awaiting the outcome of Derrick's criminal charges in Lake Charles before making any decisions about disciplinary actions. In June, with the promise of no jail time and the dismissal of the resisting arrest charge, Derrick pleaded guilty to one count of peeping. The Salvation Army theft charge was continued indefinitely.

Although Phares classified Derrick's conduct on parole as "poor," Derrick received only a reprimand for the new conviction rather than a return to jail.

His continued freedom allowed him to enjoy the money Jackie soon collected for her father's death.

The Lees bought a $57,000 house on the outskirts of Saint Francisville at the top of a hill on Highway 61. They paid off their bills, bought themselves a big TV, and discussed returning to school for further training.

Derrick worked a few weeks in April and May for his old employer, JE Merit Constructors, at the ExxonMobil plant, but the jobs did not last. He resented the men who stood above him at the plants. He was a good pipe fitter. He could look at the schematics of a job and know immediately what went where and how to best do it. He was a hard worker, too. He was called to handle the tough jobs, the heavy lifting, and what laborers call "back work." He sweated for his pay, and not like the men who stood on the edge of the ditch, barking orders down below. He felt overworked and underpaid.

Now he could tell them to go to hell. He didn't need the pay.

Derrick's stepfather Coleman held a steady job driving trucks for a Saint Francisville concrete company, and Derrick's biological father also drove trucks for a living. Derrick liked the idea of spending his days on the road, out from underneath the watchful eyes of a foreman.

In January 1998, he enrolled in the Diesel Driving Academy in Baton Rouge. And on February 19, he earned his commercial truck driver's license. But work was not really on Derrick's mind.

\*   \*   \*

When the money came in, Jackie's family urged her to invest it wisely. Instead, she dropped it into a bank account and gave Derrick free rein with the checks.

Suddenly his life was what he always wanted. He was the man with the money. He bought himself a brand-new 1997 black and silver extended cab show truck in December. Traded in his old clothes for a new wardrobe of tight jeans, silky dress shirts, snakeskin boots, and a tall, stiff cowboy hat. At night, he hit the bars and clubs carrying more than a thousand dollars in his wallet. He stored another thousand or two in his glove box.

With his new look, he found it easier to impress women. The ladies he picked up admired the thick gold chains around his neck and the diamond studded rings he wore on both hands. He reveled in the attention he was getting. What he didn't expect was to fall in love.

The first time Derrick saw Consandra Green was at a parade in Saint Francisville. He watched her as she passed by his flashy show truck. She was wearing shorts, showing off a lot of leg. She was a big, dark woman, with thick bones and solid flesh, just like he liked them.

He saw her again later at a roadside store. He spoke to her this time. He smiled at her. She told him she had a boyfriend, but he was giving her trouble. He had cut up her car's tires. Derrick offered to drive her to the service station.

The next time they crossed paths, Derrick was outside Saint Francisville's Highland Bar. He liked to sit in his truck before going inside, watching who came and went, drinking beers from the cooler he had installed in his cab. He saw her walking inside.

"Hey," he called to her. "I know who your boyfriend is." He offered the name.

"How'd you know that?"

"Don't you worry about it," he said.

"We've split up," she told him, and they went inside together.

Derrick bought her and her friends drinks. They got to talking, and things just went from there. They started spending a lot of time together, inside and outside of the bars. But her ex was still harassing her. She was tired of it. She told Derrick she was leaving town.

He didn't believe her until he went to her house one day to see her. She was gone, but she had left Derrick a letter. He drove off, then pulled over to the side of the road to read her note. She told him she enjoyed their time together, but that she had problems she wanted to escape. She needed to leave. The words brought him to tears. He was surprised by his emotions.

"Lookie here," he said to himself. "I just met this girl. Why I got water in my eyes?"

She left a phone number for him. He used his cell phone to call her. She was in Alabama, but she wasn't planning on coming back, she said. He believed her. A few weeks later, he got a strange call.

"I'm back home," a woman's voice said and hung up.

Derrick didn't know who it was. His phone rang awhile later when he was out.

"Do you know who this is?" the woman's voice said.

"No, not really."

"I told you, I'm home."

"Who is this?"

"This Consandra."

Derrick hung up and went straight over to her house. From that day, they were together. "We was like gravy on rice," as Derrick put it. "When I was with her—it was like fire. I'd say, girl, you must be from heaven."

They spent their nights in the local bars. He played pool, while she sat nearby and watched. They danced and drank and left for home together. Derrick didn't care who saw him with his new girl, a woman he called Cat.

He didn't care that people were talking about them at the bars. When the drunks at the roadhouse put on a song about a woman dating a married man, they sang along.

Jackie was not deaf to stories of Derrick's nightlife. She heard about Cat from her own husband.

"I've got a woman who doesn't give me this kind of trouble," he'd tell Jackie if she fussed at him.

Then he began to disappear for days, preferring to stay at Cat's house in Jackson. Jackie was heartbroken, but she simply moved on with her life. She went to work and came home to care for the kids.

"After a certain amount of things happened between us, I just stopped caring," she said.

Derrick would return a few nights a week, but their relationship was strained and distant.

"We were married, but not really together," she said. "We would have sex whenever, but [there was] no real communication or much intimacy."

She did, however, purchase a .25 caliber handgun in September 1996, which she began to keep by her side in the bedroom.


Derrick found fun and comfort in Cat. With Jackie's money, he threw parties and barbecued for large groups at Cat's house. Sometimes, he and Cat drove to Baton Rouge, where they stayed in expensive hotels and gambled on the riverboats. Other nights, they passed the time playing cards, renting movies, and cuddling together on the couch, talking about their feelings for each other. In the fall, they went horseback riding, breathing in the air, noticing the leaves changing.

"I thought being in love was only for rich people," Derrick said. He never thought he could love someone the way he did Cat.

Driving around, he could smell her scent all over him, on his shirts, in his truck.

Sometimes Cat worried about their illicit affair.

"I know its wrong," she'd tell Derrick. "God, gonna punish me. We're gonna get punished for what we're doing . . . But I can't get you out of my damn system."

He tried, too. They both tried to leave it alone, but they couldn't.

Derrick did not want to walk away from Jackie, but he imagined someday he would marry Consandra.

His love for Cat, however, did not keep him at home at night. He was still trolling the streets, covering miles and miles every day. The console in his truck was a cooler, where he kept his beer, so he could pass his days of unemployed freedom driving and drinking.

On February 11, 1997, about 5:20 p.m., Derrick was driving through Point Coupee Parish, a rural area directly across the

Mississippi from Saint Francisville, on his way to Lafayette, when a state trooper stopped him for riding another car's bumper.

Derrick stumbled and nearly fell when he stepped out of his truck and began walking toward the trooper's car. He fumbled around for his wallet, looking for his license, slurring his words as he spoke. He reeked of alcohol.

As the trooper explained the subsequent roadside sobriety tests, Derrick swayed on his feet. He was unable to stand still, tried to start the tests before the trooper was finished explaining, and when he did attempt them, he failed each one.

He was arrested and booked at the parish jail with driving while intoxicated and issued a summons for following too close. Jackie had to come pick him up.

The DWI conviction would prompt a suspension of his driving privileges and ruin his chances at a commercial driver's license, so Derrick went to see a lawyer the next day. On February 12, Baton Rouge attorney James Wood wrote the state requesting all the evidence that would be used against Derrick at the hearing to suspend his license for the conviction. The state failed to respond, so when the hearing was held the next month, the judge rescinded the state's order to suspend Derrick's license. His driving privileges went unscathed.


Derrick continued to prowl the streets and through peaceful neighborhoods at night. Few women realized he was outside their windows watching them undress. And when they did, he simply ran. By the time police arrived, he was nothing but a shadow. He felt invincible.

On February 19, 1997, the same day he earned his commercial truck driver's license, Derrick didn't even flinch when a Zachary police officer stopped him late one night walking through the Oak Shadows subdivision.

Officer Roderick Ennis lived in Oak Shadows. The night before, when he was off duty, his neighbor called to report a black man was across the street peeping in the window of the house at 1716 Job Avenue—Connie Warner's former home. The neighbor described the man as tall, well-built, with short-cropped hair and wearing a dark colored checkered pullover hooded sweatshirt and blue jeans.

Ennis walked outside toward 1716 Job, but did not see anyone in the yard. When he returned home, he called his neighbor, who said the black man had run south of the neighborhood into an open, overgrown field. Ennis then called the woman who lived at 1716 Job Avenue to ask if she had seen the man peeping into her window.

She was shocked. She had not seen or heard anything that night. But a few nights earlier, she had gone outside to empty her trash and discovered a black male in her carport. She jumped.

"Don't be afraid," the man told her and then he ran south toward the field.

When Ennis went back on duty the next night, February 19, he and his partner decided to patrol Oak Shadows and the surrounding area. While driving through the subdivision with their headlights off about 9:15, they saw a tall, well-built black man with short-cropped hair walking along in the road. He was wearing a dark hooded sweatshirt, blue jeans, and brown work boots.

Ennis pulled up alongside the man to stop him and ask for his name.

"Derrick Lee," the man responded calmly.

"Do you have any type of identification?" Ennis asked.

"Ah, I left my wallet with my license in my truck," Derrick told him. "It's broken down."

"Well, what are you doing in here?"

"I'm going to see my girlfriend."

"What's her name?" Ennis inquired.

Derrick could not provide the woman's name or address.

"Where's your truck at?" Ennis said.

Derrick told him his truck was parked in front of the Ambrosia Lounge, a cowboy and predominantly white bar a quarter mile away at the corner of Highways 964 and 64, across from the Zachary cemeteries.

By now, Ennis was out of the patrol car. On Derrick's belt was a leather knife sheath but no knife. Ennis patted Derrick down, and in his right front pocket found a large buck knife with a tan handle and a four- to six-inch blade. In Derrick's back pocket, Ennis found a pair of almost-new brown leather work gloves.

Ennis had little doubt he had just stopped the Peeping Tom who had been prowling around Oak Shadows the last several days, as well as the nearby neighborhoods of Willow Creek and Fenwood Hills. But he needed a little more proof.

Ennis asked Derrick to stand by while he got inside his car. He called his wife and asked her to call the neighbor who saw the peeper the night before. He wanted her to take a look at Derrick and tell him if it was the same guy. The neighbor did as he asked and called back to report she recognized Derrick as the man from the previous night.

Ennis, however, decided not to arrest Derrick. Instead, he drove him to his truck. When they arrived at the parking lot, Ennis noticed Derrick's truck was a brand-new Chevrolet king cab. Before letting him go, Ennis asked Derrick to provide some identification, and Derrick grabbed his wallet out of the truck.

Ennis radioed Zachary dispatch and requested they run a check for outstanding warrants and a registration on the truck. Derrick's record came back clear, and the truck was lawfully registered to him. Ennis then gave the buck knife back to Derrick, told him to go home, and warned him not to return to Oak Shadows.

Derrick did not take his advice. His life was on the upswing. He had more money than he ever imagined in his pocket, and with his new commercial driver's license, he could be his own boss on the road every day.

There were few things he liked better than cruising the highways. He clocked thousands of miles every month on his truck, just driving and sipping his beer.


In May, Derrick landed his first job as a commercial truck driver with Louisiana Ready-Mix. He started on the eighteen-wheelers, driving cement mix to Louisiana Ready-Mix plants around southern Louisiana. But he didn't take long to run into trouble. His driving was not up to par. He got into a number of accidents, including one on July 25, when he nearly ran over another employee's car—with her inside. On the disciplinary report in Derrick's personnel record, his supervisor chalked it up to carelessness. But the company removed Derrick from the roster of drivers for eighteen-wheelers. He was demoted to driving the cement trucks only. Derrick didn't take well to the discipline.

On July 31, on another stormy night in Zachary, Sergeant Keith Cranford was on patrol when he got a call about a prowler in the Oak Shadows subdivision.

Just after nine p.m., with the storm clouds still overhead, a woman on Numbers Street happened to look across from her home and noticed a black man wearing dark clothing crouching in the bushes just below a window of her neighbor's home.

By the time Cranford arrived about 9:10, the man was gone. Cranford searched the area but did not find anyone fitting the man's description.

About forty-five minutes later, another call came in from a woman who lived about a half mile up Highway 964 from the Oak Shadows subdivision. She was taking her trash outside when she walked around the corner of her house and nearly ran into a tall black man wearing dark clothing. They were almost face-to-face when he bolted.

Sergeant Danny Smith responded to call. He was hungry to catch the guy. Smith had worked on the Connie Warner and cemetery attack cases. He had begun to believe they were connected. When reports of a Peeping Tom in Oak Shadows began coming in, Smith was anxious to arrest and grill him.

He was joined by Cranford at the home on Highway 964, and they walked around the yard, shining their flashlights into the bushes and along the perimeter of her home. In the back, in the mud by the house, they found fresh footprints made since the rain stopped less than an hour earlier. But they saw no prowler.

While the officers were still searching around the woman's home, yet another call came in from the Willow Creek apartment complex, located less than a quarter mile away across Highway 964.

Jerry Stone had been inside his apartment when he looked up and saw a black man staring into his window.

"Hey!" Jerry yelled at the man, who quickly disappeared.

Outside, Jerry's neighbor saw a man about six feet tall and wearing dark clothing run between two of the apartment buildings toward the Fenwood Hills subdivision.

Cranford knew the man was on foot, leaving a scented trail that search dogs could easily pick up. The Department of Corrections kept one of the state's best teams of bloodhounds about twenty miles north. He put in a call to police headquarters and requested the dogs.

Before the dog team arrived, Officer David McDavid, who had heard about the chase on the police radio and was driving to the Willow Creek apartments, braked suddenly when he saw a black man sprinting south across the street in the Fenwood Hills subdivision and disappear behind the homes again.

Minutes later, Cranford saw the man near a vacant house that sat a few yards north of the Outskirts Lounge, a bar at the corner of Highway 964 and 64. As Cranford approached, the man darted into a field of shoulder-high weeds.

When the dog team arrived a few minutes later, Cranford sent them into the weeded area. Several Zachary officers who had joined the chase were stationed around the field's perimeter. As the hounds moved in, Officer John Steele, who had left his home to help with the search, saw the man emerge from the weeds, squatting on the side of Highway 964. Steele avoided the man's line of sight and watched him look north then south down the road before suddenly standing up and running toward Steele.

Steele waited until the man was within arm's length, then tackled him.

Soaking wet, scratched up, and covered in mud and grass, the man tried to tell police he was only looking for a phone. His truck had broken down and he needed to call a friend.

Zachary police quickly recognized the man as Derrick Todd Lee. They handcuffed him and put him in the patrol car and took his shoes. While Derrick was hauled to the police station, his shoes were compared to the prints left in the mud at the house on Highway 964. Police were sure they got a match, and Derrick was arrested for six counts of Peeping Tom, criminal trespass, and attempted burglary.

It had been less than a month since he was released from his parole for the Zachary burglary.

Derrick made bail and was back at work right away, but he was not getting along with his coworkers or foremen. He did not adhere well to close supervision and was belligerent with other workers. On October 30, he was disciplined for substandard work. He said he got lost on his way to a job site, but he had not contacted the dispatcher for driving instruction.

Derrick refused to sign the discipline report, even though it was still just a warning.

Meanwhile, the Zachary City Court was still processing his July Peeping Tom charges. In December, Dr. Robert Snyder, the same psychologist appointed to treat Derrick in 1989 for anger management, wrote a letter to Judge Lonny Myles with a proposal for Derrick.

"Mr. Lee had presented himself to me with a request for individual psychotherapy," Snyder wrote in the December 10, 1998, letter. "He explained that because of an arrest for what he describes as a 'Peeping Tom' offense, he is required by the court to obtain help for treatment and termination of this type of behavior."

If the judge and Derrick agreed, Snyder suggested he begin at least three months of weekly sessions for evaluation and therapy as part of Derrick's sentence in the case.

"The evaluation phase will consist of a full psychological evaluation including current intellectual, educational, and psychological status," he wrote.

On January 14, 1998, Derrick pleaded guilty to six counts of Peeping Tom. As part of his plea bargain, he received no jail time, just two years' probation and an order to seek psychological testing.

A month later, Dr. Snyder sent a follow-up letter to the judge at Derrick's request informing the court that Derrick had completed two therapy sessions.

"I have reviewed certain court documents Mr. Lee presented me with and based on what appears to have been the court's determination, I have altered my proposed program of therapy to be two therapy sessions only," Snyder wrote. "Please be advised that Mr. Lee did attend two therapy sessions with me, one hour each, with him alone in my St. Francisville office for which he paid private money.

"In my opinion, Mr. Lee cooperated fully with the intent of the therapy and he was sincere and honest," Snyder said in closing. "I was pleasantly surprised with the extent to which he is a good verbal therapy participant at this time in his life."

Two months later, on April 16, Derrick mouthed off to his supervisor at Louisiana Ready-Mix. On his termination report, the company noted Derrick was fired because he caused two accidents with his truck in the same week and was insubordinate to his foreman.

# CHAPTER 20

# Randi Disappears

In April 1998, Randi Mebruer was twenty-eight and ready to settle down again, find another husband and father for her three-year-old son, Mike Jr. She still looked young, acted young, even felt young—she wore fuchsia bows in her dark hair to match the pink laces in her tennis shoes—but she was also weary of the single life. As much as she loved to flirt, to show off her trimmed-down figure, to enjoy attention from the opposite sex, she was tired of the drunken bar scene and late nights and regrettable errors in judgment with men, including her ex, Michael Mebruer.

Randi had been divorced for more than a year, yet the romantic side in her was still unable to resist him. He was tall—six-two—and handsome—blue eyes and built. Just before Easter that year, after dropping off their son, Michael lingered at her house as he often did. They sat on the porch and smoked and drank her Diet Cokes and talked.

"I miss you," she told him.

The next morning, when he was gone and she was alone again in the life he left behind, she scolded herself for sleeping with him, as she did almost every time she repeated the mistake.

*That was the last time,* she promised herself. *Absolutely. I deserve better. I've got to move on.*

Michael was a hot-tempered husband who skipped from job to job and woman to woman. When they married in 1993, Randi was madly in love with him. She believed she could save him. She got him to quit drinking and encouraged him to stay sober. She supported his ambitions to become a medical technician and agreed to pay most of their bills so he could attend school for the training.

With her savings tucked away from years on a paltry registered nurse's salary, she bought their house, a small brick and frame ranch in the Oak Shadows subdivision, and soon she was pregnant. In her mind, she was on the road to a happy, normal family life. Her parents' divorce had been tumultuous, and her relationship with her mother was strained and distant. She and her father talked on the phone often, but he lived more than 1,500 miles away in Staten Island, New York. She wanted her life with Michael to be perfect, and she hoped pouring all her love onto him would work.

But her pregnancy proved difficult. She developed toxemia and nearly died from kidney failure. Two months after Mike Jr. was born, Randi, once a cute and petite young woman, was bloated twice her size. Her face was so swollen from her medicine, she was almost unrecognizable. Then the insults began.

She called her father, crying.

"He tells me I'm fat and ugly," she told her father.

Michael's subsequent affair with another woman ended the marriage. He wanted his freedom, and Randi did not contest it. She was heartbroken, but she wasn't up for the fight. They split custody of Mike Jr., but any money Michael promised to pay usually failed to materialize. He, however, continued to appear at length at her house, and in Randi's lonelier moments, she succumbed to old habits with him.

But after that last April 7 encounter with her ex, Randi was determined to make a change, and on April 10, she met the man she hoped would be the catalyst. Randi was instantly attracted to Brian Duby when she met him at Ricky B's, a bar on Sherwood Forest Boulevard in Baton Rouge. They hit it off immediately. Randi was a bubbly girl. She was chatty, friendly, and flirtatious, even with strangers. To her, men were easy come, easy go. But Brian seemed different. She got the feeling he was someone she could hang onto. She didn't go home with him that night, but before she left the bar, he invited her to dinner for the next night.

When he arrived to pick her up at her home in Zachary, he brought a dozen roses and got a super-big smile on Randi's face. He took her to Mike Anderson's, a Baton Rouge seafood restaurant, then to Glen's Bombay Club, and later to the bar Affects. When they drove back to her home, she invited him in for a few hours.

Brian, a construction worker, was previously scheduled for an out-of-town job in Fort Dodge, Iowa, the following week, but he called Randi several times from the road, which she took as a sign that her date had not been a one-night stand.

He was due back Sunday or Monday, April 19 or 20, so going into that weekend, Randi was giddy with anticipation. Her good friend, Betty Bergeron, talked to Randi the preceding Thursday.

"She was crazy about him," Betty said. "He was like a breath of fresh air for her. She believed finally she had found someone decent."

As they spoke, Brian beeped in, and Randi hastily got off the phone with Betty to speak with him.

"Gotta go," she said. "It's him."

Neatness was not one of Randi's strongest traits. Her bedroom was strewn with clothes, clean and dirty. Her drawers acted more as shelves, staying open all the time, with underwear and shirts and jeans draped over the edges. Her dressers were covered in receipts and jewelry and random knickknacks accumulated over the years. The rest of the house, basically, was equally as messy: dishes in the sink, food unpacked from grocery bags, and trash waiting to be dumped.

But that weekend, Randi wanted to make her house sparkle by the time Brian returned. She got out the disinfectants and sponges and paper towels and went to work scrubbing and straightening and putting away her clothes and papers and videotapes and CDs and everything else that usually stayed for weeks collecting dust exactly where she happened to put it down. The spring cleaning was refreshing, like a spring cleaning of her life, when she could dream of a brighter future.

Michael spoke with Randi at about seven p.m. on Saturday night, April 18. She seemed particularly confident and determined.

"I've met someone," she told him. "I really like him."

That meant, Randi told her ex, that their occasional sexual relations must end.

Michael didn't protest, and the two made plans for him to pick up Mike Jr. at Randi's house Sunday night. Michael was supposed to have custody of Mike Jr. all weekend, but that Friday, Michael had an operation on his foot and was confined to his house with a large cast on his leg.

"See you Sunday," he said before hanging up. It was the last time he spoke with Randi.

Saturday night, April 18, Randi and Mike Jr. drove to the Zachary Blockbuster and rented a movie. On her way home, Randi stopped to buy a lottery ticket. She never gave up hope that good luck would come her way.

She and Mike watched the movie in the living room that night, and after she put him to bed, she made a call to a psychic hotline. She was curious about her future with Brian. He seemed so perfect. Just the kind of guy she could settle down with again.

Unfortunately, her future did not include winning the lottery. After watching the 10 p.m. Powerball drawing on TV, she crumpled up the lottery ticket and threw it in the kitchen trash can. A few minutes later, she called to talk with a friend. Randi usually went to bed before midnight when she wasn't out, but that night another call originated from her home a few minutes after midnight, an unusual time for Randi to make a call.

Randi's neighbor, Cathy Morris, was asleep when the phone rang in her home. Groggy and moving slow, she got to the phone after several rings, but by the time she picked up the receiver, the line was dead.

The next day, a Sunday, at about two p.m., a boy living next door to Randi found Mike Jr. playing alone in his front yard. The boy went back inside his house and asked his mother if Mike could come over to play.

"If his mother says it's OK," Cathy Morris told her son.

"He doesn't know where she is."

Cathy went outside to talk with Mike.

"Hi, Mike," she squatted down to talk with the toddler. "Where's your mom?"

"She's lost," he said. "I can't find her."

Concerned, Cathy walked over to Randi's house. Randi's car, a Mitsubishi Eclipse, was parked in the carport. Cathy knocked on the carport door that leads into the kitchen. When she got no answer, she tried the knob and discovered it was unlocked. She swung the door open and immediately saw blood on the linoleum floor. At first, she thought Randi must have cut herself.

"Randi," she called out. "You here? It's Cathy . . ."

She got no reply. She guessed Randi might be in the shower, so she walked farther into the kitchen, which opens up to the living room. What she saw there seemed so unreal. A long streak of blood was on the living room carpet, as if something bloody was dragged across it from the bedroom area.

Cathy hurried out of the house to get her husband. He took one look at the blood inside Randi's house and called for the police.

Zachary Police Detective Ray Day arrived a few minutes later. He was told a woman was missing, and blood was found in her home, but nothing prepared him for what he saw that day.

He was not worried when he opened the door to the kitchen. Police get calls every day about missing people. He knew the routine. The so-called missing usually show up in a few hours. But when he saw the blood in Randi's kitchen and the drag marks across her living room, his gut seized up. He knew, *Something really bad has happened here.* He drew his gun and told Cathy and her husband to get out of the house.

"This is the Zachary Police," he called out. "Anyone in here?"

He tried to step over the bloodstains, but there was so much of it. He followed the dark red streaks toward the bedroom area and into Randi's bedroom.

The room was in disarray. A pajama top was on the floor just outside the door, and a pair of pink panties were at the foot of the bed. The sheets were pulled off and rumpled on the middle, and lying on top of the mattress was a steak knife.

When he looked back toward the bedroom door, he was sickened by what he saw. On the walls, arcs of blood spatter stretched from one side of the door to the other. A bloody towel lay on the floor nearby. And on the carpet next to the bed were two large, dark pools of blood. Embedded in the bloody rug fibers at the center of the smaller stain was one of Randi's blue eye contacts.

*You have to hit the dog shit out of somebody to knock out their contacts,* he thought.

But Randi was gone, and in Ray's mind, probably dead.

The trail of blood originating in the bedroom continued through the living room and into the kitchen. Clumps of Randi's hair lay on the floor. The carport door and countertops and refrigerator were also spattered with blood, although much of it had been smeared from an attempt to wipe it away with paper towels. A pair of pajama pants were on the floor near the kitchen trash can and inside the trash can were the shriveled roses Brian had given Randi a week earlier. Just outside the kitchen door, on the carport floor, several pink garbage bags were piled up, some smeared with blood.

From there, a trail of large, quarter-size dried blood

droplets led across the cement to a large pool of blood. It was not difficult to see Randi's body, dripping with blood, was probably carried outside, wrapped in garbage bags, and placed on the ground before being lifted into a vehicle and hauled away.

Ed Cleslewsicz, Randi's father, got the call about eight thirty that night. He was at his parents' house in Staten Island, and they had just settled in for a movie, *The Bridge on the River Kwai*, when the phone rang. It was his ex-wife, Nancy, calling from her home in Florida.

"Ed, I've got to tell you something." Her voice was quavering. "I hope you're sitting down . . . Randi's missing."

"Missing? What do you mean missing?"

Nancy told him what she knew about their daughter. That police found blood in Randi's house and Mike Jr. wandering in the yard alone. Nancy stressed that everyone was hoping Randi simply had an accident, cut herself, and had a friend take her to the hospital. But to Ed, that idea was foolishly wishful. He knew that immediately. Why would Randi leave Mike Jr.?

He called the Zachary police, who confirmed what Nancy said and provided more details about the amount of blood, the drag marks, the contact lens on the rug, and the trail of blood disappearing in the carport.

"I knew after that first phone call she was dead," Ed says. "There was no doubt in my mind."

Nevertheless, he stayed by the phone, hoping against logic that Randi would turn up somewhere alive. But by the next day, that shred of hope disappeared. He was sure his daughter, his only child, was dead.

She was the only delight he had left in life.

He remembers the day she was born, March 18, 1970, on a snowy day in Brooklyn. She was a cheerful child, always playful, always looking for the funny angle in life. The family's doorbell was constantly ringing from all of Randi's friends. She was a naturally dramatic and creative type. When she was eleven, she won a story-telling contest, a title bestowed upon the best narrator in all of Staten Island. It was one of Ed's proudest moments as a father.

Soon after, however, Randi's mother, who had divorced Ed the year before, remarried and moved to Louisiana with Randi. He visited with her when he could, and they tried to keep their relationship close over the phone, but it was difficult. He never stopped wishing she would move back to New York. After her divorce, as her financial situation deteriorated, she seemed to contemplate the idea of moving back to New York where her father could help her make ends meet, but she decided to keep Mike Jr. near his father. She knew how painful it was to grow up without hers.

Randi stayed in Zachary, where she worked seven days a week when she didn't have Mike Jr., four days a week when she did. She didn't mind the long hours. She enjoyed visiting with her patients. And despite her dire situation, she found happiness in each day. She marked her medical charts with smiley faces and did extra errands for her patients. Sometimes, when they couldn't afford their medicine, she paid for it out of her own pocket.

Her greatest joy, though, was Mike Jr. She was the kind of mom who climbed onto the kiddie play set with her son at McDonald's and felt no shame singing along with him to the Barney song:

> *I love you*
> *You love me*
> *We're a happy family . . .*

Ed's last memory of Randi was at the Baton Rouge airport when he was about to fly home from his last visit in September 1997. She started crying as he was leaving. He turned back to give her a hug.

"Don't worry," he assured her. "We'll get together again real soon."

Zachary Police Officer Lewis Banks was off duty that Sunday and on his way home about three p.m. when another officer stopped Banks's car and motioned for him to follow. Banks lived in Oak Shadows, not far from Randi, and his heart skipped when he saw the line of patrol cars in the neighborhood.

His relief that the crowd was not at his own home was quickly replaced by another kind of worry. He did not know Randi, but her brutal abduction from her home frightened him. His own wife and children lived just around the corner.

After seeing the pools of blood in the carport and the drag marks inside her home, Banks got the cold, sick feeling Randi was dead. But his mission that day was to focus on trying to find her alive.

He started interviewing the neighbors, hoping they could provide some clue to Randi's whereabouts, while other officers began searching the overgrown fields surrounding the neighborhood for her body.

Banks quickly learned that Randi was recently divorced, but her ex-husband still regularly visited her house. He also learned Randi had the reputation as a party girl, often out late in the local bars drinking and dancing and sometimes bringing home new acquaintances.

Banks suspected Randi might have known the man, if only for a few hours. Her home showed no signs of a forced entry, meaning either Randi's attacker got in through an unlocked door or window, or she had opened her door to him. When Banks walked through the house, he also noticed her wallet on the kitchen counter, jewelry on the bedroom dresser, and a $600 blank money order out in plain view. The only things missing from the home were Randi's keys and an eight-pound dumbbell—a potentially deadly weapon—from her bedroom. Clearly robbery was not the motive.

The blood trail—droplets, not drag marks—also led into Mike Jr.'s room. Someone had stood next to the boy's bed, dripping blood. Blood was also smeared on the outside of the boy's bedroom door and doorknob, as though an attempt was made to wipe the blood away with paper towels.

But Mike Jr. could not remember seeing or hearing anything during the night. When Banks questioned him, the boy could not even say when he went to bed. All Mike Jr. knew was that his mother was gone when he awoke Sunday morning.

Neighbors could not offer much more help. A few nearby neighbors heard a loud thump, like a hatchback slamming shut, between midnight and one a.m., but none saw anything unusual when they looked outside. The best information Randi's neighbors could provide was the recognition that her Mitsubishi was not parked where she normally left it.

Randi habitually parked her car in the center of the carport, even if she was expecting guests; they just had to park behind her in the driveway. But on Sunday morning, Randi's car was parked tightly to the left side of the carport, away from the house, leaving enough room for another vehicle to pull in alongside the kitchen door.

Whoever attacked her obviously was not in a rush to leave her house afterward. He took his time, possibly made sure Mike Jr. was asleep, tried to clean up, and probably moved her car to make removing her body easier and less conspicuous. This guy did not panic.

Banks knew he needed to track down all of Randi's male friends and acquaintances. Perhaps she had brought home the wrong guy. Banks also needed to interrogate Michael Mebruer, get him to take a polygraph. Husbands and ex-husbands statistically are often involved in such cases.

When Banks told Michael about the blood inside Randi's home, the drag marks, Banks was struck by Michael's muted emotions. Randi's neighbors had told Banks about Michael and his temper, so Banks began to think of the ex-husband as a possible suspect, even with the large cast on his leg.

But from the moment he walked inside Randi's house, Banks's gut was growling the name of another suspect. A man Banks himself had seen driving through the neighborhood recently. A man Banks and several other Zachary officers knew well.

When his colleague, Detective David McDavid, showed up on the scene, Banks could tell by the look on McDavid's face that he was thinking the same thing.

"You know who it is, don't you?" McDavid said to Banks that day as they surveyed the bloody mess.

Banks did not have to answer. He knew, too.

"We've got to go find Derrick Todd Lee," McDavid said. "We need to talk to him."

# CHAPTER 21

# Spotlight on Derrick

Detective David McDavid knew exactly where Derrick Todd Lee lived. For years, he was eyeing Derrick, keeping tabs on his habits and whereabouts. The guy was bad news. McDavid did not like seeing Derrick in his town. He knew his rap sheet, knew Derrick was a Peeping Tom and a brazen burglar, willing to walk into a stranger's home. But he also suspected he was violent, a predator. Like others in the department, McDavid suspected Derrick of the cemetery attacks and maybe even Connie Warner's murder. He just couldn't prove it.

Now he was sure Derrick was responsible for Randi's disappearance, and he was anxious to nail him. After night fell that Sunday, he headed to Saint Francisville to check on Derrick. The drive from the Oak Shadows subdivision up Highway 964 to Port Hudson Plains Drive, then north six miles on Highway 61 to Derrick's ranch house took less than fifteen minutes.

McDavid rolled slowly past the home. He saw Derrick's

tan Chevy truck and Jackie's red Mitsubishi Eclipse in the driveway. In his heart, McDavid felt strongly that Randi's killer was sitting inside the house. He wondered what Derrick was doing. Was he watching TV? Drinking a beer? What was he thinking? Was he nervous? Did he care?

McDavid drove by the house a few times that night. He knew Derrick was a night crawler, and if he left, McDavid wanted to follow him. But Derrick stayed put that evening, and eventually McDavid returned to Zachary.

The next morning, police returned to Randi's house and began searching the surrounding fields.

Overhead, Mayor John Womack joined Detective Lawrence Kling for a helicopter search of Zachary, flying over the open fields and roadway ditches and river tributaries that wind through the area. After circling the city a few times and finding nothing, Kling directed the pilot south toward Baton Rouge, to the industrial area where Connie Warner's body was dumped. Connie's case was too similar and too close to Randi's to be ignored. But again, they spotted no signs of Randi.

Their next area of interest was north to Saint Francisville. Derrick Todd Lee was already on their minds, so they flew over his house, their eyes focusing on nearby Thompson Creek and its wooded, marshy fishing grounds.

If Derrick had dumped her in the vicinity, he had done an excellent job of hiding the body.

Kling and Womack returned to the police station later that afternoon to discuss their next steps in the investigation with McDavid and Banks. All agreed Derrick was their target, but they were not sure how best to snare him. Should they simply watch his movements or go talk with him? Should they try to obtain a warrant or ask for his voluntary consent to search his home?

Womack and McDavid felt so strongly about Derrick's involvement, they wanted to question him immediately and not wait for an uncertain judge's order to get inside, especially because they were sure they had no probable cause to obtain a warrant.

So the detectives loaded into their cars, contacted the West Feliciana Sheriff's Office for assistance, and drove out to Derrick's house that afternoon.

Derrick was not happy to see a crowd of police officers on his front porch when he came to the door. And he didn't like the sound of their request: "We need for you to come into the station to talk with us."

"What you want to talk to me for?" Derrick said.

McDavid did not want to explain until they got Derrick off his own territory and onto theirs. He wanted to make sure Derrick was read his rights in an official police environment before the questioning began, just in case he said anything incriminating.

The officers only told Derrick that they needed to ask him a few questions about the case they were working.

Derrick was agitated, but agreed. He said he had nothing to hide.


The men gathered inside a West Feliciana Sheriff's Office interrogation room. Derrick remained calm, almost cocky. He was read his rights, which he shrugged off. "I understand," he said, waiving the presence of an attorney, and McDavid began with the questions.

"We're investigating a missing white female from Oak Shadows in Zachary," he told Derrick.

"What's this got to do with me?" Derrick demanded.

"You've been arrested in that area for unauthorized entry and Peeping Tom," McDavid reminded him. "Do you know anything about her disappearance?"

"No," Derrick said. "You've got the wrong man."

"What did you do Saturday night?" McDavid asked.

"I went out."

"Where?"

Derrick was tight-lipped. His answers were short, requiring McDavid and Banks to pry out details.

Derrick started the night with a girlfriend, Consandra Green, at the Highland Bar in Saint Francisville. After a few drinks, Consandra got tired of Derrick talking to another woman. She picked and picked at him for flirting. They argued, and Consandra stormed out about ten thirty to go home, leaving Derrick alone, seething. After awhile, Derrick left the bar, too, and drove twenty miles down Highway 61 to the Hideaway Lounge in Alsen, Louisiana, just south of Zachary.

After midnight, he said he left the Hideaway and drove straight to Consandra's home in Jackson, Louisiana, a route that took him through Zachary on Highway 964 right past Oak Shadows' entrance.

"But I didn't go down that street," Derrick volunteered when the conversation began to focus on his route to Jackson.

"I didn't ask you that," McDavid said.

McDavid could not believe what he was hearing. Derrick was saying he drove past Randi's subdivision between midnight and one a.m., the same time Randi most likely disappeared.

The room went silent for a few moments. McDavid stared hard at Derrick, who suddenly seemed ready to go home. Their eyes met, but Derrick was not cowering. He appeared more defiant than ever.

"I know what you've done." McDavid hoped the words burned into Derrick's conscience.

But Derrick only shook his head and stared back at McDavid with a confident smirk. He had been to prison before. He knew the routine. The police had no body. He knew they must have no evidence against him. Otherwise, they would have arrested him by now.

The detectives were running out of questions, and they wanted to get inside Derrick's house before he completely clammed up. They hoped to collect the clothes he had on Saturday night. Look for Randi's keys. Find anything that might link him to the crime.

"If you've got nothing to hide, mind if we come back to your house and look around?" McDavid said. "I'd like to see the clothes you were wearing Saturday night."

With just a hint of agitation, Derrick agreed. He acted as if he knew the police would find nothing there.


The driveway to Derrick's brick ranch house juts directly off Highway 61 at the top of a hill overlooking Thompson Creek and a Swifty's truck stop below. He had only one close neighbor, whose house is one hundred yards behind his in an open field. His other neighbors, living in a middle-class subdivision just north on 61, are located on the other side of a wide swath of trees. So, despite the home's prominence on the highway, it is well isolated from watchful eyes.

The detectives parked a small caravan of police units in the driveway behind Derrick's truck and followed him inside. The officers, who numbered more than six, split up and began looking through each room.

Derrick followed them in every direction, pacing through the house, taunting the police as he hovered over their backs: "You find what you're looking for?"

When Kling reached for a box at the top of a hall closet, Derrick called out, "Hey, I thought you said you were just going to look . . ."

"I'm just moving it out of the way," Kling told him.

In the bedroom, McDavid opened the closet. He could see which side belonged to Jackie and which to Derrick. To one side, the clothes were disordered and rumpled. But on the other, several pairs of work boots, shoes, and decorative cowboy boots were lined up side by side. The shirts and jeans were starched stiff, some still hanging in their plastic dry cleaning bags. And neatly folded clothes sat on the shelves.

*This guy's a neat freak*, McDavid thought.

As he looked through Derrick's wardrobe, McDavid felt the hairs on his neck stand up. Derrick had been pacing and fidgeting since the cops came into his house. But now Derrick was standing so close behind McDavid, trying to see what he was doing, that McDavid could feel his breath. It startled him.

"Hey, you need to back up," McDavid told him.

McDavid didn't know what he might find in Derrick's house besides Randi's missing keys, but so far he could see nothing suspicious.

"Where are the clothes you were wearing Saturday night?" McDavid asked.

Derrick disappeared into his laundry room and returned with a black pair of jeans.

"I want them back," he said.

Derrick did not, however, supply the shirt he wore the night before.

As the minutes ticked by while officers passed through

every room, opening each closet and cabinet, looking under the beds and sofas, Derrick became increasingly nervous and less cooperative. He called his mother, who showed up with her husband a few minutes later. Derrick spoke with them outside in the yard.

A few minutes later, Derrick was back in the house.

"Look, I want y'all out of my house," he said. "I want y'all out of here."

The officers knew they had to leave. They had no search warrant. When they regrouped at Swifty's truck stop after the search, they also agreed not to try to get one. Crime scene technicians were processing Randi house, but at the time they had no hard evidence to link Derrick to Randi's disappearance. And they did not think Derrick's record of arrest in the vicinity of a suspected murder was enough to claim probable cause. No judge, they thought, would allow them to search a man's home based on the vague and circumstantial evidence that gave them their gut feelings. They would just have to wait until more evidence might turn up to help nail Derrick for the crime.

They would have to wait a long time.

# CHAPTER 22

# Enter Dannie Mixon

In January 1999, Zachary got a new police chief. Drew Burk was a wiry, determined man. He came into his elected position with a mission. He wanted to solve the Oak Shadows murders and bloody cemetery attack.

For nearly a year, suspicions ran high in Zachary that the three cases were linked, that the little town might have a brutal serial killer lurking in its midst. The idea was solidified by a speculative column in the *Advocate* published after Randi's disappearance.

Then on Halloween 1998, *America's Most Wanted* aired an hour-long program on Zachary's unsolved mysteries, linking them not only to a possible serial killer but also to the legend of the cemetery witch. It left a bad taste in the locals' mouths.

During his first few months in office, Burk learned the Louisiana Attorney General's Office had a staff of investigators available to assist small police departments with tough criminal cases, like the ones in Zachary.

By early 1999, Randi's case was stone cold like the others. At the one-year anniversary of her disappearance, detectives still did not have her body. Technically, she remained classified as a missing person, but no one in the department doubted Randi was dead.

They were less confident, however, about who killed her. Derrick Todd Lee was still a prime suspect, but so was Randi's ex-husband.

A few weeks after Randi disappeared, Michael Mebruer failed a polygraph test during one of his interrogations. He then hired a lawyer and quit cooperating with the investigation.

By the end of April 1999, the case was at a standstill. Detectives did not have the evidence to make an arrest of either suspect. Their investigation had deteriorated to occasional checks on tangential and usually dead-end leads, and for McDavid, regular drive-bys of Derrick's house.

Burk hoped a fresh set of eyes looking at the case might help crack it open.

In late April 1999, Burk requested the assistance of Attorney General Richard Ieyoub's office. And on April 27, Zachary's three unsolved cases were assigned to Attorney General Investigator Dannie Mixon.

Mixon was not a guy fresh out of the police academy. In 1999, he was a hard-bitten, irascible, white-haired, plodding detective with more than forty years of investigative work behind him.

He got his first taste of police work at seventeen in the Louisiana State Police Crime Lab, where he helped process photographs and fingerprints. His mother, who worked there, got him the job after he married straight out of high school.

When he started college at LSU in Baton Rouge that fall, he continued to work at the lab full-time. After earning a history degree, he contemplated law school but quickly realized he needed a job pronto to support his wife and five kids. He was set to go to the state police academy, where he'd receive training as a state police trooper, but was offered a better job as an East Baton Rouge Sheriff's deputy.

He began duty on August 1, 1960, as a juvenile detective, but the title says nothing about the work required. As a detective, he handled everything from patrolling the streets to drug arrests to triple homicides.

His territory was Scotlandville, a gritty, impoverished, and predominantly black community on the northern outskirts of Baton Rouge. The area offered low-rent housing and after-hours drinking in the cinderblock roadhouse bars and pool halls that held sway on the landscape.

"We busted up a lot of fights," Mixon recalled. "Saw a lot of gun violence."

Street stabbings were a nightly affair. Barroom brawls often turned deadly. Mixon once arrested a man who shot up a bar, killing a man after the two argued over who won a pool game.

It was a tough environment. But Mixon reveled in it. He liked his rough edges. People skills were for politicians, not cops. And he was not out to make friends. On the streets, he got a reputation as a hassler, the kind of cop who won't leave his suspects alone, haunting them, harassing their friends and family and neighbors and coworkers until he got his arrest. He was hated in Scotlandville, earning his rep as The Scoundrel.

Mixon didn't mind the title. He kinda liked it. Still brags about it today. He was never ashamed of throwing bad guys behind bars, even if it required a little roughing up. Through the years, he racked up dozens of good arrests on tough cases, sometimes gliding the edge of legality.

In the early 1990s, he was called to a gruesome murder scene in a quiet middle-class Baton Rouge subdivision. A young married mother was raped and stabbed to death in her home—the killer had bitten off one of her breasts—while her two children, both under three, slept in a nearby room.

The day after the murder, when Mixon stopped for lunch at a nearby barbecue restaurant, a man approached him and described a wild-eyed, unstable man wearing headphones that he had seen the day before in a convenience store near the murder scene.

The tip was a long shot, but Mixon wanted to check it out. He and his partner went to the store, and while they waited to speak to the cashier, a wild-eyed, scrubby looking man wearing headphones walked in.

When the man saw Mixon, who was wearing a badge, he bolted out the door.

"There's the son of a bitch right there," Mixon said.

He and his partner got in their car and began following the man down a busy thoroughfare. The man was walking so fast he was almost running. He clearly was not going to stop.

As Mixon and his partner, who was driving, pulled up behind the man, Mixon's partner warned, "We can't stop him; we don't have any probable cause."

"Whoever murdered and mutilated that woman was a crazy, psychotic son of a bitch," Mixon shot back. "And this guy is a crazy, psychotic son of a bitch. Pull over!"

Mixon jumped out and cuffed the man. Hours later, after gently sharing a Sprite and a bag of Cheez-Its with the man, acting like an understanding minister, Mixon got the suspect to confess.

"That was one of my proudest moments," Mixon says.

The man had escaped from a mental hospital sixty miles away a month earlier and made his way to Baton Rouge. He had spent time in the house where the woman was killed when his sister used to live there with her family.

Soon after breaking that case, Mixon was offered a job with Louisiana Attorney General Richard Ieyoub's office as an investigator. It's not a big department—just a dozen detectives are on staff—but they specialize in difficult cases. When small police agencies are confronted with tough investigations, crimes they do not have the staff or experience to handle, they can call in the attorney general's troops.

Zachary was more than willing to get the help.


On April 27, 1999, Mixon met with Zachary Detective David McDavid, who was the lead investigator on the Randi Mebruer case and had reopened the Connie Warner and cemetery attack cases in recent years. McDavid briefed Mixon on what police knew about their two suspects in Randi's case— Michael Mebruer and Derrick Todd Lee. But he stressed his suspicions about Derrick.

He told Mixon the Zachary police had been chasing Derrick Todd Lee through their neighborhoods for years. They had caught him peeping, breaking into homes, and wandering the streets of Oak Shadows in dark clothing and carrying a knife and gloves.

Everyone on the department suspected him of killing Randi. They did not have to stretch to imagine he was also responsible for Connie Warner's death and the cemetery attack.

For the last few years, McDavid had been trying to rework Connie's and the cemetery cases, and his suspicions always came back to Derrick. Just two months earlier he believed he caught a break.

Michele Chapman, one of the cemetery attack victims, came in on March 1, 1998, to try another photo lineup. This time, McDavid put Derrick Todd Lee into the mix.

Michele looked at the six photos, three in a row on two lines. They were all black men with medium-colored skin, wide noses, short-cropped hair, oval faces, and almond-shaped eyes. They all looked so similar.

Michele examined each face carefully. When she got to number five, she began to tremble and tears filled her eyes.

"That's him," she said. She told McDavid she remembered his nose, his forehead, his short hair, but mostly his eyes. She still sees his face at night while trying to sleep.

Mixon listened to McDavid, but he quickly realized it was too late to do anything with the case. McDavid had missed his chance to arrest Derrick for the crime. The teens were attacked on April 3, 1993. It was now April 27, 1999. The six-year statute of limitations had just passed. Even if they caught the guy, nailed him with fingerprints and a victim ID, they could not prosecute.

Connie's case was another story. Murder carries no statute of limitation, but nearly seven years had passed since she was killed. Memories fade. Witnesses move away or die. Investigators change jobs. Mixon knew her case would be difficult to resolve.

His best bet at solving any of the three crimes fell on Randi's case. If the cases were connected, he knew, then catching Randi's killer would also solve the others.

Kurt Wagner, one of Mixon's assistant investigators at the

time, recalls Mixon's return to the attorney general's office from the meeting with Zachary police that day.

"It's a slam-dunker!" Mixon said. "It's a black man who's been caught peeping in the neighborhood."

He asked Wagner to collect background information on Derrick Todd Lee: arrest records, job history, anything he could dig up. Mixon is a paper trail investigator. He likes to know what his suspect was doing before, during, and after the murder. Was he unemployed? On parole? Broke? What kind of car was he driving?

Zachary shared their case file on Randi's murder, but it was thin, and Mixon wanted to start over, from the beginning, in case something was missed on the first go-round. He preferred to rely on his own investigative steps.

The documents Wagner began pulling in piled high: Derrick's arrest and prison record, the list of cars he owned, his sketchy work schedule, his financial woes, and the 911 calls his wife made about his abuse, which did not always lead to arrests.

Mixon and his investigators were getting a clearer picture of Derrick, and he was looking more and more like the man they wanted for Randi's murder.

In mid-May, Wagner thought he struck gold when he asked the East Baton Rouge Parish Sheriff's Office to run Derrick's name through the local pawnshop records.

"Bam!" Wagner said. "We got him pawning a .22."

When Derrick got low on cash, especially after he burned through Jackie's inheritance money, he visited the pawnshops. One place he frequented was EZ Pawn & Gun Shop at 6074 Airline Highway in north Baton Rouge.

His first trade with shop owner Robert Hubbard was a nineteen-horsepower Craftsman rider lawn mower for $375 in January 1999.

Hubbard remembers a neatly dressed, friendly young man. "He was a smooth talker. Real clever. We had a good rapport."

Derrick never complained about the price Hubbard offered, never tried to talk him into giving more. And even though Derrick was at the shop for money, he never appeared desperate, not like some of Hubbard's customers who came in with grungy old clothes and a fidgety demeanor. "He was not a dirty-looking guy."

Derrick was also the type to come back for his property.

Three months after he cashed in the lawn mower, Derrick returned to EZ Pawn with money to buy the machine out of hock.

Three days later, though, on March 29, 1999, he was back again to trade in something else: a Marlin Model 60 .22 caliber rifle.

From Derrick's criminal records, Wagner knew Derrick was still on probation in May 1999 for the 1997 Peeping Tom arrest in Zachary. Derrick was also a two-time felon, and under federal laws, that meant he could face several years in prison for simply possessing the gun.

Wagner had him. He wanted to arrest the son of a bitch. The records were irrefutable. Derrick had used his driver's license for the pawn. Hubbard kept the original pawn receipt with Derrick's signature, and Wagner was able to match Derrick's signature to his signature on his parole reports.

Even though Hubbard was unable to pick Derrick out of a photo lineup, Wagner believed it was a slam-dunk gun case. He asked the federal Bureau of Alcohol, Tobacco and Firearms to run a trace on the rifle's serial number. The gun belonged to a Leonard Washington from Jackson, Louisiana. But the ATF had no record the rifle was reported stolen.

That was a surprise to Washington, who had called the police the previous October after realizing his rifle was missing from his Jackson home. When Mixon and Wagner interviewed him, Washington insisted the cops took his report. They came to his house, but no record existed of his complaint. Either it was lost or never filed.

But Mixon wasn't interested in the missing police report. He wanted to hear more about Washington's ex-girlfriend, Gloria.

Gloria had been living with Washington just prior to the gun going missing. And Gloria had a cousin, a Derrick Todd Lee, who often came over to the house to visit. He knew the home's layout, knew where the gun was kept, and knew Washington's schedule.

**ST. MARTIN SHERIFF'S OFFICE**
400 St. Martin Street
St. Martinville, LA 70582

**St. Martin Composite**
May 23, 2003

*Suspect Vehicle*
Gold 1997 Mitsubishi Mirage Four Door

*Hampton has it!*

Suspect vehicle had a Hampton Dealership plate on the front of the vehicle.

Suspect is wanted by St. Martin Sheriff's Office for questioning in an Aggravated Rape. Suspect was described as a light skinned black male, possibly in his late 20's to early 30's approximately 5'09" to 6'01", muscular build, approximately 220 pounds, short hair and clean shaven

**To Report Information, Please call the**
**MULTI AGENCY HOMICIDE TASK FORCE'S TIP LINE**

# 1-866-389-3310

On Friday, May 23, 2003, the task force released this sketch after linking the serial killer's DNA to a July 2002 St. Martin Parish attack. The picture brought in several tips about Derrick Todd Lee. *(Photo by the St. Martin Parish Sheriff's Office)*

*Courtesy of Jack and Betty Brooks*

*Courtesy of the Yoder family*

*Courtesy of the Colomb family*

*Courtesy of the Pace family*

Clockwise from top left: Connie Warner, Carrie Lynn Yoder, Charlotte Murray Pace, Dené Colomb.

*Courtesy of the Barr family*

*Courtesy of the Wilson family*

*Courtesy of the Boisfontaine family*

*Courtesy of the Kinamore and Piglia family*

Clockwise from top left: Geralyn DeSoto, Gina Green, Pam Kinamore, Eugenie Boisfontaine.

The purple chair where Connie spent most of her evenings. Her family suspects she placed her needlepoint on the floor in front of her, perhaps to see who was at the door, in the moments before she was attacked.

*(Courtesy of the Louisiana State Attorney General's Office)*

Police suspect Connie's mattress was knocked off the box springs in a struggle with Lee. Her family believes she probably tried to reach her can of mace, which was in the open drawer of the bedside dresser.

*(Courtesy of the Louisiana State Attorney General's Office)*

Above: Randi Mebruer's small brick and frame ranch in the Oak Shadows subdivision of Zachary, Louisiana. *(Courtesy of the Louisiana State Attorney General's Office)*

Left: A bloody pink garbage bag from Randi Mebruer's kitchen was found outside her home in April 1998. Lee's semen was found on the bag five years later when DNA tests were finally conducted on the bag. *(Courtesy of the Louisiana State Attorney General's Office)*

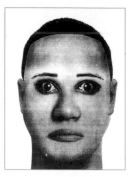

Left: Michele Chapman provided this composite sketch after she and her boyfriend were attacked by a man with a machete in a Zachary cemetery in April 1993. *(Courtesy of the Zachary Police Department)*

Below: Derrick Todd Lee's rap sheet printed out as a suspect in Randi Mebruer's murder. Baton Rouge Police detective Keith Bates suggested Zachary Police detective David McDavid compare Lee's face to the composite sketch of a suspect in a 1993 cemetery attack. *(Courtesy of the Zachary Police Department)*

## Suspect Rap Sheet

| | |
|---|---|
| SID: 001392984 | ATN: 17001 |
| LBN: 97003256 | |
| Last Name: LEE, | Initia |
| First Name: DERRICK | Suffix: |
| Address: 4273 S HWY 61 | |
| ST FRANCISVILLE | LA 70775 |
| Race: B Sex: M | Height: 6' 1 We |
| DOB: 11/5 /1968 | Birth Place: LA |
| Booking Date: 08/1 /1997 | |
| SSN: 439270426 | |
| FBI No.: | |
| DLN: 5496332 | State: LA |
| Charge Agency: PDZK | |
| Gang Affiliations: | |

| Mustache: Medium | Skin Tone: | Hair Color: BLK |
|---|---|---|
| Beard: None | Body Build: Medium | Hair Length: Above ea |
| | | Eye Color: BRO |

| Scars: Type: Location: | Tattoos: Type: Location: Litteral: | Marks: Location: |
|---|---|---|

Notes:

MCDAVID,

COMPARE THIS ONE
TO YOUR COMPOSITE
FROM "FACES"

*Keith Bates*

The shoe tread marks left near Denė Colomb's body were linked to this style of Adidas sneaker. (*Photo by the Baton Rouge Police Department and Serial Killer Task Force*)

Front: Dannie Mixon. Back, left to right: Ricky Murphy, Todd Morris, Chris Ribera, Jeff Bergeron, Ray Day. (*Courtesy of MaKeisha Johnson-August*)

Suspect is wanted for the *SERIAL MURDERS* of at least five south Louisiana Women. Suspect is to be considered Armed and Dangerous. Anyone with information on the whereabouts of this suspect is encouraged to contact their local law enforcement immediately or the

*Multi Agency Homicide Task Force*
**1-866-389-3310**

On Sunday, May 25, 2003, the DNA sample taken from Lee by Louisiana Attorney General Investigator Dannie Mixon and Zachary police was matched to the serial killer's DNA profile. The next day, the task force notified the public. *(Photo by the Baton Rouge Police Department and Multi Agency Homicide Task Force)*

When Washington and Gloria split, and she moved out—with the help of her brother and Derrick—she took more than just her possessions. Washington noticed his gold Timex watch and a gold chain also disappeared with her. He always suspected Gloria and her family.

After talking with the investigators, Washington was sure Derrick had taken his rifle, too.

Investigators needed only to file the paperwork and present the evidence to the proper state and federal authorities to pursue prosecution against Derrick.

McDavid, with the assistance of Baton Rouge City Police, went to the EZ Pawn & Gun Shop to confiscate the rifle and the original pawnshop receipt.

"They were very interested in that gun," Hubbard said. "I never got it back."

But Wagner's boss, Ronnie Black, the director of criminal investigations at the Attorney General's Office, was not so interested. He wanted investigators to focus on Randi's murder, not a gun.

"We don't want to mess around with a gun charge," Wagner recalls Ronnie telling him. "This is a murder investigation."

Likewise, when McDavid asked Mixon if he should pursue the gun charge, Mixon echoed Black's orders and suggested he "hold off for now."

So the case faded away. The gun and pawnshop receipt sat untouched in McDavid's office for over a year. And none of the agencies involved—the Attorney General's Office, Zachary Police, the Baton Rouge Police, the East and the West Feliciana Parish Sheriff's Offices, or the ATF—actively pursued any charges against Derrick.

Once again, he slipped through the cracks.


Rather than arrest him, investigators on Randi's case put Derrick under surveillance in early June 1999. It was an exercise in barhopping and high-speed driving.

Every night, Derrick traveled from bar to bar to bar in Saint Francisville and Zachary and Scotlandville and places in between. More than once he left with a woman in tow to visit a motel or her home.

"He did not stay home in the evenings," Wagner said. "It was clear that he had the kind of marriage where he could do whatever damned thing he wanted to do, and he had a hell of a sex drive."

Just before nine p.m. on Friday, June 4, investigators followed Derrick to the Lane Memorial Hospital in Zachary, where his girlfriend, Cat, was recovering from a cesarean section. She had just given birth to their son, Dedrick Tyquan Lee.

But Derrick did not stick around long to coo over his new baby. By 10:20, he was out the door and driving his wife's 1997 maroon Mitsubishi Eclipse south to Alsen, where he stopped at Club Destination for a few minutes, then headed to another nearby bar for twenty minutes, then another for twenty minutes, and then he sped back to Club Destination.

Again, he only stayed for about twenty minutes, but it was long enough to find a woman. She was drunk. She and her boyfriend had just broken up. She was angry and ready to let loose. She was supposed to go out with her girlfriends that night, but they canceled at the last minute, so she went out alone. Derrick bought her a few drinks, then asked her to go to a nearby motel. She did not refuse.

They drove to the motel, but after Derrick walked inside for a few minutes he returned to the car without a motel key. They drove back to the bar, where the woman got in her car, and Derrick followed her home.

He disappeared inside with her for an hour, then walked outside to his car and drove home.

The next night, June 5, investigators followed Derrick from his home on Highway 61 to his mother's home on Blackmore. He stopped in only for a few minutes, then headed north on Highway 61, driving like a bullet train. Investigators could not keep up without revealing their tail.

"He drove like a maniac," Mixon says.

Even with up to six cars following Derrick at a time, investigators could not keep up with his speeds of eighty to ninety miles per hour along the twisting, two-lane rural roads he knew so well.

When tailing him, investigators used a technique called leapfrogging, which required a caravan of investigators behind Derrick. The idea is to ensure the same car is not following behind him all the time. The lead car followed Derrick for a few minutes, then turned off the road, allowing the next car to pull into the lead behind Derrick.

The car that pulled off the road, however, then had to turn around and catch up with the caravan. The process works when driving at normal speeds, but when the tag is flying at eighty miles per hour on an empty country road in the middle of the night, the job can be risky.

One night, as he tried to catch the caravan, Wagner reached one hundred miles per hour on Highway 964, just outside Zachary. As he rounded a curve, he could not keep the car on the road. He went airborne as his car hit the shoulder and went over a small hill, landing in a field of weeds. Unharmed, he revved the car in reverse and managed to get back on the road with little damage to the car but plenty to his ego.

He had been racing to Saint Francisville, where investigators watched Derrick pull into a Chevron station, but not for gas. He parked and walked several blocks to the Saint Francisville Square apartment complex.

By the time Wagner arrived, Derrick had already slipped into the buildings' inner courtyard.

"I'll follow him on foot," Wagner said over the radio. His adrenaline was still rushing. He wanted to stay on Derrick's back.

But Mixon and Black, sitting in another car, feared Wagner might blow their cover.

"Sit tight," Wagner was ordered.

And the men sat back as Derrick prowled through the complex.

# CHAPTER 23

# Stalked

When Collette Walker moved into the Saint Francisville Square Apartments in early 1999, she was trying to pick up the pieces of her life after the end of a second marriage. The first had lasted fifteen years and gave her two teenage children. The second, which she rushed into after her first husband left her for an eighteen-year-old schoolgirl, lasted less than a year.

But she still believed in the goodness of people. She had grown up in rural Louisiana, just outside Zachary, where people were friendly with strangers. She was trusting and felt immune from the dangers of big city life.

In April of that year, she was working long hours as a cashier at a fresh seafood store that doubled as a local gas station in Saint Francisville. The job provided more than just a paycheck. The position behind the counter allowed Collette, a buxom blond with big blue eyes and an easy smile, lots of socializing time. She chatted all day with customers, some of whom habitually stopped by the store just to see her.

Collette is not sure how many times Derrick came into the store before she noticed him, but that April, she recalls the moment he first spoke with her.

She was ringing up one of her regular customers, telling him about her dream car, the Mitsubishi Eclipse. In midsentence, a well-dressed black man standing in line a few customers back jumped into her conversation.

"My wife has an Eclipse," he blurted out.

Collette looked up at the man. On his feet were spit-polished snakeskin boots and atop his head, rising high above his flirtatious smile and winks, was a big black cowboy hat.

"It's for sale," he added.

Collette was a little stunned. Not by the information, but by his behavior.

"Usually black men don't cut right into your conversation like that," she said later.

Barely able to buy clothes, Collette smiled and thanked the man and explained she could not afford a new car. Two days later, however, Derrick showed up at the gas station in a gold Eclipse. He strode inside the store and pointed out the window at it.

"There it is . . ." He told her, again with that flirtatious, friendly smile.

Collette politely begged off again, telling him she could not buy the car. But Derrick does not like the word no. Besides, he wasn't really interested in selling Collette the car.

He began to stop by the store regularly to see her. Then, in early June, as she returned home from work about eleven p.m., she ran into him at her apartment complex. He was walking toward her. He smiled and said hello as he passed. She assumed he was visiting a friend.

But the surprise encounters began to increase in frequency. And the smile and friendly greetings soon became a passing whistle or over-the-shoulder suggestion he seemed to know would not be accepted: "Wanna go get a drink?"

She tried to shrug off his advances, rationalizing it as harmless flirting. She was accustomed to men hitting on her. She was a good-looking woman, and she knew men sometimes got the wrong idea from her friendly, playful banter. He would get the hint soon enough, she thought. He would fade away.

But the man, whose name she had yet to learn, was not fading away. He was trying to get closer. Collette did not know at the time, but he was stopping by the store when she wasn't there, trying to figure out her schedule. He also grilled her coworkers, two black women, if she was prejudiced. He wanted to know if she dated black men.

On June 12, 1999, a Saturday night, Collette left work just after ten p.m. She parked her car in front of the apartment complex five minutes later. A male friend stopped by for a few minutes, then left again about ten thirty. A few minutes later, she, too, left the apartment with plans to visit friends at another local gas station. She often passed the late-night hours sipping on a fountain Coke and catching up on the local gossip with the other cashiers, an event that counts as a night on the town in Saint Francisville.

She shut her front door and turned toward the parking lot. She didn't see him, didn't even feel his presence. But when she looked up, he was right there, just four feet away. Her heart jumped.

Derrick was as still as stone. He smiled, as if he was surprised to see her. "Oh, hey," he said. "You live in that apartment?"

Collette didn't have time to respond before he pried further. "Is that your boyfriend who just left?"

"No," was all she could get out. She began walking to her car. Derrick kept pace with her. This time, he wasn't going away.

"He has a nice truck," Derrick said.

"Yeah." She kept walking.

"Where you going?"

"To the store."

"How about we go for a ride across the river and get a beer?"

Across the river is across the Mississippi from Saint Francisville. A small ferry carries cars over to the little town of New Roads, where the bars provide a notorious frolicking ground for cheating spouses.

"No, I'm not going anywhere but to the store and back," she told him.

"But it's the weekend . . ."

"Yeah, well, I'm not going out this weekend."

"What about Sunday? Do you want to go out Sunday?"

"No, really, I'm not doing anything this weekend."

"OK, but at least give me a ride to my truck. I was just visiting a friend, and I need to get back to my truck. It's right over there . . ."

He pointed in the direction she would be going, just up the street.

"Sorry," she said as she slipped into her car and shut the door.

Collette stayed at the gas station for more than an hour. She wasn't sure what to think about the man's more aggressive pursuit of her, but she was comforted by the presence of a local police officer on duty at the store.

She finally left to go home sometime after midnight. She pulled into her parking space at the complex. In the beam of the headlights, she could see all along the walkway stretching between her and the front door to her apartment. Her eyes strained to see behind the shrubs and trees. Everything looked still. She got out and hurried to her front door. Her keys jingled as she inserted them into the lock.

"Hey." Derrick moved like a cat from around the corner of her building and was instantly standing within arm's reach.

"Can't you give me a ride to my truck?"

"No, I'm going to bed." She hustled inside and shut the door as he persisted with the request, which she could hear through the closed door.

"You gonna make me walk?"

Collette was uncomfortable with the attention this man was focusing on her, but at the time, she did not think he was dangerous. Irritating, yes, but she reminded herself that this was safe, friendly little Saint Francisville. Murders didn't happen there. The town sees less than one murder every couple of years. Besides, he was a local. People knew him. People had seen him at the store. He couldn't possibly want to harm her, she thought. That's not logical. He'd get caught. He just wanted a date.

She didn't see Derrick for two days, and by Monday, she had almost stopped looking over her shoulder. That night, she returned home from work about ten thirty p.m. She unlocked her door and was about to step inside when Derrick brushed past her, pushed open the door, and walked into her home. He flicked off the lights, knowing just where to find the switch, as he strutted toward the kitchen.

Standing at the doorway, Collette was dumbfounded, but she was determined not to let him get the best of her. *Don't show any fear,* she told herself. *Stay in control.* She did not call the police. The thought did not even cross her mind. She believed she could handle him on her own. That was her new motto. Taking care of herself. She turned the lights back on and saw he was peering into her refrigerator.

"Do you have any beer?"

"I don't keep beer."

He shut the door and opened the cabinets, finding himself a glass. He walked to the sink, turned on the kitchen faucet, and filled the glass.

"I've been watching you," he said as he moved back into the living area and sat down on the couch.

Most women assume they would immediately run to a phone and dial 911 if a man walks into their home uninvited. But violent crime statistics are filled with victims who were more concerned about seeming rude than protecting themselves. Nearly 80 percent of rapes are committed by people the women knew: friends, neighbors, acquaintances. No matter how tenuous the relationship, many women are compelled to be polite to rather than suspicious of someone they know, even when he unexpectedly shows up at their front door.

Collette has a hard time explaining why she didn't walk away from her apartment that night, but she admits she did not want him to think she was prejudiced against black men.

"I don't have anything against blacks," she said. "I just don't date black men."

She also did not feel threatened, not overtly. She felt uncomfortable, but not in danger. She figured he just wanted to talk with her. She could handle that. She knows herself as a kind and generous person. She would hear him out, then let him down easy. He would eventually go away. At least that's what she told herself.

"I've been wanting to ask you out for a long time," he told her that night. "You've seen me in the store, right? That's why I've been coming in so much."

"Oh, yeah?" Collette sat down in a chair right next to the front door, which she left wide open.

"We should get together . . . You ever date black guys?"

"Black guys ask me out, but I don't date blacks," she said. "We can be friends, though."

"Because of your family? 'Cause of what they'll think?"

"They'd probably disown me."

The man laughed and shook his head. "The last white woman I dated said the same thing . . . She picked me up and took me to her apartment for the whole weekend. No one knew about us. We'd go out of town together, where no one knows us."

"I'm sorry, I just don't date black men."

Her words were not having the effect she intended. With each new refusal, he seemed more insistent, confident that his flirtatious arguing would win her over.

"I know white women have fantasies about dating black men . . ." He smiled.

"I don't."

"If you were with me, no one else would matter anymore; you'd only want me."

"I've got a boyfriend."

"I'd take good care of you if you need money or help or whatever. I always take good care of my white women because they know how to make a black man feel like a real man. Black women don't treat their men right. They just want their men to pay the bills . . . Come on, let's go out of town tonight, across the river . . ."

"No, I can't."

"Why?"

"You could be one of those crazy people who would kill me and throw me on the side of the road."

The man laughed again, only this time he gave her a hard stare.

"You seem nervous. Are you scared of me?"

"Should I be?"

"If I wanted to hurt you, I could do it right now. Your neighbors aren't home, and your kids aren't home. I could rape you right now, and no one would know."

He was right. Her children were with their father. The neighbors were out. She was suddenly afraid. She realized she was not in control of the situation. She stood up and moved toward the open door.

"You really need to go now. I have to go to the store."

"Can I ride with you?"

"No."

"Can you give me a ride to my car?"

"No, you need to go."

Before leaving, Derrick grabbed a Post-it pad off the coffee table. His thick hands deftly flipped past the first several sheets and scribbled his number deep inside the stack of paper.

"Call me. My name is Todd. But don't tell anyone about me. I like to keep my business to myself."

"I'm not going to call," she said.

"Can I at least have a hug?" He was walking toward her. Without waiting for an answer, he put his arms around her. She stood still with her arms at her side, her heart racing, her body paralyzed with fear, her mind waving giant red flags.

"You didn't hug back," he said.

He was not moving toward the door, so Collette stepped quickly out and didn't look back.

When she returned two hours later, the door was locked, and Derrick was gone.

The next night, Collette was at home with her twelve-year-old daughter and thirteen-year-old son. She was glad she was not alone. She double-checked the door to make sure it was locked. She did not tell her children about the previous night's encounter because she did not want to scare them. But when her daughter wanted to go outside to the car for her fingernail polish, Collette insisted on going with her.

It was after eleven p.m. when Collette was standing at the door as the lanky girl hurried from the apartment to the car twenty feet away. She watched her daughter dig through the car. No one else was around, but she sensed someone was staring at her. She looked around the apartment complex, trying to see into the shadows all around her. She could not see anyone, but the feeling did not go away.

"Hurry up!" she called to her daughter.

"I am . . ."

The girl slammed the car door shut and walked briskly toward the apartment. She gave her mom a raised eyebrow when she saw Collette peering intently into the darkness.

"What are you looking at?"

Without a word from her mother, Derrick stepped out of the shadows of a small tree, startling gasps out of both of them.

"Is that your daughter?" he asked as he moved closer to Collette. "She looks just like you. She's very beautiful."

Collette quickly ushered her daughter inside and locked the door.

Now Collette was not only worried, she was angry. "You can mess with me, but don't mess with my daughter," she said.

The next day, Collette told her boss, the owner of Feliciana Seafood, and a friend who was a former cop, about her run-ins with Derrick. She had previously mentioned his flirting to coworkers but never in detail. They both told her to report him to the police.

In Saint Francisville, like many small towns, going to the police doesn't always mean going to the police station. Cops are often just neighbors or friends with badges and the power to throw someone in jail—or not. Police went to elementary school with the local criminals. Their parents go to bingo together. Or they all attend the same church. Enforcing the law in small towns is often done with a personal touch, like a call made first to a suspect's mama to find his whereabouts or a "talkin' to" instead of an arrest.

Collette's coworker took her to the home of Randy Metz, a Saint Francisville police officer, who knew Derrick from his multiple run-ins with the local law. Metz suggested Collette talk with another officer, Archer Lee—no relation to Derrick—about her complaints.

Archer had heard from the Attorney General's Office that they were looking at Derrick as a suspect in Randi Mebruer's disappearance, and Collette's story concerned him. But when he reported her complaints to the attorney general investigators, Archer said he was told they would handle it.

Collette asked if she should file a restraining order against Derrick, but she recalls police telling her it would be a waste of money. The order was just a piece of paper offering no protection from Derrick if he truly wanted to harm her.

Instead, Archer promised Collette the police would keep an eye on him.

Trusting the police, Collette agreed to wait. But in the weeks that followed, Derrick seemed to be at the apartment complex more than ever, although he did not try to get inside her apartment again. She assumed the police were doing their job as best they could, but she could not understand why they had not arrested him.

Her answer came to her door in the form of two men in dark suits, identifying themselves as investigators from the Louisiana State Attorney General's Office. Mixon and Kurt Wagner wanted to talk with Collette about her relationship with Derrick Todd Lee.

"You're originally from Zachary, right?" Mixon asked. "He must know you from there? Maybe you met him at a bar down there?"

"I don't go to bars," Collette told him, and she didn't like what he was implying.

"Do you know about the murders in Zachary?" he asked.

"I've heard of them."

"Derrick's our best suspect. We have him under surveillance."

Collette was stunned. No one had told her this before.

That night, she and her children moved in with a friend. But every time she went back to the apartment, she seemed to run into Derrick. She felt helpless, frustrated. She had done everything she was advised to do by law enforcement. The police told her a restraining order would not help. Mixon said Derrick was under surveillance, but he was still stalking her. He was still roaming free.

By August, her female neighbors began complaining about

him. He was now watching them, standing behind their bushes, and staring at them as they worked in their small yards. He was even peeking into their windows.

"Collette, that man was here creeping around again," a neighbor, Diane Halloway, said. "You've got to do something."

"I have," Collette shot back. "I've told the police. They want more evidence. Why don't you report him?"

On August 16, 1999, Halloway filed a complaint with the Saint Francisville police about Derrick, and police told her he would be arrested.

Three days later, believing Derrick was arrested, Collette moved back into her apartment. At the time, she had just started a new job as a dispatcher at the Saint Francisville Fire Department.

She was at work when she got the call from her daughter, hysterical.

The girl saw Derrick crouching in front of the apartment window, peering inside. When she screamed, her thirteen-year-old brother ran outside with a baseball bat, scaring Derrick off.

Collette was home in minutes.


"I was pissed. I thought he was in jail. My kids were in danger." She called Archer. "I told him, 'Somebody's going to pay if my kids get hurt.'"

He quickly assured her they would arrest Derrick immediately.

"We'll take him in as soon as we find him," Archer told her.

Now Collette demanded to know why Derrick wasn't arrested before, when she first made her complaint in June. Archer did not try to make excuses. He candidly told Collette his officers held off on arresting Derrick at the request of the attorney general's investigators.

"They wanted us to back off," Archer said years later. "They were on a case. We always try to work with these guys."

But by mid-August 1999, things were getting out of control. Clearly, no one was watching Derrick, and he needed to be stopped.

"They were going to be pissed at me for arresting him, but if something happened to Collette or her family, we'd get blamed—not them. It would be *our* fault for not arresting him."

That night, August 19, 1999, a warrant was issued for Derrick's arrest for stalking and unlawful entry into Collette's apartment. The date cited as the day of Derrick's illegal offense: June 12, 1999.

The next night, Archer Lee and another Saint Francisville police officer, Randy Metz, pulled into Derrick's driveway off Highway 61 at about eight thirty. His wife, Jackie, answered the door. On her heels came Derrick, storming to the door bare-chested and barefoot, in cut-off jeans.

"Derrick, we need to talk with you," Archer Lee said.

Derrick was already in a rage. "I don't have to talk to you."

"We've got a warrant."

"I didn't do nothing. Get out of my fucking house. This is my fucking house."

Derrick tried to slam the door shut, but Metz stuck his foot in the door, and Archer pushed it open. Metz, a man with arms solid as steel, grabbed Derrick by the forearm and pulled him outside.

"We've been watching you," Archer told Derrick. "We've got you on tape over at the Saint Francisville Square Apartments, harassing those women."

"I can go over there. I can fucking go wherever I want."

Archer was bluffing about the surveillance and videotape, but he elicited a confession of sorts from Derrick, who admitted he had been at Collette's apartment complex. As Derrick yammered on about his innocence and the unjust police harassment, the two officers cuffed him and took him to jail.

Bail was set at $150,000. Derrick could not pay his way out from behind bars this time. Instead, his family began collecting contributions from friends and relatives. Florence put up her home to secure $30,000 of the bond, and Jackie took out a loan on her house to help. Finally, in December, they had enough, and Derrick was released—with no alert to Collette.

In mid-December Collette got a call from a former coworker, one of the black women Derrick used to grill at the seafood store. She socialized in Derrick's circle of friends and wanted to pass on the news of his release.

"Derrick's out of jail," she told Collette.

"No, Derrick's in jail," Collette said.

"No, I'm at a party with him, and he's pissed. He's running his mouth about you. You better be careful."

Derrick pleaded guilty to charges of stalking and unlawful entry. Judge George Ware sentenced him to six months in jail but gave Derrick credit for time served and ordered the remainder of the sentence suspended as long as Derrick successfully completed two years of probation. Ware also ordered Derrick to stay away from Collette and complete fifteen days of community service.

"No one called me," Collette says of Derrick's day in court and sentencing. "They never took my case seriously."

# CHAPTER 24

# Derrick Escapes Scrutiny

By the fall of 1999, just a few months after he was assigned Randi's case, Mixon was losing interest in Derrick Todd Lee as a suspect. He had moved on to someone else, Michael Mebruer, Randi's ex-husband.

Mixon's change in course was not instigated by newfound evidence exonerating Derrick. On the contrary, when Derrick was arrested for stalking Collette, Mixon and his boys rushed up to Saint Francisville to interrogate him at the jailhouse.

Derrick was illogical, evasive. He denied he was a Peeping Tom. He insisted he did not remember being arrested in Zachary for peeping in the Oak Shadows subdivision. And he swore he knew nothing about Randi's disappearance. He said he didn't even understand why he was in jail for hanging around the Saint Francisville Square Apartments.

Investigators got nothing from him.

But Mixon was already beginning to look closer at Michael Mebruer. Mixon's initial feeling that Derrick was the killer faded when he began to get a better picture of Randi's ex-husband.

Michael had access—Randi would have let him inside. Motive—Randi had broken off their sexual relationship, they were fighting over child support payments, and Randi had a $30,000 life insurance policy with his name as beneficiary. And possibly means—he had been emotionally abusive to Randi in the past, and according to police, he had once threatened to kill his first wife.

The more Mixon dug around, the more dirt he uncovered about Mebruer. His coworkers said he was always looking for a quick and easy buck. He had a reputation as a womanizer and a cheat. And his temper was notorious. Even Randi's father, Ed, thought Mebruer was capable of killing Randi.

Most damning was the polygraph Mebruer had failed a few weeks after Randi disappeared. But then another nail hammered Mebruer to Mixon's cross.

Zachary gave a copy of the case files of the three unsolved attacks to the FBI's Behavioral Science Unit. Investigators hoped one of the agency's psychological profilers could tell them more about the man or men they should be looking for in the unsolved cases.

The profilers reviewed details of each case, looked at the crime scene photos, and examined each potential suspect, including Mebruer and Derrick.

In its 1999 report, the FBI determined that the cases were not linked. The man who attacked the teenagers lost control, he attacked randomly and in a rage. Connie, the report says, was likely killed by a spurned coworker who had acted nervous when interrogated and clammed up after hiring a lawyer.

In Randi's case, the FBI report notes that the killer took time to clean up after murdering Randi, suggesting he must have felt comfortable in the house, like he felt safe enough to stick around and wipe away his bloody prints.

The best suspect in her case, the report concluded, was Michael Mebruer.

With all those arrows pointing at Mebruer, Mixon was convinced he was guilty. For the next several years, he hounded

Mebruer, determined to uncover that one piece of evidence linking him to the murder.

As an old-school detective, Mixon believed in shoe leather investigations, paper trails, and witnesses. He was not the type to rely on the crime lab to drop DNA evidence into his lap. He and his investigators collected everything they could about Mebruer: his phone records, his bank records, his work records, his driving and car records. Investigators interrogated everyone Mebruer knew. They followed him for days at a time.

"If he farted, I knew about it," Mixon said.

The investigation bordered on harassment as Mixon plodded forward. But every new lead came to another dead end. Mixon and his team could find nothing to link Mebruer to his wife's murder.

"I've never put so much work into a case for so long and not break it," Mixon lamented to his assistant Wagner.

Countless hours were spent pursuing Mebruer, often at the exclusion of following other leads, including some investigators' continued suspicions of Derrick Todd Lee.

In Zachary, McDavid was frustrated with the overwhelming focus on Mebruer. He wanted to continue investigating Derrick. But a few months into the investigation, he was removed from the case. He was dogged with accusations that he had loose lips about details of the investigation that police wanted to keep secret.

Attorney general's investigators also alleged he failed to share important information about the case with them, which McDavid denies. He says he handed over the entire file.

Regardless of why, the investigation shifted focus from Derrick to Michael. And from late 1999, Derrick was no longer under much scrutiny from the Zachary police or the attorney general's investigators in the Zachary cases.


Meanwhile, the State Police Crime Lab was just finishing with the pieces of evidence submitted in Randi's case in the fall of 1999. Nearly eighteen months after bloody and stained items from Randi's home were submitted, the lab issued a report confirming the existence of blood and seminal fluid on several items.

The comforter on Randi's bed tested positive for seminal fluid. Blood was found on Randi's pajamas, her underwear, a towel, and the pink trash bags that were obviously wrapped around her body when she was removed from the home.

At the time, the crime lab was not conducting DNA tests. If police agencies wanted DNA testing of evidence, they had to hire private companies to do the work, often an expensive endeavor.

Consequently, no DNA analysis was completed by the state crime lab on the blood and seminal fluid found in Randi's home. But in the crime lab report, the forensic analyst, Carolyn Booker, said if investigators wanted further information from the evidence, they should seek DNA analysis of the comforter, trash bags, and other bloody items. Several years passed before Zachary followed the suggestion.

# CHAPTER 25

# An Angry Man

Derrick was pissed off when he walked out of the West Feliciana Parish jail in December 1999. He had been held behind bars just because that white bitch Collette didn't like him flirting with her.

While he was on the inside, he lost his job as a truck driver for Ascension Concrete. The bank won a $1,507 judgment against him for nonpayment on a loan. His wife had to take out a $30,000 second mortgage on the house to cover their bills and help pay his bond. His show truck was about to be repossessed. And worst, he thought his girlfriend, Cat, was running around with another man.

She was starting to give him as much trouble as his wife. Just a few days after he was set free, she gave him an ultimatum. Leave Jackie and move in with her and their new son, or it was over between them.

*Fuck her,* he thought. He had given her so much already. Hell, he had given the boy his name—Lee. That's more than

Derrick's father had done for him. When Cat got pregnant, his sister Tharshia advised against claiming the child as his own. He had no legal obligation. He didn't even know for sure if the kid was his child. But Florence's pain whispered in his ear.

"Don't do her like your father did to me," she said. "You know how that feels."

Derrick resented his father's neglect. He hated what Sammy had done to him.

Less than two years after Derrick was born, Sammy Ruth skipped out of the picture, returning to his wife and other children, who had moved to the New Orleans area.

Growing up, Derrick saw his father occasionally, but the two were not close. Sammy was a troubled man, and by the mid-1980s, found himself committed off and on to the psychiatric ward, where he was diagnosed at various times with major depression and manic depression and placed on antidepressant and antipsychotic drugs.

Like Derrick, Sammy was born into a poor and crowded household. He was the eighth of nine children. When he was only seventeen months old, his mother died giving birth to her last child. The children were then passed on to relatives, and Sammy was raised by an aunt in New Orleans.

He dropped out of school in the tenth grade and married his sweetheart, Rosetta. The couple and their five children were living in Long Beach, California, when Sammy began his relationship with Florence Lee and refused to return home.

In May 1968, when Florence was six months pregnant with Derrick, Rosetta sought the Louisiana court's assistance in collecting $1 a month alimony and $60 for child support from Sammy, who was then arrested for criminal neglect of his family. After pleading guilty to the charge, however, he was ordered to pay Rosetta only $25 a month to raise their children.

Sammy stayed with Florence off and on for nearly two years, then split for good after Tharshia was born. For much of Derrick's life, his father was absent, making only occasional trips up to Saint Francisville to visit. He was unapologetic. He was a rambler. A ladies' man. He did not like to be tied down, and was physically threatening to women. By 1973, after fathering a sixth child with Rosetta, the couple divorced and Sammy remarried—to another Rose—and fathered two more children.

He made no effort to help Florence financially, and as a boy, Derrick often thought bitterly of his father on the nights his mother came home exhausted from the sweet potato factory, her feet swelling out of her shoes, and collapsed on the sofa for a long cry. Derrick wiped away her tears and swore he would never treat his women that way.

As the years passed, Sammy's mental condition and health worsened.

In 1986, he was forced to retire from his City Park Police job because of a nerve problem, inflammatory neuropathy, that impeded his ability to move. Left to his natural inclinations, he felt the call of God, and he began preaching in 1988.

His godly ways, however, did not shine light onto his second marriage. In 1991, Sammy's instability had so strained his relationship with Rose, the couple had separated.

His behavior was becoming increasingly unpredictable and psychotic. In May, he was arrested twice, once for refusing to pay a cab fare and once for impersonating a police officer.

On May 7, at 9:30 in the morning, he chased a man through the streets of New Orleans while driving his 1991 Chrysler New Yorker. When the man stopped his car, Sammy got out and began yelling, "I'm a police officer! Get out of your car!"

Five months later, he pulled a gun on his wife.

It was on October 15. Rose had let Sammy borrow her car for the day and was driving him home that evening when he pulled a .38 caliber revolver out of a paper bag and pointed it at her. Terrified, Rose grabbed at the gun, wrecking her car into a utility pole in the process.

Sammy was arrested for attempted second-degree murder, but he was soon found incompetent to proceed to trial and was sent to a state mental hospital.

Months later, a court-appointed psychiatrist, Richard Richoux, found Sammy's condition was regressing, possibly because he was cheeking his medicine—hiding the pills in his mouth instead of swallowing them. Consequently, Sammy was still "psychotic and very unstable," suffering from a severe form of manic depression.

Richoux and another court-appointed psychologist agreed that Sammy was still too unstable to proceed to trial and not safe enough to release to the public. When the doctors reviewed Sammy's case again in November 1993, they found no improvement and felt he would not regain his sanity anytime in the foreseeable future.

Ironically, Sammy's incarceration at the mental hospital brought him closer to Derrick. The state housed its criminally insane at the Feliciana Forensic Facility, which happened to be in Jackson, Louisiana, just thirty miles from Saint Francisville.

Although the rest of Sammy's family abandoned him, Derrick visited his father a number of times in the hospital, bringing him such comforts from home as slippers and a robe. But it was too late to build a relationship. Sammy no longer had the mind for it, and Derrick no longer had the heart.

Now Cat was trying to take his son away. Derrick was sure all that bitch wanted was money. That's all black women ever wanted from him. So what if he hadn't given her a dime in months? He was in jail. When he was out, he regularly bought her diapers and dropped off cash now and again. If she tried to pull anything, he told her, he was going to fight for custody of their son.

He'd show her. He stopped by her apartment one night and took the boy, despite her protests. He was gone several hours, and she called the cops, but he knew she was too afraid to press charges.

Despite their split, Derrick could not let her go. He started following her. In mid-December, when Consandra was leaving a Saint Francisville hotel, Lee confronted her, cursing at her and calling her a slut.

On December 17, the day after Lee pleaded guilty to stalking Collette and earned two years' probation, Consandra called the police to report Derrick was threatening to kill her. Then on January 19, she sought a protective order from the court. But before it was issued, she ran into Derrick at a bar in Solitude the two used to frequent together.

On January 22, just after midnight, Consandra pulled into
the parking lot of Liz's Lounge. When she opened the door to
get out, Derrick was standing a foot away.

"I want to talk to you," he said.

"I don't want to talk to you," Consandra shot back, trying
to get out of her car.

Derrick pushed her back into her seat. She struggled to get
out. He smashed the car window, then grabbed her hair and
pulled her out onto the ground. He started punching her in the
face. He sat on top of her and pummeled her head.

"Derrick!" she screamed. "Please stop hitting me!"

As she begged him to stop, screaming for help, he continued to pound away.

Another bar patron pulled Derrick off Consandra, but as
several people rushed over to hold him, he started stomping
and kicking her face with his cowboy boots. He had gone
wild. He broke away from the people trying to hold him and
was on top of Consandra, again beating her in the face.

When he was pulled off her a second time, Consandra
grabbed her cell phone and dialed 911. She ran inside the bar
and, with the help of the other customers, hid behind the DJ on
the floor, before Derrick came barging inside looking for her.

Derrick ran when he heard the sirens. The West Feliciana
Parish Sheriff's deputy tried to block the roadway when he
saw Derrick was driving his way, trying to flee. Derrick did
not slow down. If the deputy had not jumped out of the way,
Derrick would have plowed him down.

Everyone at the bar knew Derrick, so it was only a matter
of hours before he was arrested and booked for aggravated
battery on Consandra, criminal damage to property, flight
from an officer, and attempted first-degree murder of a police
officer.

Consandra went to the West Feliciana Parish Sheriff's Office and filed a complaint. She seemed prepared to go as-
sertively forward with charges. But by April, she was refusing
to testify. The aggravated battery and criminal damages
charges were dropped. And as part of another bargain, Derrick pleaded to the lesser charge of aggravated flight from an
officer instead of attempted murder.

He could not avoid jail this time, however. His probation

for the stalking charge was revoked and, in addition, he was sentenced to serve one year in parish jail.

While he was inside, he wrote to the judge, pleading for an early release:

"If given this opportunity by you to have my sentence shortened, I will not let you, my family, society, or myself down," Derrick wrote. "I will be a productive citizen, an asset to all."

The judge denied his request.


When Derrick was released in January 2001, he returned to construction work, applying at his old employer JE Merit for a job. He had already burned through the money Jackie received from her father's accidental death. In early March, he was hired on to a temporary position in the solvent section at the Dow Chemical plant just south of Brusly, Louisiana.

Derrick would not have taken the job if it wasn't for his parole. He still felt overworked and underpaid. And he didn't like being under the thumb of a foreman again. His boss at Dow treated him like a kid, at least that's what he told his coworkers after blowing up at the man.

But Derrick had to be good, at least until his parole officer took the monitoring bracelet off his ankle. He needed to save some money to buy transportation. He relied on others to drive him around until April, when he and Jackie bought a 2001 goldish Hyundai Accent. And a few weeks later, he took Consandra to a Baton Rouge car lot where he signed a loan for a 2000 maroon Dodge Neon. By then, she was back into Derrick's arms, despite the scars he left on her face.


Two women were never enough for Derrick, though. Within a few months of his release, Derrick was looking for Collette again.

He stopped by the Feliciana Seafood store, not to buy anything but to snoop around. Store employees recognized him and his intentions when he popped his head around the corner to peer in the back to see who was working. He also began hanging out at the Saint Francisville Square Apartments until he realized Collette had moved.

Collette did not need the warnings from former coworkers and neighbors to know Derrick was on the streets again. She began receiving heavy breathing phone calls with the number blocked on her caller ID box. The person on the other end would not speak when she answered, but whoever it was remained on the line until she hung up. She was sure the caller was Derrick.

Collette again sought police help but was told the number was untraceable. She was getting nervous. She was now living with her fiancé and children on a large wooded tract of land with no close neighbors, no one in earshot.

Later that summer, her son awoke in the middle of the night to see Derrick's face peering in the window at him. The teenager jumped out of bed and ran outside. Derrick was standing in the moonlight holding a beer. When he saw the teen charging at him, Derrick threw the can to the ground and ran. A few weeks later, when Collette and her husband were out of town, the son again awoke in the middle of the night when the family dogs began barking wildly.

He looked out the window and saw a black man on their property walking toward the house. This time, he called the police before running outside. When officers arrived, however, the man had slipped away into the woods.

Collette was a wreck. She felt as if she was being followed everywhere she went and watched inside her home. She was afraid to go out. Her fiancé started carrying a gun. And they kept a shotgun nearby when inside the house. It was like living in a state of unending terror. She knew he was dangerous, but she didn't realize how dangerous.

Derrick continued working at Dow through the summer of 2001, showing up for work every day and on time, but when the monitoring bracelet around his ankle was removed, he began to arrive late and skip days.

Then, on September 27, he stopped showing up. He had been arrested the night before—just three days after Gina Green was murdered—for simple battery on his wife. Jackie called the West Feliciana Parish Sheriff's Office to report she was "having trouble" with Derrick again and wanted an officer to come out to their house and talk with him.

Derrick was hauled to jail for the night, but charges were later dropped.

Once he was free again, JE Merit sent him back to Dow Chemical in mid-December. The job was over fast. On January 11, he was laid off. He was so angry he walked off the site before the end of the day. He needed someone to take it out on.

# CHAPTER 26

# Dreams Slaughtered

January 14, 2002, began as a good day for Geralyn DeSoto. Change was in the air. Her December graduation from LSU was still fresh in her memory. She was looking forward to starting summer classes at the university's top-ranking occupational therapy program in New Orleans, a final step in steady pursuit of a career as an OT. And early that Monday morning, Sissy, as her friends and family knew her, was asked to interview for a job at an office not far from her home in the West Baton Rouge Parish town of Addis.

"Can you be there at two thirty today?" the job recruiter asked her.

"I'll be there," Geralyn promised.

All her hard work was paying off. For three years, the pretty brunette tomboy from the small country town of Simmesport, Louisiana, maintained a full class load at LSU's Baton Rouge campus, even through the summers. She also worked twenty hours a week at the campus Accounting Services and, every evening, made sure she was home to cook dinner for her husband.

Darren DeSoto was a demanding spouse. He kept tight tabs and high expectations on his wife. He bought her a cell phone so he could check in on her all day, sometimes every fifteen minutes. He wanted Geralyn to stay at their trailer home except for her outings to work or school or the grocery. If she left, he wanted to know with whom, to where, and for how long. At night, when he returned from his job at the Kaiser Aluminum plant, where he X-rayed pipes for minuscule fractures, he expected a freshly cooked dinner on the table.

Geralyn put up with it. He was her husband. They had been married for almost three years. His jealousy and control, she told herself, only reflected how much he loved her.

But sometimes, especially when he roughed her up, she thought about leaving him.

Like the time he ripped a tight blouse off her body, telling her she looked like a slut. Or when he grabbed her by the hair and forced her outside to her car.

"See those ashes!" he screamed, pointing at what he believed were cigarette ashes on the driver's window. "You were smoking!"

"No, I wasn't," Geralyn said. She knew how much he hated it. She had promised him she had quit.

But Darren didn't believe her denials, and he shoved her head down toward the car window, pushing her closer and closer to what he believed was irrefutable evidence.

"I'm not stupid!" he shouted. "You can't tell me that's not ashes. Just admit it !"

Later, she told friends she'd like to escape his violent temper, his constant control, but she was afraid.

"He'll find me," she'd say.

Despite the difficulties of her life, however, Geralyn kept a smile on her face and a steely determination never to let go of her career dreams.

"When she decided to do something, she continued down that path until she accomplished it," her mother, Melanie Barr, says.

In high school, where she played on the basketball team,

Geralyn decided she wanted a life in sports—not as a player or a coach, but as someone who could help the athletes in another way. She would train as an occupational therapist and come back to athletics to help injured players return to their games.

When she first applied for the occupational therapy program, she was rejected. Her grades and test scores were high, but not high enough. The school was highly competitive.

After she received notice of her rejection, however, she wrote the admissions board a letter. In it, she expressed her lifelong dream of becoming an OT, she wrote of her dedication and determination to accomplish her goal.

When the board read it, they did something they did not normally do. They were so impressed with Geralyn's passion and gumption, they let her into the program for a probationary semester. If she could handle the work, she could stay.

To Geralyn, the crack in the door shined gold into her life. She believed this was her ticket to happiness, to a good salary, a more exciting life. And going to school in New Orleans would offer her new freedoms. She knew she was about to start a whole new chapter in her life, and she was thrilled about it.

Before she could start the school's summer program, however, Geralyn needed one last prerequisite class in Baton Rouge that semester. And on January 14, she was bumping up against the deadline to pay her tuition.

She drove the ten miles to campus from her home in Addis, a speck on the map across the Mississippi from Baton Rouge, and after paying the bill, at about nine forty-five, she stopped by her old job to see a good friend.

She and Jonathan Soileau had worked together on campus at Accounting Services for three years. He had not seen her since she left in December after graduating. They went outside to smoke a cigarette together. She was in a good mood. Her blue eyes sparkled as she chatted excitedly about her upcoming classes and her job prospect. Jonathan was glad to see her so happy, to watch her wide, animated face light up so brightly.

Geralyn was home by 11:30, when she logged onto the Internet using the phone line. With her future so much on her mind, Geralyn wanted to send Professor Eve Taylor, the director of admissions for the occupation therapy program, a heartfelt note of gratitude.

"I just wanted to thank you and the faculty for allowing me to attend summer classes," Geralyn wrote in an e-mail she sent at 11:41 a.m. "Becoming an OT is a desire like no other to me. I intend to do everything necessary to fulfill this dream."

A few minutes later, at 11:50 a.m., she signed off from the Internet. Someone was at her door. He needed to use the phone.

Geralyn was a trusting person. She was raised by devout Baptists. Her parents had worried about her moving to Baton Rouge, but when she and Darren settled into a small, one-lane trailer park way outside the city limits, they believed she was safe. So did Geralyn. The trailer park was a neighborly spot. People looked out for each other. Crime was not a problem—not even theft.

Geralyn let the man use her phone. He dialed a number at 11:51 a.m. The call went out to the ExxonMobil plant in Baton Rouge, but the stranger at her door did not really need to reach anyone. He only wanted to get inside Geralyn's home and past her defensive guard. And that's when he attacked.

He hit her hard on the head with the phone, making his intentions suddenly nightmarishly clear. But Geralyn, still a tough athlete, was not going down without a fight. She ran for the back bedroom, where her husband kept the shotgun. She reached for it, wrapped her hands around it, pulled it out of its place in the corner, but she didn't have time to point it. The man who seemed so friendly just moments before was now in her bedroom, fighting her in a death match for the gun.

He was big, six foot two, and at least two hundred pounds, so much bigger and stronger than Geralyn. He punched her repeatedly in the face, breaking her nose, bloodying her lip, blackening her eye. As they struggled, the barrel of the gun went up and scraped hard against the ceiling, ripping down parts of the tiles. She had no chance. He overpowered her. With a four-inch-bladed knife, he stabbed her twice in the back. He grabbed her around the waist and jerked the blade backward twice into her rib cage, just below her breast, puncturing her lung. He jabbed the knife at her throat, making a few superficial wounds, but she was wiggling, still fighting, trying to get away.

She was breathing in blood now from the puncture wound in her lungs, gasping for air. She was losing strength. She weakened in his arms. He got her where he wanted her. He pulled the blade hard across her throat from ear to ear, slicing through the flesh, the taut muscles in her neck, through her trachea, her arteries, back to her vertebrae, nearly severing her head.

He knew he killed her even before she stopped breathing. He watched Geralyn grab at her throat and attempt to run out of her bedroom, blood gushing from the arteries in her neck. Her bloody hands pressed against the wall and slid down the doorframe to the floor as she fell.

As the last drops of Geralyn's blood and life gushed out, the stranger stepped over her body, stomping his boot down hard on her backside, before walking out the front door into a bright, sunny day.

Darren spoke with Geralyn about ten thirty that morning. She told him about the job interview at two thirty and promised she would call him right afterward. He radioed her again when he went to lunch at eleven thirty, asked if she had eaten yet—no—and wished her good luck on the interview. When he clocked back in at the plant just before noon, he got busy. He knew Geralyn would be at her interview until at least three thirty, so he didn't think about contacting her until around four when a coworker needled him for going more than an hour without speaking to Geralyn.

Darren used his handheld radio, which did not have phone capabilities, to reach Geralyn on her cell phone, which also took radio calls. He got no answer, so he paged her. At four thirty, he began wondering why Geralyn had not returned his call. He tried again and again but got no answer. He tried twenty minutes later, then several times back-to-back. Geralyn was not answering. Darren knew that was not like her.

He felt a little angry, thinking she might be ignoring him. He knew his unanswered radio calls to her phone would set it beeping every few seconds. She should know that she had missed his calls.

By five thirty, with no word from Geralyn, Darren began to worry. He feared a car wreck or something worse. He left work about six fifteen and sped to the gas station down the road. His office was not equipped with a phone, so he had not been able to call Geralyn on their home phone. Using the gas station pay phone, he called their house. No answer.

He was beginning to feel sick to his stomach. He knew something was wrong. He could sense it. He raced home, driving the fifty miles in less than forty-five minutes.

When he turned into the trailer park, he could see his driveway. There was Geralyn's car. He breathed a sigh of relief.

*Thank God. She's home.* He thought.

He parked his truck and walked toward the house. As he climbed the front stairs, he noticed the front door open a crack. From inside, he could hear Geralyn's phone beeping. He rushed inside. Her phone was on the table by the front door next to the computer. He picked it up and turned off the beeping.

He first noticed she had not started supper, which was un-usual.

"Sissy?" he called out to her.

He turned toward the hallway and took a few steps before he saw her body in the doorway of their bedroom. She was ly-ing on her side in a pool of blood, her jeans and white T-shirt stained red, her left hand in a tight fist.

He ran to her and knelt at her side.

"Sissy!" He touched her arm. Her flesh was stiff and ice cold. He cringed back. He looked around the room and saw the shotgun on the bed. He stood up and grabbed it. "Oh, God, what happened?" He shouted, thinking she had accidentally shot herself or committed suicide. "What did you do?"

He cracked the shotgun open and saw no empty shells. The gun had not been fired. He was confused, in shock, crying. He did not understand what had happened, why she was dead. He felt like he was having a nightmare.

He knelt back down by his wife's side. He lifted the back of her shirt and saw two wounds in her back. He turned her and lifted the front of her shirt, thinking maybe she fell on something and it penetrated through her. He saw no wounds in her chest.

He stood up and paced around the house, not knowing

what to do. He knelt back down by her side, this time by her face. Then he noticed all the blood was seeping from her neck, and he saw her face was swollen and bruised.

He turned her head, and that's when he realized her throat had been cut wide open. He screamed. He stood back up and ran out of the house, suddenly furious, punching the wall before he left.

The news traveled quickly to Simmesport, Louisiana, the central Louisiana town seventy miles away where Geralyn grew up.

Darren's father made the phone call to Geralyn's family home. Her mother, Melanie Barr, answered.

"We just talked to Darren," he told Melanie. "When he got home from work tonight . . . he found Sissy . . . She's dead."

Melanie dropped the phone. She collapsed on the couch. She was barely able to ask her eldest daughter Heather to find her father.

Heather went to the Simmesport Town Hall, where John Barr, Geralyn's father, was attending a meeting as town alderman.

He was surprised to see his daughter walk into the meeting room. "Daddy!" Heather cried as her knees buckled and she began to fall to the floor. "It's Sissy . . ."

John Barr had three daughters. He loves them all deeply, but Geralyn was his baby. She was such a tomboy, he often thought of her as the son he never had. She was so special to him. She was everything he wanted in a daughter. Even after she married they stayed close. They talked often. They played golf together regularly. When she came to visit, she liked to sit close to him on the sofa and hold his hand just like she did when she was small. Despite growing up, she was still Daddy's little girl.

When John saw Heather's face that night, he knew: *Sissy's dead*. He moved across the room to Heather, to hold her, help her stand up, but he fell to the floor, too, and they both cried.

John has no memories of how he got home, but he recalls his family gathered there that night to await more information from the West Baton Rouge Parish Sheriff's Office. At that point, the family still did not know if Geralyn was murdered or had shot herself, either by accident or in a suicide. All they knew was that she was dead.

John's head was in a rage. He wanted to destroy something, tear up the furniture, scream and beat his fists into a wall, but his heart was too heavy. He could barely move. His chest tightened, and he wondered if he was having a heart attack.

He thought about driving to Geralyn's house, but he could not bear to see the police lights, the yellow tape, the crowd of neighbors hoping to get a better look inside his daughter's trailer. He did not want to see her dead body. He could not stomach seeing her blood.

No, he wanted to remember his daughter the way she was, beautiful, fun, strong, and so alive. A jokester, always laughing and cheering others. She was the perfect child, rarely needing discipline, a great student, eager to work hard and learn new things. And helpful.

"She always wanted to help someone," John says.


West Baton Rouge Parish Sheriff's Detective Freddie Christopher was the first detective to arrive at the trailer. Walking in, he saw no signs of a struggle in the living room and kitchen. No one had jimmied the lock to get in or broken down the door. A dirty coffee mug sat on the counter. A screwdriver was placed next to the open waffle iron. But nothing looked out of place. No dishes smashed on the floor, no framed pictures hanging askew on the walls. The TV and VCR and computer were untouched. And Geralyn's purse, with her wallet inside, was still in there. The only thing missing was the handset to the home's cordless phone.

The peacefulness of the front half of the trailer was in stark contrast to what Christopher found in the back. The walls in the hallway were covered and dripping with blood from arterial sprays, and just inside the doorway of the back bedroom, Geralyn was lying on her left side in a pool of blood, her right arm bent backward behind her.

Christopher had never seen such brutal violence, so much blood from one body. This was not a typical murder for West Baton Rouge Parish.

*This is bad.* He thought. *This was a crazy rage.* In his mind, he went over the possible motives.

Geralyn was fully clothed, still wearing jeans and a white

T-shirt, so rape did not seem likely. Nothing of value was taken; her murder was not the result of a robbery. Clearly, whoever killed her was enraged, and she was the focus of his anger. Usually, that type of crime is personal, a crime of passion.

Christopher needed to find out who might hate her enough to slaughter her. He thought about Darren. Spouses are always the first suspects.

Darren stuck to his story from the beginning. He was at work all day. He had been trying to reach Geralyn since four that afternoon. When he arrived home, he found her dead. He was crying, distraught like any loving husband would be. As word of Geralyn's bloody murder passed down the one-lane line of trailers, however, all eyes looked with scorn at Darren, the new widower. They watched him sobbing as he spoke with police, but among themselves, they commented that they could see no tears on his face.

When Christopher interviewed the couple's neighbors, he got a hot earful about Geralyn's so-called loving husband. The DeSotos' troubled marriage was an open secret in the trailer park. Loud arguments from the couple's trailer spilled out into the night air, and sometimes so did the fight.

"He dragged her outside by her hair," Sandy Geautreaux said, describing the night Darren wanted Geralyn to admit she was smoking. "He was beating her head on the car because of the cigarette ash."

The neighbors knew about Darren's temper and Geralyn's complaints about his need to control her every move: the music she listened to, the clothes she wore, the people she hung out with.

When the police came knocking, no one showed any hesitation in expressing their suspicions of Darren. So within the first few hours of the investigation, Darren became the most viable suspect.

Darren was interrogated for hours that night and the next morning at the West Baton Rouge Sheriff's Office. He answered every question about his relationship with Geralyn, admitting, "I slapped her once, and I've regretted it ever since."

But he insisted he could never kill her. He loved her too much.

Detective Ned Horner, the chief of detectives at the time, was not convinced. He had been on the force for more than twenty years. He was a Marine. He trusted his gut, and his gut told him Darren was guilty.

In the interrogation room, he explained to Darren the workings of a little black box that sat on the table nearby.

The Computer Voice Stress Analyzer, as it is called, reads the voice for signs of stress and deception. When people lie, Horner told Darren, the machine picks up on the increasing microtremors in their voice and detects when they are lying.

"Do you mind if we give you this test?" Horner asked Darren.

Darren agreed, and they went through a list of questions before beginning.

The first few were easy. "What's your name? What color is that wall? Do I have on a tie?"

Horner needed to record how Darren's voice sounded when he told the truth. Then he asked, "Do you know who killed your wife?"

"No."

"Did you kill your wife?"

"No."

When the test was over, Horner showed Darren the results.

"They show deception," Horner informed the young man.

Horner let Darren see for himself, letting Darren compare his voice frequencies results to textbook pictures of voices telling the truth and lying. Darren's results matched the liars.

"Do you want to tell us anything?" Horner asked Darren.

Darren looked confused. He cried. He swore he knew nothing about Geralyn's murder. He never changed his story. He insisted he arrived at the Kaiser Aluminum plant at seven twenty-six Monday morning and stayed until after six p.m. He claimed he left only for a short lunch break that did not give him nearly enough time to drive the fifty miles to Addis and back.

"Look at my time card," he said. "I have a receipt for lunch . . ."

He gave detectives a register printout from a Sonic Drive-

In near the Kaiser plant showing a meal was purchased at about eleven forty a.m., January 14.

He seemed to have a tight alibi, but investigators remained suspicious. Perhaps he had someone else clock in for him or maybe he snuck away. Besides, they thought, who keeps their fast-food restaurant receipts? To them, it seemed too convenient, maybe even planned.

Detectives tallied up what they knew:

• No forced entry

• A history of violence in the marriage

• A murder committed with intense rage

• No theft

• No rape

The detectives agreed, everything pointed to Darren as the most obvious suspect. But they could not make an arrest without more direct evidence. So they spent the next several months searching for it, tracking down every tip or lead they received about Darren, his threats to Geralyn, his work habits, his friends.

They were confident they would turn something up. But every trail they followed hit a dead end.

Darren DeSoto's time card at Kaiser Aluminum showed him clocking out for lunch on January 14 at 11:32 a.m. and clocking back in at 11:52 a.m. Twenty-two minutes. Not nearly enough time to drive fifty miles home, kill his wife, and return to work. What's more, Darren had a debit card receipt showing a hamburger purchase for lunch that day at a fast-food Sonic Drive-In not far from the Kaiser plant.

Detectives wondered if he hired someone to kill Geralyn, but they could find no evidence of that either: no unusual numbers on his phone records, no unusual money withdrawals, nothing.

And while Horner put his faith in the voice stress analyzer, other detectives were wary of the machine's accuracy. Some studies have shown it works no better than a random guess.

There were other facts about the crime that didn't fit if Darren was the killer.

A phone call was made from the trailer just before noon at the estimated time of Geralyn's death. The number dialed belonged to the ExxonMobil refinery. Darren never worked at ExxonMobil, and he insisted he knew no one there, but the number was only given out to ExxonMobil employees.

Also, the trailer was not disturbed except for the bedroom. "We looked at kitchen and living room area, but there were no signs of an attack," Detective Bryan Doucet, who was assigned the case said. "If it was the spouse, usually you'd see signs of rage in the house. The fight, the trigger mechanism that sets it off. An argument ensues before the murder actually happens. We didn't see that."

Then there was the phone. Investigators noticed the handset to the couple's cordless phone was missing.

"Why would Darren take his own phone?" Doucet wondered. "It didn't make sense. That was the $20 million question."

The other frustrating obstacle in the case was the lack of witnesses. Often, the neighbors heard Geralyn and Darren fighting. But on that Monday, no one heard or saw any activity at the DeSotos' trailer, not even the trailer park's watchdog, a disabled man who lives near the entrance and keeps an eye on the comings and goings every day. On January 14, the day his eyes would have been most useful, he was on a rare trip out of town.

# CHAPTER 27

# So Close,
# but Not Close Enough

With less than 23,000 people living within its borders, West Baton Rouge Parish is still considered mostly rural—or industrial. The western banks of the Mississippi are crowded with oil refineries and chemical plants, belching acrid plumes of burning toxins into the air.

Recently, the parish began billing itself as a cheaper alternative to the leafy eastern suburbs of Baton Rouge, but the majority of West Baton Rouge residents work where they live, usually in the plants or in the surrounding farmers' fields.

Crimes in the parish still reflect its small-town character; rapes and robberies happen, but they are rare, while murders are even more uncommon, maybe three or four a year. And most are usually the result of bar fights, domestic violence, or dirty drug deals—with a fast and easy arrest.

Geralyn's murder stood out as one of the worst.

"It was the biggest case in West Baton Rouge because of the violence," Doucet recalled. When he first walked in on the scene, saw all the blood, the brutal nature of Geralyn's murder, he knew he was not looking at a typical crime scene.

*For somebody to do this,* he thought at the time, *with so much violence, with that much rage, if it wasn't Darren, then whoever did it, they've either done this before, or they'll do it again.*

But detectives were not thinking of a serial killer. No one was thinking of a serial killer in January 2002. They were thinking of Darren. He looked like a perfect suspect.

For the next several months, Doucet exclusively pursued him, hoping to either clear him or arrest him for the murder.

They questioned Geralyn's family about his abusive behavior and relationship with his wife: "Did you see any signs of abuse? Bruises? Unexplained scratches? Did she talk about his temper?"

Melanie and John Barr were stunned.

"She was very secretive about her private life," Melanie says. "We thought everything was fine. She was always smiling. You never knew it if she was unhappy."

The Barrs always believed Darren was perfect for Geralyn. The two had been together since Geralyn graduated from high school. Now police were saying he killed her. While Melanie was suspicious, particularly after Darren quit cooperating and hired a lawyer, John never believed it.

He knew his daughter too well.

"There would have been marks on him," John said. "She would have fought back. She was tough. She was in good shape. She would have wanted to make some marks on that boy."

John was blunt with detectives when they expressed no doubt that Darren was guilty.

"Y'all looking in the wrong place," he said.

But detectives were unwavering.

In the months following Geralyn's murder, the Barrs called the West Baton Rouge investigators regularly, hoping to hear about new evidence, new leads in the case that might lead to an arrest, but the only word they got from detectives was: "We're working on it."

The investigators did not have much. The State Police

Crime Lab processed several pieces of evidence from the DeSotos' trailer, but nothing provided the kind of hard proof police needed to make an arrest.

The autopsy told investigators what they already guessed: Geralyn bled to death from her neck wound. The autopsy also found no signs of rape, so no swabs were collected from her body to test for seminal fluid and DNA. The pathologist, Dr. Alfredo Suarez, clipped Geralyn's fingernails for DNA tests, but the results came back inconclusive. Geralyn's blood overwhelmed any suspect DNA that might have been there.

Dozens of fingerprints were lifted from inside the trailer, but most came back as matches to Geralyn or Darren. No third person's prints were clearly identified.

The best evidence came from Geralyn's own blood.

Kim Colomb, a fifteen-year veteran of the Louisiana State Police Crime Lab who processed the scene that first night, focused her attention on the trailer floor, which was stained with two different types of bloody shoe prints.

One set, a size ten and a half Sketchers boot, was left in various positions in the bedroom, the hallway, and the living room. Later, she determined these were Darren's prints, tracing his panicked pacing after discovering his wife's body.

But another set, a size ten to eleven Wolverine boot impression, was left in a straight line from the bedroom exiting the trailer. To Colomb, that meant no blood was on the floor when this person walked inside. But when he left, he had to walk through the pool of blood to get out.

She collected several cutouts of the second set of impressions from the carpet and the hardwood floor in the hallway. She was confident that they were the killer's tread marks.

But without a suspect, investigators had no one to link to the print.

Police continued to look at Darren, but they had followed every lead to its end with no evidence to link him to Geralyn's death. Detectives were running out of tips to follow, and the investigation began to stall.

"Eventually we were pretty much at our wits' end and didn't know which way to go after four to five months of digging into Darren," Doucet said. "You put in five months, and you're still at square one."

Detectives were frustrated. So was Geralyn's family

"It got cold quick," Melanie says.

No one could understand why police could not catch a good lead. Geralyn was murdered inside her trailer, in a brutal fight; surely there was some incriminating evidence: a hair fiber, DNA, an old-fashioned fingerprint, anything.

"We couldn't comprehend there was nothing there," Melanie said. "We just felt there had to be something."

But the killer seemed to have left almost no trace of himself. To the Barrs, he was like a ghost. And they feared they might never know what happened to their daughter.


Then the news broke about the serial murders across the river in Baton Rouge. The cases seemed so similar—women attacked in their homes with no signs of forced entry and, in Murray's case, slaughtered brutally.

When John learned the handset of Murray's phone, like Geralyn's, was missing, he called detectives.

"That's the same person," he said. "Y'all see that?"

John recalls the detectives putting him off with a confident "Nah, Darren did it."

But John was convinced Geralyn's case was connected.

Not until later that year, after Darren agreed to and passed a polygraph, did the detectives in West Baton Rouge Parish also begin to suspect the case was connected to the murders in Baton Rouge.

In the weeks before the serial killer task force was formed, Doucet and others from the West Baton Rouge Sheriff's and District Attorney's Offices went to Baton Rouge for a round table meeting with city and East Baton Rouge police, as well as a few members of the State Police Crime Lab.

The West Baton Rouge investigators presented Geralyn's case, and the Baton Rouge authorities agreed her case was similar, but they did not officially link it to the serial killings.

When the task force formed soon afterward, the group drew a line in the sand. Only cases with the serial killer's DNA would fall under the umbrella of the task force investigation, and only the police agencies investigating those cases were included in the task force. Task force leaders argued they wanted to keep the investigation scientific, as well as keep a tight lid on investigative details. What's more, as the theory went, if every Louisiana police agency with an unsolved murder joined the task force or wanted their case included, the investigation would quickly reel out of control.

The DNA demarcation policy drew severe criticism from criminologists, victims' families, and the public, who argued investigators were dangerously blinding themselves.

For decades, police in other cities inflicted with a serial killer managed to link cases without the benefit of DNA. Detectives looked at the style of killing, the locations, the manner of subduing the victim, the victim characteristics, where the victims were left, etc.

Ignoring a case that looked like the work of the Baton Rouge serial killer but did not have the DNA as proof risked a lost lead. Perhaps the case had a good witness or the killer had close ties to that victim or he left a clue that could take police directly to him, maybe he was already a suspect in the case.

Besides, not all cases in the Baton Rouge region that appeared similar to the serial murders had DNA available. The murder of Christine Moore, whose bones were found scattered near a churchyard on the outskirts of Baton Rouge, could provide no evidence at all. In Geralyn's case, the killer's DNA was simply not found after several attempts by State Police Crime Lab technicians. The cases of Randi Mebruer and Connie Warner lacked DNA. Yet other aspects of all four cases seemed to link them to the Baton Rouge serial killer.

Behind the scenes, however, the task force was not ignoring Geralyn's case. They simply were not investigating it. Task force investigators stayed in touch with Doucet, asking about his progress on the case, about new leads or suspects.

And when the task force developed a good lead or suspect, Vavasseur called Doucet to determine if the suspect fit with the facts of Geralyn's case.

Neither agency, however, let the public in on their suspicions.

# CHAPTER 28

# Families Fight Back

In the first weeks after Pam's murder was linked to the serial killer in July 2002, her family gathered with the families of Gina, Murray, and another Baton Rouge woman whose 1997 murder remained unsolved five years later.

Eugenie Boisfontaine was the thirty-three-year-old daughter of a prominent New Orleans judge. She was recently divorced, had no children, and spent many afternoons walking around the LSU lakes. Then in June 1997, she vanished. Her family did not report her missing for more than two weeks, however, because she habitually left them guessing about her whereabouts. For years, she had suffered with schizophrenia complicated by alcohol and substance abuse. But what intrigued the families of the serial killer victims most about Eugenie was her address. She lived on Stanford Avenue, just one block away from Gina and the house Murray rented before moving to Sharlo.

When Eugenie was reported missing, Baton Rouge police conducted a cursory search around the lakes where a jogger found her driver's license and credit card. But they found nothing to push the case forward. Perhaps, police suggested, Eugenie had gone off with a friend. Within a week, her disappearance was just that: poof. She was gone, and police could do nothing more about it.

Frustrated by the lack of police effort, Boisfontaine's family hired a private investigator, who returned to the area of the lakes where her driver's license was found. Using a metal detector, he quickly discovered her keys in the brush just off the mowed lawn. Clearly, this indicated Eugenie was not running around having fun with a friend.

But the keys could tell them nothing about where to find Eugenie. The family would have to wait several more excruciating weeks.

On August 7, 1997, a woman's body was found dumped in Bayou Manchac, a swampy area just south of the East Baton Rouge Parish border in Iberville Parish. The coroner determined she had been dead at least a month. The deterioration was too great to provide much evidence about her death, except to confirm she was murdered.

Like so many other Baton Rouge murders, the case went cold not long after it was opened. Eugenie's life was unpredictable. She was known to sit on a bench at the lakes with a bottle of wine and mumble to herself. She attached to strangers without fear. She would have been an easy target. Detectives had several vague leads, but none proved fruitful.

Her family was forced to face the idea that her murderer might never be caught. But when Gina's and Murray's cases were linked, Eugenie's case took on new significance—not necessarily for the police—but for the victims' families.

The more recent victims' families hoped a meeting of the victims' relatives and close friends might uncover a common link between the women, something they all shared: the same hair salon, the same car dealership, a favorite restaurant, gym, carpenter, or perhaps even the same activity on the day or days before their murders.

They came up with just a few common threads in the women's lives. Other than the Stanford Avenue connection, Murray and Gina both drove BMWs, and all the women ate at the Caterie, a restaurant at Stanford and Perkins Avenues, just a few blocks from where Gina, Murray, and Eugenie lived.

The commonalities among the women brought police no closer to finding the killer, but during their discussions, the families discovered they formed a unique, albeit unfortunate, community of grief. They understood each other like even their closest friends could not. They could look each other in the eye and not shy away when the discussion turned to the brutal ways in which their loved ones died. They were comrades in arms up against the same enemies: the killer and their pain. But together they had strength.

Lynne Marino and her family had learned quickly the power of their voices. When they spoke, the media listened. The images of Lynne's strained, tear-stained face was becoming a staple of most news stories on the serial killer, especially when the task force provided little information to report.

Just two weeks after Pam's body was found, her family and friends—old and new—organized a rally on the steps of the state capitol building to remember Pam and all the other women whose murders remained unsolved in Baton Rouge. Lynne and Ann Pace, Murray's mother, spoke to the crowd about their loss and determination to seek justice for their daughters and every other daughter whose killer still roamed free.

The slogan for Pam's family was "Justice for Pam, Justice for All." They had it printed on bumper stickers, T-shirts, and buttons.

The rallies continued regularly once a month. What began as a few family members and friends of the three linked victims became a focal point for the families of a dozen or more murder victims whose cases were unsolved.

Geralyn's relatives and friends began attending. So did Connie Warner's and Christine Moore's and Eugenie's and Randi Mebruer's.

"We were lost before those rallies," said Jack Brooks, Connie's father. "We felt so alone."

The group's numbers were growing. And so was their frustration with the investigation.

Lynne and others had been urging the task force to seek advice from outside investigators with experience hunting serial killers, but the task force insisted they already had all the expert advice they needed.

Ann Pace, Murray's mother, lost significant confidence in the task force after learning about Jeremiah Pastor, a twenty-four-year-old LSU student and former Navy SEAL trainee. Three days after Murray's murder, Pastor crawled through the kitchen window of her town home and roamed around the bloodstained rooms for twenty minutes.

Frustrated by the lack of information released by police immediately after Murray was killed, Pastor told police he had planned to go by the house and simply look through the windows. When he walked into the backyard, however, a window left open by police was too inviting for him to pass up.

"I needed to do this for the safety of my family," Pastor, who lived with his sister, brother-in-law, and niece, told the Baton Rouge *Advocate*. "I've seen a lot of bad things, and I needed to know what I can about the enemy."

Ann was stunned by Pastor's trespassing when she learned of it from the newspaper in August, two months after the fact, but she was more surprised that Baton Rouge police did nothing about it. They did not arrest or charge Pastor. They investigated him as a suspect. They tested his DNA—it did not match the serial killer's—but they let him go unpunished. And quietly, without a word to the public.

Initially, when Pastor's story hit the newspaper a few months later, the Baton Rouge police would not even answer questions about it. Spokeswoman Godawa told the *Advocate*, "We're not going to discuss it. I'm not even confirming or denying anything."

A week later, under the heat of public criticism, police announced Pastor's arrest. He later pleaded guilty and received a sentence of probation.

The criticisms of the task force, however, continued.

In October, best-selling crime novelist Patricia Cornwell,

who had recently written a nonfiction book about Jack the Ripper, added her support to the families when she began working on a *PrimeTime Thursday* news report about the case for ABC television.

While speaking at the October rally, she told the crowd they should show support and offer help to police, who she insisted had "their hearts in the case." But she also took a swipe at their investigation.

After interviewing members of the task force for her television report, she said she sensed investigators might need more help but were afraid or felt unable to ask for it because of political reasons—or, more specifically, egotistical reasons.

At the November rally, Geralyn's aunt, Jackie Robert, expressed exasperation with what she saw as the lack of attention her niece's murder was receiving from the media and the police.

She was convinced authorities suspected several of the Baton Rouge area murders were connected, but they were not discussing it publicly.

"These other cases are not being put into the news," Robert said. "I'm asking for help."

Robert's frustration with the task force and the West Baton Rouge investigators spurred her to put out a petition. She collected several thousand signatures from southern Louisiana residents who wanted the serial killer investigation handed over to the State Attorney General's Office.

She presented the request to Governor Foster, who was not about to take the investigation away from the task force, which was made up of several prominent law enforcement agencies in and around Baton Rouge. But he did agree to meet with her and several other family members to hear their complaints and suggestions.

At the meeting, as always, the governor promised no expense was too much to ensure the task force got what they needed to investigate the case. He cautioned the families about their criticisms of the task force and their demands that investigators bring in outside help. Egos are involved, he reminded them.

"Is this about egos or saving lives?" Lynne shot back.

But by mid-November, media attention of the serial killer case was waning, and so was the public interest. While the families stood on the capitol steps and shouted into the wind, cautioning women to keep up their guards and urging the police to do more to solve the case, the rest of Baton Rouge was moving on with life.

"I believe the killer will find strength in our weariness and inattention," Ann Pace told the November rally's crowd.

# CHAPTER 29

# A Surprise Attack

In April 2002, just a few days after her twenty-third birthday, Trineisha Dené Colomb stood at a freshly dug gravesite in the tiny, eighteenth-century town of Grand Coteau, Louisiana, and watched her mother's coffin lowered into the ground.

Verna Colomb was not the first mother Dené had lost. In 1979, when Dené was born, her biological mother, an unmarried white woman, decided she did not want to raise her caramel-skinned baby, a child conceived with a black man.

The rejection never stopped stinging in Dené's life.

"Why didn't she want me?" the little girl wondered, pestering her adoptive parents, Verna and Sterling Colomb. "Does she live around here? What does she look like? Do I have other sisters and brothers?"

The Colombs tried to comfort Dené, tried to give her the love she needed in a gentle and supportive home, and Dené loved them dearly for it, but the void in her heart persisted.

Since she was old enough to notice different skin colors,

Dené suspected her parents were not both white, nor were they both black. Her skin was too light, too caramel-colored. People told her she looked mixed.

When Dené was sixteen, Sterling pointed out the woman— her biological mother—to his daughter. She was living not too far from where the Colombs raised Dené and an older brother, Sterling Jr., in Lafayette, Louisiana.

"You say you want to know who your mother is?" he whispered. "Well, there she is."

Dené stared at the woman. She was pretty and blond, with fair white skin. Dené thought about saying something to her, but what do you say to a stranger who also happens to be your mother, a woman who never tried to contact her daughter, who had made it clear she wanted nothing to do with her? Dené watched the woman walk away.

As she got older, Dené attempted to find her biological father, hoping he might want to know her, too. Maybe she even had more siblings. But attempts to connect with her biological family hit only dead ends and silence.

When Verna was diagnosed with breast cancer, Dené was terrified of losing her, too. In September 2001, Dené obtained an early discharge from the Army, moved home, and helped take care of her mother as the tumors spread unabated into her bones.

The two women spent a lot of time at home with a pet dachshund, Tiny, that Sterling bought for Verna when she became ill. He had heard dogs were good for helping people heal, or at least easing the sorrows as disease conquers the body.

When Verna died, however, the dog became Dené's best friend, a comfort for the loss of her mother and her vicious protector. He rarely left Dené's side when she was at home.

"You couldn't go into her room," Sterling said. "The dog would attack you."

Dené always spent a lot of time in her room, reading or watching TV alone. Since childhood, she had been a voracious bookworm, devouring dime store novels as well as lesson books on how to speak foreign languages. She was working on learning Russian.

But after her mother died, she was staying behind her closed door more often, sinking into depression. She had given college a try, twice, once straight out of high school, then again after she quit the Army, but she decided it wasn't for her.

She felt lost, unhappy with her lot in life. Most of her friends were from the Army and lived out of state. She dated, but only white men. In Lafayette, Louisiana, despite her glowing good looks, she sometimes found that difficult due to lingering racial prejudice. She used the Internet to meet men online, but after a few dates or a sexual encounter, they would go their separate ways.

At the time, Dené was struggling to find herself. She was confused about her sexuality. She began frequenting gay clubs, including the Sound Factory in Lafayette, where she gravitated to feminine white women.

But she could find nothing to heal her pain. On September 18, 2002, she tried to kill herself with an overdose of pills.

She was hospitalized, and after her physical recovery, she was admitted to a mental health facility for psychological therapy. She continued seeing a counselor after her release in October, and seemed to be more determined than ever to pull herself out of her rut and get out of Louisiana.

"I'm trying out for *Survivor*," she announced.

The television series was looking for a new set of contestants to test their survival skills in the wilds for a million-dollar prize.

Sterling laughed when she told him. Dené was a shy girl, never the one attracting attention. Her voice was so soft and quiet, Sterling often asked her to speak up.

But Dené knew she was built strong. She had survived boot camp. She was proud of her tough edge. And underneath that shy demeanor, she was spirited and ambitious.

For her audition to the show, she submitted a videotape of her wrestling in the mud with a squealing pig.

When TV fame eluded her, she decided the military was her ticket to world travel and an exciting international career as a foreign language translator—hence the Russian language studies. Instead of rejoining the Army, though, she wanted to call herself a Marine.

That meant she needed to train. She showed her father the battery of physical tests she would be facing as a grunt cadet.

She began a workout schedule, running several miles every week, and her weightlifting began filling out her slender arms.

"Look at my muscles!" She'd say, grinning and flexing her biceps for Sterling. She was proud of her body, its lean, shapely stature and firm, sexy curves.

Things seemed to be looking better for Dené when tragedy hit home again for her.

Tiny died from heartworms. Dené was crushed that he was gone, too. She was angry, she felt cheated. Life seemed so unfair to her. What terrible thing, she cynically wondered, would happen next?

About six a.m. on Thursday, November 21, 2002, before he left for work, Sterling opened the door to his daughter's bedroom and looked in to see her.

"Bye, Dené," he called to her. "I love you."

"I love you, too, Daddy," she called from under the blankets, her voice groggy. "See you later."

"See you later. . . ."

Sterling left the modest ranch house where they had lived most of Dené's life and drove to his job at SLEMCO Electric Company in Lafayette.

He wasn't one to keep track of Dené's schedule, but he assumed she was going to work later that day.

What Dené had not told him was that she had stopped showing up for her job at a local answering service two weeks earlier.

Late that morning, Dené visited the Lafayette Parish Library, where she often went to use the Internet because she did not have access from her home computer. She logged onto her Yahoo.com account at 11 a.m. to check her e-mail. She did not stay long at the library, because she was home again by 12:23, when Sterling called to check on her during his lunch break.

"How's it going?" he asked.

"Fine . . ."

"What are you doing today?"

"I'm going to work. I'll see you tonight."

She did not tell him she planned to visit her mother's grave in Grand Coteau. She never told him, even though she went to the cemetery often, where she sat for hours and left gifts by the headstone. He only knew because when he went, he found the gifts, including a Tweety Bird cartoon, Dené's favorite character.

Sterling arrived home a little after six p.m. Dené was not home, but he was not worried. She could be at the store, with a friend, or still at work. Her absence did not begin to eat at him until later that night, after the ten p.m. news.

She had not called or left a note. That was unlike Dené. She rarely went out on weeknights, and when she did, she let him know if she would be late.

When 2 a.m. rolled around, he was not only worried, he was angry.

"I'm going to kill her," he said to himself, thinking she was being irresponsible for staying out too late.

As he tossed and turned that night, he tried to convince himself that Dené must have fallen asleep at a friend's house. He wished she had a cell phone.

He woke up before the sun rose. He walked to her room and pushed open the door.

"Dené?" he called into the dark. But she did not respond. She was not in her bed. He was concerned but not yet frightened. Lafayette, with a population of 110,000, was a relatively safe town. Like all cities, certain areas are inflicted with urban blight and violent crimes, but Dené kept herself away from trouble. Her friends were mostly clean-cut, smart, straight-edged people.

Sterling told himself she was safe. He was not going to panic. He did not call the police. He went to work, figuring Dené would come slinking home soon to explain her absence.

At 10 a.m., he was about to call home when the phone rang for him. A Grand Coteau police officer was on the line.

"Do you own a black 1994 Mazda MX3?" the officer said.

That was Dené's car. Sterling owned it, his name was on the title, but Dené drove it.

The car, the officer told Sterling, was abandoned on Robbie Road, an isolated gravel road just a few blocks down from the Saint Charles Catholic Church cemetery where Verna is buried. The driver's door was slightly ajar, the window rolled all the way down, and the keys were in the ignition. On the front passenger seat, police found Dené's purse with her wallet inside.

A local man in Grand Coteau first saw the empty car at about three thirty p.m. the day before. When he drove by it again Friday morning, he notified police.

Sterling was stunned, confused. He did not understand why her car would be parked on that road. His first thought was that she had taken her own life. But Dené seemed so excited lately about joining the Marines. He did not know what to think. How could she be gone? Where could she be?


Dené was a special gift to Verna and Sterling, the answer to their prayers. Verna had nearly gone blind carrying their first child, Sterling Jr., and her doctors recommended she not have another child. But the Colombs dearly wanted a daughter. Unfortunately, they could not afford to adopt. Then one day in April 1979, their neighbor asked if they wanted to take in a newborn girl. A woman at the Charity Hospital wanted to give hers up for adoption.

Within two days, baby Dené was home with her new family. The little girl, Sterling's "little rascal," had grown up so fast. Suddenly, she was graduating from Lafayette's Northside High and off to college in northern Louisiana, then to Texas for the Army. Despite Dené's occasional moodiness, Sterling enjoyed having her back home. She kept his spirits lifted after Verna died.

He dreaded the thought of losing her, too.


He left work and drove quickly to Grand Coteau, an old town best known for its all-girls' Catholic boarding school. The Academy of the Sacred Heart was founded in 1821 by French nuns and was the finishing school of choice for the daughters of wealthy landowners in the nineteenth century. Even into the twentieth century, the school continued to attract the offspring of the state's upper classes.

The campus sits at the northern end of town, at the end of Church Street, several blocks past the Saint Charles Catholic Church and cemetery. Dené's car was also found at the northern end of town, around the corner from the academy, past where Church Street ends and becomes Robbie Road.

Robbie Road itself winds back into an isolated wooded area where a metal gate to the local water plant entrance sits at a curve leading around to an old farmhouse. Dené's car was found parked facing into town on the side shoulder not far from where Robbie Road begins but far enough back that she was isolated from easy view.

When police learned from Sterling that Dené was missing, the local Saint Landry Parish Sheriff's Office took a description of Dené, which included details about her tattoos, a yin-yang symbol, a heart with the name Dené written over it, and a Tweety Bird.

Saint Landry police also took a closer look at the Mazda, dusting it for prints and swabbing the steering wheel for DNA. As they examined the outside driver's door, officers could see the dust was smeared off in places as if someone was leaning against the car or was struggling next to it.

The news media was alerted to Dené's disappearance on Friday afternoon. Soon her picture and car were appearing on television screens across southern Louisiana. Lafayette police were notified, too, and the search was on throughout the mostly rural regions around Grand Coteau and Lafayette Parish thirty miles away.


On Sunday, Reginald Holman and a friend spent the morning rabbit hunting in rural Saint Landry Parish. But after a few hours without much luck—one rabbit and one quail—they were ready to give up. About ten a.m., Holman dropped off his buddy at home and headed to his house.

On his way, he passed through the little town of Scott, Louisiana, in Lafayette Parish about twenty miles from Grand Coteau. He remembered a wooded field in those parts that his brother-in-law told him was good rabbit hunting grounds. He was still trying to get used to his new rifle, so he decided to stop.

The only drivable access to the field is from Renaud Drive, a two-lane, twisty road through the rural, sparsely populated landscape. The turnoff is easy to miss. Just after a curve in the road, at a small break in the trees that line the shoulder, is a grassy drive that immediately curves to the left back behind the line of trees again.

Holman parked in the grassy clearing. He didn't plan to stay long, just long enough to "mess around" a bit, try to "make a rabbit jump," he said.

A trail leads into the woods from the clearing, but several feet in, the beaten-down path disappears. The field is a shrubby area with thick underbrush. Holman rustled the shrubs with his rifle as he went deeper in the woods.

The area was quiet, except for the occasional car passing on the road. As he walked, the woods opened up onto a recently cleared strip of land for high power lines. Holman crossed the clearing and went back into the woods on the other side. After reaching what he believed was the property line, he headed back, trying to cover new ground with his steps. Before he got to the tower clearing, he noticed something several feet off to his right on the ground. Something that didn't look like underbrush. He walked toward it.

"I kept staring at it and staring at it," he said. Then the shape of it clicked in recognition. "I realized it was a body."

He did not go close, but from where he stood, he could see it was a woman, a dead woman, lying on her stomach, wearing only a gray T-shirt, white socks, and muddy white tennis shoes. Her shirt was pulled up around her head. He scanned the woods surrounding him. Near her body, a pair of sweatpants and panties were hanging on some shrub branches, as if they had been tossed off into the brush.

Suddenly, Holman was scared. He lost no haste walking back to his truck to call the police.

Scott, Louisiana, is less than five miles outside of the city of Lafayette. The town is a flat, sprawling rural landscape of less than 10,000 people. The police force employs just a dozen or so officers, enough to handle the thefts and burglaries and occasional assaults that fill their time on patrol. But murder, the department admits, is beyond their capabilities.

A Scott police officer was dispatched to the field where

Holman discovered the body, but the Lafayette Parish Sheriff's Office, which handles unincorporated areas of the parish, was called in to work the case.

Right away, Lafayette Parish Sheriff's Detective Sonny Stutes suspected the body was Dené Colomb. The department had been looking for her for three days.

When he was led into the woods to where the body was found, he was unable to identify the body by her face. She was unrecognizable.

Her face was brutalized. The flesh was swollen and bruised. The autopsy later showed her skull was cracked open by nine heavy blows that damaged her brain and left wide, gaping wounds on her face. Her killer beat her to death with a blunt object, perhaps a pipe or board or tree branch.

When the crime scene technician moved the dead woman's shirt, revealing her back, Stutes hated recognizing the tattoos from Dené's description stretched across her graying skin.

He did not need to see the fingerprint report to tell him who they had discovered.

Looking around the wooded field, investigators began to piece together Dené's last few moments.

From the clearing just off the road, police found a muddy tire impression and two sets of footprints side by side, walking into the woods, one much larger than the other. A few feet in, the smaller set appears to break away into a run, a longer striding gait for a few yards before disappearing into the brush.

Several more feet into the woods, past the clearing for the power lines, Detective Kristen Bayard noticed an area of smashed-down thick brush that was covered in dried blood. A nearby tree trunk was splattered with what looked like blood cast off from the beating.

Bayard suspected this was where he killed her, where he beat her head in either before or after stripping off her pants and raping her. From there, Bayard could see where he dragged Dené along a bloody trail marked by smashed underbrush to an overgrown grassy area. Dené's body was tucked slightly under a shrub, and her fleece pants and white underwear were tossed into a nearby briar patch. She was covered in mud, particularly her legs and tennis shoes, which had thick clumps of it. Pieces of vegetation were stuck in her hair, and the skin on her back was torn up from being dragged by her feet.

She had one wound on her side that looked like a burn.

Detectives knew immediately they were looking for a brutal sexual predator. Lafayette was not immune to murder, but few were this vicious. They took extra precautions when collecting evidence at the scene, and within hours, investigators were tracking down possible suspects.

During the next few weeks, Detective Stutes and Detective Renee Speyer spent countless hours following up on tips, including a few witnesses claiming to have seen a white truck parked behind Dené's car that Thursday, and interviewing potential suspects in both Saint Landry and Lafayette Parishes.

The fact that Dené's killer drove her twenty miles from her car to an isolated field suggested he planned to take her life. He knew what he was doing. Perhaps he had followed her to the cemetery, watched her park her car on the lonely road for a few minutes of quiet time, before making his move. Maybe he knew her, police theorized, maybe he was a spurned suitor stalking her.

Stutes and Speyer went first to Dené's family to learn more about her life and develop a timeline of her last few days. From what they could piece together, Dené went to the Lafayette Wal-Mart between nine and ten Wednesday night, came home, and in the morning stopped by the Lafayette Parish Library, returned home by twelve thirty, then left again soon after and drove to Grand Coteau.

Detectives searched her bedroom but found nothing significant. They tried to track down the men she had recently dated, including the ones she met online, obtaining DNA swabs from several if they could not be eliminated otherwise.

One of their best leads came from a traffic ticket issued to a man driving a white truck on Robbie Road the same day Dené disappeared. The man claimed he stopped on the road to urinate, but when pushed about his whereabouts during the rest of the day, he was evasive but agreed to provide a sample of his DNA for testing.

\*    \*    \*

In Baton Rouge, reports of Dené's murder got some initial coverage from the TV news and papers, eliciting the public's typical furrowed brows of sympathy, but the story did not inspire a renewed media frenzy about another possible serial killer victim. No one suspected her brutal rape and murder were linked to the others.

Dené's murder was too unlike the serial killings. She was abducted from her car, not attacked in her home.

Besides, Lafayette Parish is sixty miles from Baton Rouge, an hour's drive west on Interstate 10, over the Atchafalaya Swamp and through miles of rural Cajun country. The crime seemed too far removed.

Soon, reports about Dené's murder faded from the news in Baton Rouge. Thanksgiving came and went, and the city turned its focus to the upcoming holidays. The last serial killing was more than four long months earlier.

The panic of that summer was falling away. The extra self-defense classes were canceled. Gun and mace sales dropped back to normal levels. And more women began running alone again along the LSU lakes. Even the tips to the task force hotline tapered off.

By early November, the task force stopped hosting daily press conferences in lieu of weekly ones. By December, the task force decided they would call in the media only when investigators had something important to report. Several weeks passed without a news item.

Some people even speculated the killer had moved on. Too much attention, too much police heat had scared him off.


On December 18, Stutes put in a call to Lieutenant Lynn Averette of the Louisiana State Police. Averette was the state police representative on the Baton Rouge serial killer task force, and Stutes wanted to share details about Dené's murder to determine whether the same man might be responsible.

Averette, however, was skeptical. He told Stutes that the serial killer's three victims were all white and had been stabbed or strangled, not beaten. Further, they were attacked in their homes, with the last being removed and dumped elsewhere. Dené's murder, Averette said, could not be related, because the killer's method was so different.

Stutes was not so sure. But he did not have the DNA to say otherwise. At the time, Stutes knew only that the Acadiana Criminalistics Lab, which was processing evidence in the case, had obtained semen from Dené's rape swabs and they hoped to develop a DNA profile of it soon.

Meanwhile, Stutes had an interesting conversation with a detective from a neighboring parish.

At a December 19 round table discussion of several area police agencies, Stutes presented the details of Dené's case to other detectives from the Acadiana region, which includes Lafayette, Iberia, Saint Martin, and Saint Landry Parishes. Afterward, Saint Martin Parish Detective Arthur Boyd told him he was investigating the brutal attempted rape of Diane Alexander in Breaux Bridge, about twenty miles east of Lafayette.

The case was so unusual, so brutal and random for a parish that rarely sees such violent crime, that Boyd was on the lookout for similar crimes elsewhere. He suspected Dené's might be related.

Stutes agreed, and the two men spoke with one of the crime lab's ace DNA analysts, Carolyn Booker, about it. They hoped she might be able to get a DNA profile from crime scene evidence in Diane's case, which had so far been fruitless.

The two men kept in contact for the next several months, and Stutes often checked on the progress of Diane's case with the crime lab.

Then, on December 23, Booker found a DNA profile in Dene's case that no one expected to see.

Booker was in the lab trying to finish some work before the Christmas holiday began. She had promised Stutes she would try to get him a good DNA profile from the semen found on Dené's vaginal swab.

Early that Monday morning, Booker put the semen sample from Dené's rape swab through a machine that reads the chemical compounds of the genetic markers and spits out the results from each of the thirteen loci.

Before the process was complete, a unique marker from the sperm found on the rape swab caught her eye.

At the loci called VWA, Dené's killer had the genetic markers of sixteen and twenty-two. One number was inherited from his mother, the other from his father.

The twenty-two was extremely rare, so rare, Booker and her colleagues at the lab had never seen it before at that loci—except once. And she had been on the lookout for it ever since.

She walked quickly to her desk where she had taped a portion—not the full thirteen—of the Baton Rouge serial killer's profile to her shelf. She put the two profiles side by side and compared. They matched. She took a deep breath. She needed to see the rest of the serial killer's profile to be sure.

She called Angela Ross at the Louisiana State Police Crime Lab in Baton Rouge, and Angela read the serial killer's full profile to Booker over the phone. Booker checked each marker as they went down the list. Her heart was racing by the time they got to thirteen. All loci matched.

Dené was another victim of the serial killer.

Booker called her boss, who had already left for vacation, then she called Stutes.

"Are you sitting down?" she told him. "The semen on Dené's vaginal swab matched the serial killer in Baton Rouge."


Later that day, Lafayette Parish Sheriff Mike Neustrom and the serial killer task force made the stunning announcement: Dené was beaten to death by the same man who had murdered Gina Green, Murray Pace, and Pam Kinamore.

The news shot across the region like wildfire, and its implications were immediately obvious.

The serial killer was mobile. Suddenly, the whole region—not just Baton Rouge—was his hunting grounds. He was traveling Interstate 10 between Baton Rouge and Lafayette, and Interstate 49 between Lafayette and Grand Coteau, stopping who knows where along the way.

Research suggested repeat murderers stick to a similar method of killing. But this guy, this ghost Louisiana police were chasing, was breaking all the rules. He was flexible. He was unpredictable. He did not require the privacy of a victim's home to attack. He was more brazen than that, grabbing Dené off the street. And he had crossed racial lines, a rarity for serial killers.

The faceless predator was all over the map—literally. He could be anywhere, watching anyone, ready to attack at any time. No woman in southern Louisiana, if she was paying attention to the case and realized the killer's breadth, felt immune from his threat.

# CHAPTER 30

# The Serial Killer
# Spreads His Wings

The news that the serial killer had struck again was less than a day old when Mari Ann Fowler set off from Baton Rouge on Christmas Eve 2002 to visit her husband in federal prison in Beaumont, Texas, about two hundred miles west.

Jerry Fowler, the former state elections commissioner, was serving a five-year sentence for bribery. He was one of several Louisiana politicians, including former Governor Edwin Edwards, who was prosecuted on a host of corruption charges in 2000, but Fowler was one of the few who pleaded guilty. He admitted to taking up to $8 million in palm-greasing money from the owners of a voting machine company awarded a lucrative state contract.

Despite the public humiliation, though, Mari Ann was sticking by her husband's side. At sixty-five, she was a savvy veteran of Louisiana politics, both as a wife and in her own professional capacity. For years, she worked within the tumultuous state Department of Education, including a stint as the as-

250

sistant superintendent, and she carried herself with the smooth, polished look of having thrived in an accomplished life.

That Christmas Eve, with a pile of wrapped presents in the back of her car, Mari Ann headed west on Interstate 10 toward Texas. On her way out of the Baton Rouge region, she exited at Louisiana 415 just past Port Allen and pulled into a brightly lit strip mall to grab a few deli sandwiches to go. She parked directly in front of the Subway restaurant.

A few minutes after she went inside, a dark-colored truck pulled into the space to the left of her car. The Subway employees remember Mari Ann walking outside, because she was their last customer before closing early for the holiday. But they did not see what happened next.

They did not hear a scream or the screech of tires peeling out of the parking lot. They only noticed Mari Ann's car was still in front of the store several minutes after she left. On the ground by the driver's side door, the employees saw the sandwiches Mari Ann had just purchased, her purse, and her car keys.

As they looked around, confused about what had just happened, one of the cashiers noticed several false fingernails on the asphalt near the sandwiches; they had popped off of Mari Ann's fingers in her struggle with an abductor.

When the West Baton Rouge Sheriff's deputies arrived, they quickly ruled out robbery. The Christmas presents were still in the backseat, and Mari Ann's wallet was still in her purse.

Her relationship to Jerry Fowler, a man with a history of dirty political dealings, raised suspicions that her disappearance might be linked to her husband's troubles. Perhaps she was kidnapped in retaliation for his loose lips during the criminal investigation. Maybe she faked the abduction and disappeared with her husband's alleged ill-gotten millions.

But the possibility that the serial killer struck again was high on everyone's minds, and the task force sent its troops in right away.

Mari Ann Fowler was a professional, smart, good-looking brunette. She was older than the other victims, but she looked much younger than her age. And something else about her looks shocked one of the victims' mothers.

When Lynne Marino saw Mari Ann's picture flash across the TV screen, she felt as if she might be looking at herself. The two women are almost spitting images: high cheekbones, big brown eyes, petite narrow chins, and full lips. They were also almost exactly the same age. Lynne could not help but wonder if the serial killer had mistaken Mari Ann for Lynne, the outspoken victim's mother who was often on TV and in the newspapers, calling him a monster, a cretin who does not deserve to breathe. She had been trying to piss him off, to let him know he was hated, that she would never stop harassing the police, would never let their investigation die until he was behind bars, on death row, and ultimately dead.

Maybe, Lynne thought, the killer had spotted Mari Ann and, thinking she was Lynne, followed her, and when he saw an opportunity, snatched her to shut her up, to teach her who was more powerful.


Dozens of police officers were called out of their homes that night, away from their families just as many were sitting down for Christmas Eve dinner, to begin searching the area around the strip mall. From the scene, however, it was easy to see Mari Ann was taken in a vehicle. The mall's proximity to Interstate 10, just a few blocks away, also suggested her whereabouts would not be easy to trace. Louisiana 415 is the last exit before the westbound interstate begins its long stretch over the Atchafalaya Swamp and into the bayou country of Louisiana.

Detectives, however, hoped they might finally get a break in the case when they learned the cigarette store next to the Subway kept security cameras running on the interior and exterior of the building. Perhaps the video recorded Mari Ann's abduction, or maybe even caught her abductor's face or his vehicle plates on tape.

They watched with anticipation when the store owner rewound the tape and pressed play:

They could see Mari Ann walking out of the store at about five forty. She was carrying her sandwiches and her purse as she walked between her car and a dark truck. She turned to unlock her door, when a large, big-chested man grabbed her from behind.

The abductor was right there on the screen in action. Investigators were so close to getting a face, a profile, some semblance of what he looked like, but the screen was cut too short.

An awning outside blocked the camera's view, blacking out the man's body from his chest up. Investigators also could not tell if he was white or black. And the recording was too dark to make out details on the truck and its plates.

Investigators sent the tape to the FBI for enhancements, but it never produced the kind of leads they had hoped for.


An intensive search for Mari Ann went on for several days and continued, albeit with less urgency, for weeks. The helicopters were brought out, dogs came in, and police used four-wheelers to search several areas that might offer isolation and an ideal body dump site throughout West Baton Rouge and neighboring Iberville and Point Coupee parishes. But she did not turn up, and soon the search was called off.

Without a body and evidence to follow, her case hung in limbo. Within a few months, the investigation went cold. Her disappearance was a mystery and might remain so forever.

# CHAPTER 31

# More Misleads

The man's piercing stare was unforgetable. But not until she heard about Dené's murder did she realize she might have seen the killer. In late December 2002, the woman, Angela, called to report what she and her sister saw less than two blocks from where Dené's body was found.

On New Year's Eve, Lafayette detectives met with the Lafayette area woman who described the man she saw in a parked truck on the side of the road on the day Dené was abducted.

One month earlier, on November 21 about midday, Angela and her sister were driving north on Mills Street, which intersects with Renaud Drive not far from the entrance to the field where Dené was killed. After passing the Renaud Drive intersection, they saw a white truck stopped on the shoulder, halfway off the road.

At first, Angela thought the truck, a late-model 1990s pickup with a metal toolbox behind the cab, had gone into the ditch. She could see no one in the cab. But as they pulled up on its back bumper, she realized the truck had simply pulled over.

The truck was jutted too far out into the road to easily pass, so Angela's sister, who was driving, had to wait for a southbound car on Mills Street to pass before she could maneuver around it. Then, as they drove around the truck's cab, a man sat up in the driver's seat. He met Angela's stare with an angry, intimidating glare.

Angela noticed a black woman at the man's side. She was lying on the passenger seat with her head resting against the door. Angela's first thought was the couple were probably having sex.

Angela did not think of it again until she realized it was the day of the murder and just around the corner from the murder site. She tried to provide a good description of the man, but could only say he was a white man, medium build, in his late thirties to forties, with dark hair that was graying on the sides.

She agreed, however, to submit to hypnosis, during which she provided details for a composite sketch of the man to a Lafayette forensic artist. Her sister, who did not see the man well, could say only that he was white.

That night, details about the truck and a picture of the sketch were released to the public, but the man was described only as a "person of interest," someone investigators wanted to question. Police also held back on releasing the information about the black female seen in the truck. It was a tightly held piece of information.

The sketch, however, was the first image a terrified public could latch onto as the possible face of the killer. The picture was published in the paper, shown nightly on the TV news, spread far and wide by e-mail, and plastered on telephone poles, bulletin boards, and store windows throughout the region.


Meanwhile, FBI profiler Mary Ellen O'Toole hoped to learn more about the killer from his latest victim and murder. She visited the sites where Dené was abducted and killed. She read through the details of the case and talked with investigators. Then, on January 17, the task force released an update to the killer's behavioral profile:[1]

As with the other murders, Dené's abduction, rape, and murder indicated the killer was willing to take enormous risks to do what he wanted with these women. He got Dené into his car in the middle of the day, when people were around and could have easily seen him and noted a description of his vehicle. As with Pam, he drove with Dené at least thirty miles to kill her, again risking witnesses, when closer locations were available. What's more, the field where he killed her is open to hunters, something he most likely knew by familiarizing himself with the area. Yet he was undeterred by the randomness of when someone might show up.

To the profilers, the killer's behavior suggested his need to heighten the thrill of his attacks; he needed to take immense risks that were unnecessary to get more of a rush. His acts were impulsive, without care for the consequences, and they reflected an intense rage.

"These attacks involve a very unique type of violence," the profile states. "It is an unprovoked violence . . . People who know this offender may be intimidated by him because of his erratic, spontaneous temper."

One personality trait added to the killer's new profile was a distinct lack of empathy.

"There is an obvious disregard for these victims," the profile says. "His coldness and lack of regard for others would be noted in other areas of his life especially by family members who have been hurt by his lack of concern. His emotions are usually shallow and even inappropriate at times."

Basically, they determined, this man is an ice-cold brutally violent man who would kill when the impulse struck him and feel not a shred of empathy when his victims cried and screamed and begged for their lives.

[1] FBI's Serial Killer Behavioral Profile—Addendum (see Appendix B)

# CHAPTER 32

# Evidence Tells a New Story

While task force investigators tracked down new leads produced from the composite sketch and the updated profile, analysts at the Acadiana Criminalistics Lab in New Iberia, Louisiana, were focusing on Dené's crime scene evidence. They knew something sitting on their laboratory desks might be the piece of evidence to help crack the case.

Trace evidence specialist Mark Kurowski was particularly interested in a cast of a shoe print that crime scene technicians made of prints left in the mud by whoever dragged Dené to her final resting spot.

After eleven years at the crime lab, Kurowski was still the kind of scientist who lived every day for the thrill of a *gotcha* moment, when two pieces of evidence—one from a crime scene and one from a suspect—match at microscopic levels.

A microscope, after all, was what got him into the field to

begin with. He was a chemistry major in college at the University of Florida until he happened to wander upstairs from his department to the forensic science lab. On the table was a "really cool microscope," a comparison microscope, and when he looked through the lens at a split screen, showing two slides side by side, he was hooked.

Now he was working on one of the biggest cases of his career, a mystery that had stumped the entire region, and in his hands was possibly a crucial piece of evidence to help solve the puzzle.

The shoe cast was a solid one, almost complete from heel to toe and sized between a ten and eleven. The work took several hours, but after examining the tread patterns and comparing them to hundreds of soles, Kurowski determined the killer was wearing an Adidas brand shoe. But Adidas makes dozens of styles of shoes, leaving Kurowski with the task of finding the right one.

The best way to determine which style carried that sole was to look at the shoes themselves. So late one morning in early January, he took a Polaroid of the cast and drove out to the Lafayette mall, hoping that the killer, if he lived locally, also bought his shoes locally, preferably with a credit card.

Kurowski got a routine down quickly, learning how to deftly explain to the employees why he was fascinated with all the Adidas shoe bottoms in the store. He picked each one up and flipped it over. He looked at basketball high-tops, running shoes, and walking sneakers.

He worked his way from the indoor mall to local strip malls and on to the shoe warehouse stores. By the time he stopped at Academy Sports, a superstore of sporting goods and footwear, he no longer needed to refer to his Polaroid of the sole treads. The print was burned into his mind. He had been looking at shoes for more than three hours.

Inside the Academy store, Kurowski began his routine, meticulously flipping over every Adidas. When he picked up the Give-N-Go basketball shoe, the recognition was immediate.

"It was obvious," he said. "It was just a rush."

He hated not being able to tell anyone what he had just

found. But imagine the looks if he had shouted: "I found the serial killer's shoes!"

Back at the lab, Kurowski called Adidas and asked for information about the Give-N-Go style shoe. The company told him that only twenty-five to thirty shoes of those styles in sizes ten and eleven were shipped to Louisiana, and only in one color: white.

It was a promising lead.

Detectives immediately got busy tracking down the sales records. In Lafayette, the shoe was available at Academy Sports, and records showed only seven pairs had been sold. Six were bought with a credit card, and all six people were found. The shoes were located, and the owners were eliminated as suspects. But the owner of the seventh pair, purchased with cash, was never found.

In Baton Rouge, the shoe was available at Academy Sports and JC Penney department stores. The task force told Stutes that detectives there also tracked down all the purchasers who used a credit card and eliminated the owners as suspects, but they too, had several unknown buyers in Baton Rouge who used cash.

Once again, investigators had hit a dead end.

But Kurowski still felt the shoes had more to tell about the killer.

Give-N-Go were not typically a white man's shoe. They were billed as basketball shoes, but the design was more toward fashion—hip-hop fashion. They were inexpensive—about $44—and buyers were primarily young black men.

*What if,* Kurowski thought, *the killer is a black man?*

The idea contradicted everything the task force was reporting about their suspect. Task force investigators were focusing exclusively on white men. They had put their faith in witnesses who said they saw a white man in a white truck exiting Interstate 10 at Whiskey Bay with the body of a nude woman in the front passenger seat the night of Pam Kinamore's abduction. More recently, on the day Dené was abducted, two women saw a suspicions white man in a white truck lying on top of a black woman in the cab just a quarter mile from the field where Dené was killed.

But another piece of evidence, a trace amount, was bothering Kurowski.

A Negroid head hair was found on Dené's body. The strand was still unidentified. It did not belong to Dené, her brother, or her father, and it was covered in blood. By itself it meant little.

But Kurowski knew trace evidence like hairs and fibers are usually transient, meaning they tend to stick to a person for only a few hours before falling off. That suggested the head hair belonged to someone who had contact with Dené not long before she was killed. He wondered if it belonged to the killer.

Meanwhile, his colleagues working with the killer's DNA at the Acadiana lab discovered something about his genetic profile that gave the black suspect theory more weight.

The serial killer's profile showed rare markers at three loci, including the twenty-two marker at loci VWA that was particularly rare.

When the DNA analysts at the lab conducted further research on the probabilities of finding a twenty-two at the VWA loci, they learned that the marker was seen predominantly in blacks.

From experience, the analysts knew the VWA loci was not one of the spots on the genetic code that determines any racial characteristics, so they could not say the killer was definitely black. But they knew it was a good possibility.

Good enough, they argued in January 2003, for the task force to include black suspects in their search.

"We just wanted them to keep an open mind," said Carolyn Booker, of the Acadiana lab.

Her colleague George Schiro, the DNA technical leader at the lab, was more blunt: "From our end, we felt the investigation should be expanded," he said.

The Lafayette detectives agreed and began submitting DNA swabs from black suspects in the serial killer investigation. Based on the color of Dené's skin alone, they already had their doubts that her killer was white.

But in Baton Rouge, the suspicions from Lafayette went unheeded. No information was released to the public about the possibility the serial killer might be black. No changes were announced in the investigation. Not even the FBI's profiler, in her addendum about Dené's murder released January 17, suggested the killer could be black. Instead, Baton Rouge investigators continued to swab white men exclusively.

"We were wondering, *Why are they still focusing on a white guy?*" Schiro said. "But we didn't know what other information they had."

"We kept telling them he's not white," Kurowski said. "But who are we? We're just a little lab in the country."

The scientists at the Acadiana lab realized they would need better proof if they wanted to alter the course of the task force investigation.

In late January that year, Schiro got an anonymous e-mail about a Florida company that claimed the ability to ascertain racial characteristics, such as skin color, eye color, and hair color, from DNA codes.

This was brand-new, cutting-edge science, and at first Schiro did not believe it.

"I had never heard of it before," he said.

Schiro read through all of the company's validation studies, which appeared to show the company's claims were true. But first he wanted to test them in a blind study.

Several lab employees with different ethnic backgrounds— Asian, Italian, German, and American mutts—submitted their DNA to the company. Sure enough, the company reported accurate results in line with what the employees knew about their genetic heritage.

He wanted to send in the serial killer's DNA immediately, but the Acadiana crime lab's sample from Dené's rape swab was a mixture between the killer's DNA and Dené's DNA. DNAPrint needed a pure sample with only the killer's DNA, which the Louisiana State Police Crime Lab in Baton Rouge possessed.

In mid-February, Schiro told Julia Naylor at the State Police Crime Lab about DNAPrint, and she said they would take it from there.

Meanwhile, the killer was already trawling for another victim.

# CHAPTER 33

# A Skydiver Falls Prey

The first weekend in March 2003 was the height of Mardi Gras season in southern Louisiana, particularly in New Orleans, where the locals call the weeks before Mardi Gras day Carnival, a time of flamboyant festivities, when loud, raucous parades overrun the city streets and twenty-four-hour parties loosen inhibitions and invite public debauchery.

In Baton Rouge, news of the serial killer investigation had faded from the headlines. No new clues had surfaced, and the task force was not holding regular press conferences. The victims' families continued to rally each month on the capitol steps, but they got little media attention.

Life was moving on, and the public, it seemed, was more interested in *lassaiz les bons temps roulez*.

Carrie Yoder, a twenty-six-year-old doctoral student at LSU, certainly wasn't thinking about the serial killer that weekend. She and her boyfriend, Lee Stanton, packed up her car, picked up her friend, and road tripped it sixty miles south from Baton Rouge to New Orleans on Saturday, March 1.

With the million or so other revelers who flocked to the city for Mardi Gras, the trio chugged their drinks street side and begged for bright, colorful plastic beads tossed from the towering parade floats rumbling by. They took in two super-sized parades, Endymion on Saturday and Bacchus on Sunday, and partied for hours in between. On Sunday evening, they headed back to Baton Rouge.

After dropping off her friend, Carrie and Lee drove to Lee's condo and fell into bed, wiped out, dead tired.

The next morning—the day before Mardi Gras—was a holiday for LSU. Most southern Louisiana schools give students Monday and Tuesday of Mardi Gras week off, so the streets around campus were quiet. Lee, also a doctoral student at LSU, planned to spend the day finishing construction on a laundry room behind his condo. All he had left to do was wire it for electricity to hook up his new washer and dryer.

As she sipped her morning tea, reading the paper at Lee's kitchen table, Carrie said her only plans that day were to visit her lab at the biological sciences building. By 9:30 a.m., she was dressed and walking out the door. When she got to the gate at the end of Lee's front walkway, she turned to look back toward the condo. Lee was standing at the door watching her. He waved. She looked so pretty in the morning, her dark ringlet hair still a mess. She gave him her big, mischievous, flirty grin, her darks eyes twinkling, and slipped out of his sight.

Just before five that evening, Lee's phone rang. Carrie said she was on her way to the Winn-Dixie grocery store less than a mile from her house, a little blue two-bedroom rental just a few blocks from the south campus gates.

"Do want to come over for supper?"

Carrie and Lee had dated off and on for three years. They were intensely attracted to each other, but they were also both intensely independent souls. When they got close, too close for comfort sometimes, they'd take some time off, reclaim their space. They dated other people, but after a few weeks apart, they would end up back together. Most recently, they had split in October and didn't see each other for a month. Lee was going nuts.

"I realized I liked myself better with her in my life," he said. So he wrote her a love letter and hoped she'd respond. She did, and since then, they saw each other almost every day, waking up together, meeting for lunch or an afternoon ice cream, having dinner. Only rarely did they not spend the night together at his or her place. The relationship was settling into such a relaxed, comfortable routine, the idea of marriage no longer felt so foreign to them. Lee began to think of planning his future with Carrie.

On the night of March 3, however, Lee was only interested in his laundry room. He was almost done. In the fifteen years since he left his parents' home, he had lived without a washer and dryer of his own. He was so close to finally changing that. He and Carrie had spent the entire weekend together, so one night apart seemed inconsequential.

"I'll eat something here," Lee told Carrie that evening. "If I don't talk to you later tonight, I'll see you tomorrow."

Carrie was fine with that. She told Lee she would spend the evening with her laptop, downloading the Mardi Gras pictures they took with her digital camera. She wanted to put the photos into a PowerPoint presentation for her parents.

"They'll love it," she said.


At the grocery, Carrie bought a steak for her dinner. She was feeling adventurous. For years, the idea of putting a bloody red slab of flesh in her mouth was frightening. She had stopped eating meat at thirteen when her high school biology teacher ordered the class to dissect a pig. But since moving from her home state of Florida to Louisiana, where good eatin' and drinking is a family value, she had begun eating seafood, then chicken, and recently a little pork.

Just a week or so earlier, she came home from the grocery and while unpacking the bags in her kitchen, she called to Lee in the living room, "I think I need your help making supper tonight," she said. "I bought something I'm not sure how to cook."

She appeared in the doorway with a package of thinly sliced chops and that cheeky grin. After Lee fried up their dinner, which she decided she enjoyed, Carrie announced she might try steak next.

She was like that, always evolving, acquiring or discarding new interests and tastes and hobbies. The first time she jumped out of an airplane, she was eighteen years old, not long after her birthday, which made her legal to skydive without her parents' permission.

She told her parents afterward, when she was back on the ground, with a fiery gleam in her eyes.

"What a rush," she said. She lived for the thrill of freefalling, watching the earth rush toward her, feeling her body glide through the air. No drug could provide such a high. During the next several years, she leapt into the open blue sky a mile above the earth sixty-one times.

But by 2003, she had sold her dive gear and parachute; she was moving on to new interests. She was ballroom dancing, performing with a partner at gala events in the blue lace princess gown she sewed for herself. She had begun researching her genealogy, putting together several generations in a family tree.

But Carrie did not have an abundance of free time. She was busy conducting field work for her dissertation. She was studying the effects of floodwater on coastal wetlands. She spent days out in the swamps and mucky marsh of Weeks Bay Reserve, Alabama, collecting proof for her theory that humanmade flooding—the result of rising sea levels based on global warming—left more damage than natural calamities, such as hurricanes or fire. She was almost done. She had completed her course work and was about a year from graduating.

On the night of March 3, 2003, she prepared a steak with mushrooms, carefully cutting off the fat from her filet before throwing it in the pan. She took her dinner to the living room sofa to eat in front of her laptop computer. She knew Lee would have been proud that she ate every bite, leaving only juice on the plate before setting it on the coffee table in front of her.

By the time the sun went down, she was deep into the

photo story of her Mardi Gras weekend that she was preparing for her parents.

The next day, Mardi Gras day, Lee stayed busy finishing work on his new laundry room. By 4:30 p.m., he had installed the washer and dryer and was sitting on his back deck, relaxing in a lawn chair, his feet propped up on a cooler, appreciating his handiwork.

He called Carrie to find out what she was doing for dinner. Her got her voice mail.

"Guess what I'm doing," he said in his message. "I'm sitting on my deck, drinking a bourbon and Coke, and washing my first load of clothing."

He was surprised Carrie did not answer. She always carried her cell phone. But then he remembered she mentioned she might go with a friend to a Mardi Gras celebration in Mamou, Louisiana, a small Cajun town that throws a wild rural-style Mardi Gras party. Maybe her cell phone was out of range, he thought.

He tried her again about seven p.m., trying both her home and cell phones, but got only her voice mail. "I went ahead and ate supper here," he said on her voice mail. "But call me when you get this message."

By nine, he was beginning to feel a little worried. Since they had gotten back together in November, they stayed in touch, usually talking on the phone a few times a day. He wondered if she was out with another guy. He fought the urge to go by her house. He didn't want to look like the crazed, jealous boyfriend.

*Carrie's a big girl.* He told himself. *She can take care of herself.*

Carrie had traveled the world, keeping track of her stops with stickpins in a world map she kept on her wall. She had hiked across glaciers in Alaska, looked for new frog species in the jungles of Panama, skied in Switzerland, and backpacked across much of Europe.

Rationally, Lee knew he need not worry about his savvy, sophisticated girlfriend, but his gut was in knots anyway. He could not sit still. He drove to her home. Dobson Street is only one block, and even though it's less than a half mile from campus, surrounded by student housing, the street feels isolated. Across from Carrie's house is an overgrown wooded area. Her backyard was encased in a high, wood plat fence, with an unlocked gate giving anyone entrance.

As soon as Lee turned onto Dobson, he saw Carrie's white Chevy Nova in her driveway. When he parked right next to it, he noticed the lights were on in the house. He climbed the stoop to her front door. He looked at the peephole he installed for her a few weeks earlier. But his knock went unanswered. He walked around the house but could see no one inside and nothing out of the ordinary.

*She must be out with a friend.* He thought. *I'm overreacting.*

He went home bothered but arguing with himself that she was fine. She had to be. This was Carrie. She was too smart, too dynamic, too special for anything terrible to happen to her.

He had a hard time falling asleep. When he awoke at two, he tried her again.

"Carrie, I'm really, really worried about you," he told her voice mail. "Please call me."

He tried to fall back to sleep, vowing to go to Carrie's first thing in the morning if she didn't call, but he tossed most of the night.


He awoke suddenly to banging on his front door. The sun was up, and Lee's phone had not rung.

He opened the door to the property manager, who was dropping off some paperwork.

"I've got to go . . ." Lee told him, as he threw on a sweatshirt and shorts.


Carrie's house looked the same as the night before. He knocked on the front door again, but he really didn't expect an answer this time. He walked around the side of the house, into the fenced backyard.

Carrie's bedroom window was partially cracked open. He lifted it higher and climbed inside.

"Carrie?" he called out.

Looking around her bedroom, then the living room, he could see nothing out of the ordinary, nothing out of place, but it felt as if Carrie had simply disappeared from the scene.

Her laptop computer was still on, still open and sitting on the right side of the couch. A dirty plate with steak juice and a drinking glass were on the coffee table. A wedge of cheese with bite marks sat on the sofa's left arm. Bags of groceries, including a bunch of souring grapes and a Winn-Dixie receipt for 5:01 p.m. Monday, were still unpacked on the kitchen floor and counter.

He walked toward the front door, which opens onto the living room and kitchen area. He saw her purse, keys, and cell phone sitting right by the door.

When he reached to unlock the front door to go outside, he noticed it was already unlocked. Carrie always locked her door. Even when she just went outside to get her mail.

Then he noticed the key holder on the wall next to the door. Usually, two nails held it up on both ends. Now it was dangling on one nail. *That's wrong*, he thought. *That shouldn't be like that.* Lee stared at it for a few moments as his brain caught up with the facts.

He imagined Carrie struggling with someone at the door. Lee suddenly felt dizzy, confused. *This can't be happening.*

He grabbed her cell phone and used her contact list in its memory to call Carrie's best friends, the ones she spoke with every day, people who would know her routine and her whereabouts. No one had seen or talked with her since Monday.

He tried to reach her parents but did not have their work numbers.

Then he made the call he never imagined making: 911.

"I need to report a missing person . . ."

One uniformed officer arrived at Carrie's home within five minutes. Lee showed him Carrie's purse, her keys, the key holder. Told him about the unlocked front door.

The officer asked Lee to step out of the house, calling it a crime scene.

"The others are on their way," he said.

Soon, a swarm of investigators descended on the property.

"People were piling out of vans," Lee said. They cordoned off the house, began snapping pictures, dusting for prints, and snooping through Carrie's belongings.

Lee realized the police were not treating this as a typical missing persons case. He and Carrie had been aware of the serial killer investigation, but they had not been following it closely. They never imagined it would affect them. Carrie never expressed any fear. She never spoke of wanting to buy a gun or mace or take self-defense classes.

Lee did not even own a TV, so when Baton Rouge Police Chief Pat Englade walked up to him, Lee had no idea who he was or the significance of his presence. Englade introduced himself and comforted Lee. He said police would do everything they could to find Carrie, but the tone in his voice was not hopeful.

Just after three p.m., Lynda Yoder was almost through an uneventful day at work when her husband, Dave, called. At the time, they were carpooling to their jobs. He usually picked her up at four.

"I'm leaving now," he said, his voice strained. "There's a problem. I'll be there in fifteen minutes."

"What is it?" Lynda pressed.

"I'll be there in fifteen minutes."

Lynda braced herself for the worst. It's one of three possibilities, she thought: Dave was laid off. Their house was burglarized. One of their kids was hurt in an accident.

"Carrie's missing," Dave said when Lynda climbed into the car.

A friend of Lee's had tracked down Carrie's good friend, Lauren, who also happened to be dating Carrie's brother, Greg, in Florida. Lauren passed the news on to Dave.

At the time, the local Florida police were still trying to locate the Yoders and had mistakenly gone to the family's former address.

The Yoders called Sergeant R. Quibedeaux with the Baton Rouge Police missing persons bureau. Officially, Carrie was listed as a missing person, but Quibedeaux told the Yoders the department's best investigators—homicide detectives—were already on the case.

He did not need to tell the Yoders why.

Dave and Lynda were aware of the serial killings in Baton Rouge. Carrie had not told them; they had seen it on the national news months earlier.

In passing, they mentioned it to Carrie, but she expressed no fear, and they felt little need to worry. That sort of stuff happens to other people. People you read about in the newspaper and think, *How awful!*

Suddenly, the unimaginable horror behind the headlines was real for them. They were living the story, they were the distraught parents, and it was their beautiful, brilliant daughter, the one they never doubted would have a bright, happy future, the girl who seemed immune from tragic twists in life, who was making the headlines.

In a split second, the world as they expected it to turn was reeling in a distorted, nightmarish direction.

When they arrived at their home, the couple could barely function enough to pack. A neighbor stepped in, literally directing them, step by step—take your toothbrush, several changes of clothes, important records, etc.—until they made it out the door about five p.m. for the drive to Baton Rouge.

They drove all night, too pensive to talk, and arrived in the Baton Rouge city limits about four a.m. Their meeting with Quibedeaux was not until eight a.m. They had four hours of the darkest, deadest stretch of the morning to survive, alone. They felt lost, almost as if they were in a dream. The streets of Baton Rouge were empty. The traffic lights turning for no one. The businesses and homes dark.

They did not know where to go or what to do. They were strangers in an unfamiliar city. They had been to Baton Rouge only once before.

They pulled off the interstate and found an empty Denny's restaurant. They asked the waitress to keep their coffee cups full as they tried to grasp what was happening. Breaking their silence, Lynda said what they were both thinking: *"There's a good chance we'll never see our daughter again."*

Lee Stanton arranged for the Yoders and other family members to stay at a friend's family home in Baton Rouge, where they could spread out and prevent the media, which was again in a frenzy, from finding them.

Quibedeaux met with the Yoders at the house, but he did not offer much hope. Police knew nothing other than that Carrie was gone.

Officers spread out in Carrie's neighborhood to question neighbors. They hoped that months of media attention about the serial killer would cause people to pay more attention to their surroundings, notice unusual activity or strangers who looked out of place. All the police needed was one good witness to catch a license plate number, a car type, to see the killer's face.

His luck couldn't last forever, investigators told themselves. He was a man, not a ghost.

But at door after door, the police met with neighbors who had seen and heard nothing. Monday night had been rainy and overcast. People who were not out partying huddled inside all day. And many locals had left town for the Mardi Gras weekend, which stretched through Tuesday night.

The ground searches also proved useless. Dogs sniffed out the woods and ditches near Carrie's home but could get no trail. The helicopters flying overhead found no trace of her.

Interviews with Carrie's close friends confirmed the suspicions of foul play. Carrie was not the type to pick up and leave without notifying anyone. Inquiries about her emotional state revealed a strong-willed, confident, and happy young woman. The Carrie everyone knew showed no signs of depression or a desire to hurt herself. Everything in the case pointed to another abduction.

\* \* \*

Quibedeaux assured the Yoders police would call if they learned anything important; otherwise, he said, sit tight. There was nothing else they could do but wait.

That was the hardest part—waiting—especially at night, when the temperatures dropped and the rain came.

"That was all I could think about," Lee said. "She's cold."

All weekend the Yoders waited. When they met with police again on Monday, March 10, there was nothing new to report. The ground and aerial searches were ongoing, but investigators were running out of places to look.

Crime scene technicians had collected dozens of pieces of evidence from Carrie's home. They had taken the front door to the crime lab, hoping to find a good print or DNA or some other trace evidence of the abductor's identity. They tried to lift prints from the front doorframe, the wall, and back window of her house. Using a blue light, they scanned the rooms for blood and saliva and seminal fluid. But nothing proved fruitful.

Once again, the killer left the trail of a ghost.


Early on March 13, as the morning fog lifted off the Atchafalaya Swamp, Curtis Roban was at the helm of his crawfish skiff. The bow of his boat was cutting through the muddy waters underneath Interstate 10, just east of Whiskey Bay, when his eye caught on a pale white object in the water.

He motored his boat back around for a better look. The sky was overcast and dripping a light rain. He strained to focus his eyes on the floating object, doubting himself when he thought he was seeing a woman's backside. He rode his boat up upon it, and he reached over. His hand pulled back quickly when he felt her flesh. It was a woman's bloated and decaying body wearing only a black top.


An army of police and crime scene technicians arrived within an hour. The body was located in a canal running underneath and parallel to the interstate about a half mile east of the Whiskey Bay exit. From the position of her body in the water, investigators determined she did not float to that spot. But she could not have been driven there, either; the area is inaccessible by car. Most likely, investigators theorized, she was dumped there from above. Her killer likely pulled over to the shoulder of Interstate 10, pulled her body out of his vehicle, and tossed her over the rail into the swamp.

After Carrie's disappearance, Lee found himself spending more and more time with Carrie's academic advisor, Professor Bill Platt. They shared a common respect and love for Carrie. The two scientists—Lee was working on his Ph.D. in oceanography—got together to discuss Carrie's schedule, people she came in contact with, anything she might have said lately that could be construed as a clue.

On Thursday afternoon, March 13, they drove out to the botanical gardens at LSU's Rural Life Museum, where they liked to retreat to nature. Neither had watched the television news that morning, which began reporting a woman's body was found in Whiskey Bay.

Bill got the call from a student.

"They found a body . . ."

Across town, the Yoders were having a late lunch. Like Lee, they had not heard the news of the day. Instead, they began their day feeling upbeat, invigorated by the media reports coming out of Utah about another family looking for their missing daughter.

Nine months earlier, fourteen-year-old Elizabeth Smart was kidnapped from her Salt Lake City home. Many people had given up hope that she would be found alive. But on March 12, police announced she was found wandering the Salt Lake City streets with her capturers. A mentally unstable couple kidnapped Elizabeth to become the man's second wife. Except for psychological scars, the girl returned safely to her family.

*It can happen,* Lynda told herself. *Carrie could still be found alive.*

The Yoders returned to their temporary home from lunch

about three thirty p.m. They expected investigators for a previously scheduled meeting at four p.m., but a caravan of police cars was already in the driveway.

"They're early," Lynda said. She did not think the worst.

The police were already gathered in the living room when the Yoders walked inside. Lynda greeted FBI Agent Jeff Methvin with a smile.

"Jeff, I've had such a good day," she said. "They found Elizabeth Smart . . ."

He did not respond.


Investigators waited until the Yoders were seated before breaking the news.

"The body of a white female was found near Whiskey Bay this morning . . ." The next words floating through the room were drowned out by the thoughts rushing through Lynda's mind. *Maybe it's not Carrie. Maybe it's some other woman. Maybe this is still some terrible mix-up, and Carrie will turn up safe.*

The police did not have much else to say. The conversation was short. Investigators already had Carrie's dental records. They would try to identify the body and let the Yoders know as soon as they knew.


Minutes later, Lee and Bill arrived at the house. Tearful hugs went around, but hope was still present. Carrie's dance partner, a Vietnamese man, had recently contacted his uncle in Vietnam. The older man was a "see-er" and said he believed Carrie was being held in a valley somewhere, alive. The Yoders were not superstitious people, but they'd rather believe his vision than the one they were facing.

As the crowd of people at the house milled in and out, cell phones beeping and ringing, Detective Ike Vavasseur signaled to Lee to joined him outside.

"I need to ask you a couple questions," Vavasseur said, shutting the door behind Lee. He was holding a radio phone. "This is an investigator on the scene out there . . . I need for you to describe what Carrie's tattoo looks like."

At the base of Carrie's back, just below her pant line, she had a tree of life inked on her skin. The vines arose out of a flowerpot at the center and spread out toward her hip bones into a weaved Celtic design.

Lee leaned awkwardly toward the radio in Vavasseur's hand as he described the tattoo to the officer in the swamps.

"That's it," the officer's words shot back into Lee's ears like a bullet. The man's voice sounded so matter-of-fact.

Lee's knees buckled, and he nearly collapsed. Vavasseur caught him with a bear hug.

"Listen," Vavasseur said, speaking quietly but sternly. "You've got to go back in there, but you can't tell anyone. You've got to be strong."

Lee was barely able to walk. When he returned to the living room, he was shaking and rocking back and forth. His face was pale. Bill was immediately at his side.

"I need to take a walk," Lee mumbled. "I've got to walk."

They went out back and made loops around the yard.

"It's her, Bill, it's her . . ."

They decided then that something positive needed to come out of Carrie's death and vowed to work on creating a scholarship in her name.

By the 10 p.m. news, reporters were announcing that Carrie's body had been found, but the Yoders had not yet received confirmation, and Lynda desperately held onto her dying ray of hope.

She was sick with guilt about it, but in her prayers she wished the body was someone else's child.

The phone rang at about two a.m. Dave's nephew Steve answered. Lynda watched his face. He tried to look calm, but she could tell by his eyes. She knew before he hung up that it was over. Carrie was really dead. Lynda would get no more hugs from her daughter. There would be no more birthdays, no more phone calls, no more memories. Carrie would never earn her Ph.D., get married, or have children. When Carrie was killed, an irreplaceable part of the Yoders' future died with her.

\* \* \*

The following Monday, the task force called a press conference to announce what everyone in Baton Rouge already suspected. Carrie's murder was linked by DNA to the same man who killed Gina Green, Murray Pace, Pam Kinamore, and Dené Colomb. The victim count was now officially up to five.

# CHAPTER 34

# Derrick's End of Days

Two weeks of work. That's all Derrick got out of JE Merit in April 2002. Now that Jackie's money was gone, the Lees were struggling to make ends meet. Jackie was working at the U.S. Post Office in Baton Rouge, but the family's bills exceeded her salary. And Derrick certainly did not have the cash he was used to carrying in his pocket. He was out of jail, but he felt trapped. The frustration was building.

In May, he filed for unemployment and was happy to discover the government would give him $258 a week. He didn't spend it on his mortgage, though. He let that lapse the same month. He had other things on his mind. Mainly women.

He was cruising more than ever. He really knew the highways now, every road to everywhere. That was his home. He liked the truck stops, too. A place where he found lonely, lost women, some of them looking for love, especially during the night shift.

Derrick liked to try his luck at Bayou Bill's Shell Station in

Grosse Tete, the last stop off westbound Interstate 10 before the long, dark stretch through the Atchafalaya Swamp.

One of the cashiers, Elizabeth, a white woman in her late thirties, remembers the first time she saw him. He introduced himself as Todd. He was wearing a fancy gray sweat suit with nice new tennis shoes. Two heavy gold chains, one with a money sign pendant, the other with a cross, hung around his neck. On each hand he wore two fat gold rings with diamonds.

"You got a man in your life?" he asked her after he got her chatting. He asked her to go out, then he wrote his cell phone number on a piece of paper and handed it to her, saying, "I need someone to talk to."

He asked for her work number.

"It's in the book," she said. She was not comfortable with his advances.

Two days later, he called her at the station.

"Do you want to go have breakfast with me?" he asked.

She said no. Then he asked about dinner, then his apartment in Baton Rouge.

She kept turning him down, her rejections stripping away Derrick's cool demeanor. He yelled through the phone, "You fucking bitch! You'll end up regretting that!"

She hung up and went back to work. At the end of her shift, while she sat in the store's Subway restaurant area, Derrick sat down across from her.

"I'm sorry," he said. He apologized for his behavior. "I'm going through a lot."

They talked for about an hour at the station, and then Derrick walked her to her car.

A few days later, Derrick called her at the station again.

"What are you wearing?" he asked. "What color underwear do you have on?"

Increasingly, his questions were invasive, vulgar. "Do you wear a thong? What do your nipples look like? Do you shave your pussy? Do you give blow jobs?"

"I don't want to discuss what I'm wearing," she said.

"Why don't you meet me at my apartment in Baton Rouge . . ." he suggested.

"No."

Derrick persisted. He called her at the station at least every other day, leaving messages if she wasn't there. When he reached her, he only wanted to talk about sex.

"I like to get a little rough," he said. "Do you like it rough?"

"No, I don't, but some women do . . ."

"Do you like to be tied up? Do you like to be bit?"

She told Derrick she did not like any kind of bondage or role-playing. He wanted to know if it was OK to talk with women about their sexual preferences.

"No," she said. "You really shouldn't."


In July, while still collecting unemployment, Derrick began another job for JE Merit at the Baton Rouge ExxonMobil plant on Chippewa. He worked long hours, usually 6:30 a.m. to 5 p.m., hauling limestone and gravel in a dump truck on site or laboring as a boilermaker, hooking pipes together at the refinery.

As a truck driver, he left much to be desired. He often left his truck unmanned, requiring coworkers to track him down when they needed it moved. He parked in restricted areas, and when told of his infractions, he was confrontational and quick to flash his temper. But as a boilermaker, he was one of the best men on the job.

He made few friends at work. He tried to intimidate his coworkers and balked at his foremen's orders. He often arrived angry and just looking at people who were paid more than him pissed him off. Most of his downtime was spent on his cell phone, his voice sometimes flirtatious, sometimes demanding.

Occasionally Derrick would disappear down by the riverbank, an area overgrown with weeds.

"What were you doing back there?" one of his coworkers asked when Derrick emerged from the thicket one day.

"Looking at the river . . ."


The extra cash he earned still was not used to pay his mortgage. He pocketed it for his own pleasure, blowing it on drinks and clothes and gas and women. He continued to spend several nights at home with Jackie or Consandra, but other nights he was cruising for sex elsewhere.

Two of Derrick's uncles, John Barrow and Michael Barrow, worked as DJs at Club Hooks on North Acadiana Thruway in Baton Rouge, not far from Interstate 10. Every Saturday, Derrick hung out at the club until closing. He rarely sat down, preferring to stand at the bar or at the back wall. Usually, he arrived with a different woman every week or picked one up at the bar to leave with.

He stayed some nights at the run-down Vel Rose Motel on Airline Highway in north Baton Rouge, but he was also shacking up with a few regulars at their apartments.

In November 2002, he took one of his women to Millennium Motors in Baton Rouge and bought her a green Ford Taurus, putting just a few hundred bucks down. He had no intentions of paying it off. He made no further payments on the car loan he signed at 16 percent interest.

He was racing toward a cliff. Derrick was spreading himself thin, and the load was increasing. By the end of 2002, the bank was closing in on his home on Highway 61 for nonpayment on a $44,000 mortgage. The car dealers were threatening to repossess his vehicles for the same reason. Yet Derrick remained unresponsive to the moneymen. The financial mess finally forced the Lees to file for bankruptcy in late 2002.

On November 18, Derrick filed an insurance claim on Consandra's Neon, saying he hit a deer. Yet when adjusters tried to get the full story, he was belligerent and uncooperative. The next two days, he left his job at ExxonMobil early and did not show up at all on November 21. Instead, he cruised the highways, ending up in Grand Coteau the same day Dené Colomb was visiting her mother's grave.


In February 2003, Derrick began working the night shift at ExxonMobil, 6 p.m. to 4:30 a.m. By the end of the month, he took a break. He did not return to the job for more than a week. He was scheduled to work on March 4, Mardi Gras day, but he called in and reported a relative had died and he needed to be off for awhile longer. On March 6, though, just three days after Carrie was killed, Derrick showed up at the Exxon-Mobil office dressed sharp and wearing his pointed cowboy boots to pick up his check.

Earlier that week, he had met a twenty-one-year-old black woman who was shopping at the Delmont Shopping Center, 5151 Plank Road.

"You're looking good," he said.

He doled out the compliments, introduced himself as Derrick, then offered her a ride. She climbed inside his red Ford Explorer, and he drove her home to Ned Avenue in a gritty neighborhood on the opposite side of town.

He talked to her about his belief in God and the struggles of life, and he confessed he often felt like committing suicide. When he dropped her off, he scribbled his name and number on a piece of paper.

The next morning at nine, Derrick was back at her house. He was dressed in a long-sleeved white shirt, faded blue jeans, with black-and-white cowboy boots peeking out. He walked into the kitchen and placed a small knife on the counter.

"Can I watch you take a bath?" he asked.

She let him watch as she bathed. Then she got out and walked nude into the den, which was furnished with a bed and a sofa. She lay down on the bed, and Derrick sat on the sofa. While he watched her, he began masturbating. When he finished, he got up and went into the bathroom to take a shower.

He dressed in fresh clothes, stuffed the clothes he took off into a black garbage bag, and left.

Derrick visited the woman several times. When she wasn't home, he sat in his truck outside her home and masturbated. He did not care who saw him, and several neighbors did. He followed one of them, a woman who worked the night shift at Hunt Correctional Facility. He trailed her all the way to the prison gates.

At work, Derrick kept to himself. Few people liked him. He was always agitated and ready for a fight. Sometimes, he talked about his love of hunting and fishing, but he never went with his coworkers on their regular trips together.

Most mornings, he sat down in the workers' trailer with his nose stuck in the newspaper.

One afternoon in April 2003, just a few days before Derrick was laid off, a coworker was riding with him in a truck across the refinery site.

"What do you think about this serial killer?" she asked Derrick, trying to make small talk.

Derrick did not respond.

"I don't believe in the death penalty," the coworker continued, "but in this case, when they catch him, they ought to kill him."

Derrick said nothing.

# CHAPTER 35

# Color Coded

Making an abrupt about-face in the middle of a massive, intensely watched, media-whipping, eight-month investigation is never easy. But the Baton Rouge authorities tried their best to do so confidently after Carrie Yoder, the fifth victim, was linked to the serial killer.

On March 21, 2003, the task force called a news conference. The room was packed with reporters from Baton Rouge, New Orleans, Lafayette, and national media outlets. Task force spokeswoman Mary Ann Godawa was quick. The message was simple: The serial killer might be black. She explained only that a second canvass of Carrie's neighborhood led investigators to believe the serial killer could be a dark-skinned white man, a black man, or someone of mixed race.

The news was stunning.

For eight months, the task force said they were looking for a white man, probably driving a white truck. When the FBI profile was released in early September, police described the

284

serial killer as a white man likely between the ages of twenty-five and thirty-five. The media published and republished reports about the white man in a white truck.

The investigators had been focused acutely and exclusively on white suspects, taking more than 1,000 DNA swabs from Caucasian males. When a tip led to a black male, task force policy allowed detectives to rule him out based on the color of his skin.

Yet at the news conference, Godawa claimed, "We have never limited our investigation, and we're asking the public not to limit theirs."

When questioned further about the number of suspects who might have been ignored or not reported to the police because the task force was looking for a white male, Godawa responded, "a few."

For weeks, it was unclear how the new information was developed.

At the news conference, Godawa suggested the new information about the killer's race was developed from a recent canvassing of Carrie's neighborhood, but police declined to elaborate about the new information.

The task force also declined to discuss whether they had acquired information about the suspect's race from analysis of his DNA. In fact, Godawa told the media, if lab tests confirmed the serial killer's race, the information would be made public.

The task force's secrecy was particularly frustrating for a group of scientists in Sarasota, Florida.

Tony Frudakis, chief scientific officer and founder of DNAPrint genomics, was disappointed that task force investigators would not acknowledge his company's involvement in determining the color of the serial killer's skin. Using cutting-edge genetic science, Frudakis's team of scientists had analyzed the serial killer's DNA and determined he was predominantly of African descent.

In mid-March, Frudakis called Detective Ike Vavasseur with the news. Vavasseur had gathered several investigators on the conference call to hear the results of DNAPrint's analysis.

"Your guy is an African American," Frudakis told them. "Furthermore, he's very likely to be of average skin tone for an African American."

His words were met with a few moments of heavy silence. "How sure are you about this?" was the first question.

"As sure as sure can be," Frudakis said.

Investigators were skeptical. They thought they had three solid eyewitness accounts pegging the killer as a white man:

- On the night Pam was abducted, a trucker on Interstate 10 said he saw a nude woman's body in the passenger seat of a white truck that exited at Whiskey Bay, where Pam was later found. Under hypnosis, the trucker described a white male driver.

- Earlier that same night, a woman driving on Airline Highway said a white Chevrolet truck driven by a white man sped out of Pam's neighborhood and drove erratically in front of her. In the passenger seat of the truck, the woman saw a brunette woman turn and look out of the cab window with a terrified stare.

- On November 21, the day Dené was killed, a woman driving a quarter mile from where Dené's body was found said she saw a white truck parked on the side of the road. As she passed, a white male driver sat up in the seat, and at his side, with her head against the passenger door, was a black woman.

In addition to the eyewitnesses, statistics on serial killers showed the majority are white males, especially if the victims are white. The FBI profile did not determine the killer was white, but when the task force subsequently announced the killer was white, the FBI did not say otherwise.

Now some newfangled scientific test done by a group of Florida scientists with no involvement in the case was saying otherwise. It was stunning, heartbreaking, and unbelievable all at the same time. The idea that the serial killer was black meant investigators had been looking in the wrong direction since the beginning.

But Frudakis was confident in his company's analysis. DNAPrint's science was brand-new. The technique had never been tested in court. It was only recently peer reviewed by independent scientists. But so far, the results had never failed to be correct.

All humans share 99.9 percent of the same genes. That 0.1 percent is what makes each person an individual. Within that 0.1 percent are hundreds of genetic markers that provide information about the individual's biogeographic ancestry.

DNAPrint looks at hundreds of areas on the genetic code with that 0.1 percent that reveal markers seen more commonly among particular ethnic groups. For example, Asians might have a set of markers that is not commonly seen in Europeans, and vice versa.

By looking at hundreds of these markers on the serial killer's DNA and comparing it to a database of DNA gleaned from people of all ethnic heritages, DNAPrint was able to see his heritage was 85 percent sub-Sahara African and 15 percent Native American.

Unlike most African Americans, who are at least 20 percent European, the killer had inherited no European genetic markers. That meant the color of his skin would likely be at least average to slightly darker than most blacks in the United States.

The task force had heard it before from other scientists who had tried to analyze the serial killer's DNA, but none could claim the certainty of DNAPrint.

The information could not be ignored. The new information realized investigators' worst fears, alerting them to a colossal and disturbing error in their investigation. Meetings were had. Discussions began. And after careful determination, the task force decided to announce the *expansion* of their search to include black males.

In later testimony, East Baton Rouge Parish Sheriff's Detective David Smith explained, "We didn't shift focus from say white males to black males. We considered everybody at that point a suspect . . . We still looked at some white males because we didn't know. We didn't want to make the same mistake twice . . ."

That meant the task force needed to go back and review thousands of tips about black men that had been cleared by the task force based solely on the color of the men's skin.

At least one of those tips was about Derrick Todd Lee.

Collette Walker, who Derrick stalked in 1999, tried several times to report him as a suspect prior to March 2003.

On September 4, 2002, at 10:28 p.m., after hearing details from the FBI's behavioral profile of the serial killer, she called the task force and provided Derrick's name, the location of his home, and information about his criminal history as a Peeping Tom.

The task force assigned the lead to Captain Shane Evans of the Baton Rouge Police narcotics division, but it was quickly cleared and closed on September 6.

Again, Detective Smith explained during later testimony, "He was eliminated based on the fact that he was a black male, period."

Prior to mid-March 2003, the task force also showed little interest when police from nearby departments shared information about crimes similar to the serial killings when the suspect was black.

Saint Martin Parish Sheriff's detectives had informed the task force in late July or early August 2002 about the home invasion and attack of Diane Alexander. In the same time period, investigators in Zachary told the task force about the murders of Connie Warner and Randi Mebruer, including the details of one of their main suspects: Derrick Todd Lee. But at the time, the serial killer investigators were not interested; a black male attacker did not match their description of the killer.

The new information changed everything, for everybody: the police, the public, and the killer. He was no longer protected by the color of his skin.


When a number of Murray Pace's close neighbors heard the killer was black, they thought first of the suspicious man they saw watching her home in the hours and day before her murder, the man they told police about. They all agreed he had light brown skin, a flat nose, and was wearing blue work pants and a long-sleeved shirt.

But since the murder, police had never requested more information about the man. Detectives did not ask neighbors to help develop a sketch. Nor did authorities release information about the man to the public. In the ten months since Murray's death, the neighbors wondered if their reports had simply disappeared.

One of them posted a comment about the suspicious man on a *Court TV* Web site in a page dedicated to the Baton Rouge serial killer investigation. In March 2003, he was approached by a Mississippi forensic consultant who had heard about his posting from one of Murray's old roommates.

Ann Williams is a lawyer who teaches forensic investigation and consults with police departments stumped by difficult unsolved cases. Soon after Murray's murder, she spoke with a California psychic, Jeanne Borgen, about the case. Borgen told Ann she believed Murray's killer was a light-skinned black man with a broad, flat nose, who was in his early thirties and six feet tall. He was not bulky, but his arms were powerful. Initially, Ann dismissed the woman's claims because the suspect in the case was supposedly white.

But in March 2003, Ann remembered Borgen's description when she heard about the man Murray's neighbors saw. She contacted one of the neighbors, Chris Villemarette, who put her in touch with the others. After hearing about how the police had not responded to the witness accounts, Ann recognized a need to offer her assistance.

Ann had been brought into the case through the class she taught at the time in Jackson, Mississippi. Murray's mother had signed up for it after Murray's murder, and the two women had become friendly.

Shortly after Ann contacted the neighbors, they all gathered in Ann's Mississippi apartment. They, too, were eager to help.

With FACES, a computer software program used by police departments around the country, Ann helped them complete a composite sketch of the man.

The results—four individual sketches and one done together by all witnesses—were submitted to the task force in mid-April. But, again, authorities did not release the information to the public. Nor did they try to interview the witnesses again to develop their own in-house sketch.

Instead, the task force argued that police officers had already tried to track down the lead, driving through the neighborhood looking for men fitting that description, immediately after Murray's murder.

"We have investigated and interviewed men who fit this description in that area," Godawa told the media after information about the witnesses' reports became public. "We are still investigating that."

Godawa said several Hispanic people lived in the Sharlo area, some of whom were stopped by police for questioning. But the task force did not appear particularly excited about the lead.

"We have no proof he had any connection to Murray Pace's homicide," Godawa said. "We don't know why he was in the area."

The task force had no intentions of releasing the new sketch, arguing that the four individual sketches from witnesses were different from one another and therefore their combined sketch was unreliable.

Meanwhile, the task force was busy reopening old and closed-out leads of black males. They were also receiving new ones. On March 31, the task force got a fax from the West Feliciana Parish Sheriff's Office.

Captain Spence Dilworth suggested investigators take a look at one of their Peeping Toms, a man also suspected in two Zachary murders, a man named Derrick Todd Lee.

The next day, April 1, the lead sheet already in the task force database on Derrick Todd Lee was reassigned to a detective in the field. Baton Rouge Police Officer Livingston "Lee" Alfred got the job. But the tip was not assigned as high priority.

A week later, Alfred asked East Baton Rouge Parish Sheriff's Officer Michael Lockwood to go with him to Saint Francisville to collect a DNA swab from Derrick. The two Baton Rouge officers called the West Feliciana Parish Sheriff's Office for assistance, since they would be treading on foreign territory. With a West Feliciana Parish Sheriff's deputy leading the way, the men went to Derrick's home on Highway 61. But no one was home.

Alfred then gave the deputy his card and asked him to call if he saw Derrick.

No further attempts—no search warrant, no subpoena, no surveillance to surreptitiously collect a glass or bottle Derrick drank from—were made by the task force to obtain Derrick's DNA.

# CHAPTER 36

# The Country Grocer
# and the Lost Lead

Thirty miles north of Baton Rouge, in the rolling hills of East Feliciana Parish, retired grocer and former cattle rancher James Odom nearly fell out of his chair when he heard the Louisiana serial killer was not a white man. Instantly, his memory shot back to a sunny spring day in 1998 and the disturbing words he heard from one of his work hands.

At the time, James was just settling into his retirement after twenty-five years of running the local grocery store in rural Jackson, Louisiana. He had worked almost every day, babysitting its daily operations and locking her up at the end of the day. But by April 1998, his days were filled with the chores of maintaining his seventy acres of cow pasture and farmland.

On April 20, his job for the day was cutting up a large red oak that had fallen on his fence. At sixty-one, James was still fit, strong enough to do his own labor, but after a lifetime of saving and wise investment, he was also wealthy enough to hire someone to help with the heavy lifting.

Leroy Shorts, a local for hire, was usually the first man James called when he needed an extra hand. Matching his name, Leroy is a short man, and squat, making him look immensely nonthreatening. Leroy is also quiet, with a pleasant, relaxed temperament that further inspires trust from other men. He's dependable and a loyal employee, not only because he wants to do a good job but also because he needs to keep the job. He is from a poor black community in Jackson and in 1998, was struggling to take care of his family.

After years of working together, James had come to think of Shorts as a friend, although both men knew the friendship would always have its constraints because of the racial and economic divide between them.

On that sunny April day in 1998, a Monday, James's task for the day was a big red oak that had fallen on the property. He and Shorts would make firewood out of it. As the men got to work with the saw, they also got to talking, and James asked a question that would forever change his life.

"You hear about that woman who disappeared from Zachary this weekend?" James asked.

On the news the night before, police reported the disappearance of Randi Mebruer, a twenty-eight-year-old nurse, from her home in Zachary, just fifteen miles away. James was troubled by the few gruesome details that were released. Blood throughout her home and a little boy, her son, left alone inside. James shuddered at the thought of something like that happening to his own daughter-in-law.

Shorts had also seen the news, but not until that morning. And he, too, was troubled, but for a different reason. He was quiet for a moment, taking his time to think about what he would say.

"Yeah," Shorts began. "I know something about it, too."

James stopped pulling on his saw. He looked at Shorts.

"What do you mean?"

Looking up at his boss, Shorts said plain and straight, "I think I know who might of done it."

The day before, a Sunday, Shorts was visiting his next-door neighbor, Joe Green, when a man Shorts had seen around the property, but had never met, introduced himself as "Todd Lee." At the time, Derrick Todd Lee was living off and on with Joe's niece, Consandra "Cat" Green, and that afternoon, they planned to host a barbecue. Derrick invited anyone and everyone over to Cat's house that day. He and Cat had just returned from the store with more food and drink—beer, chicken, ribs, pork chops, and jambalaya—than they could eat.

Derrick presided over the grill, a beer always in hand, happy to be at the center of attention, chattering nonstop and telling jokes. The few moments Shorts got alone with Derrick, he bragged about his abilities to charm women, and even offered to bring Shorts "wild" women who would do anything for a little crack cocaine. Derrick particularly warmed to Shorts after learning they had both served time behind bars, although Shorts's most serious crime was for minor drug possession.

Sometime about four p.m., the barbecue broke up and the dozen or so guests, mostly Cat's friends, cleared out. Shorts went to his house right next door. He spent the next several hours on his couch watching TV.

Just as he was falling off into sleep, Shorts was startled by a loud, incessant banging on his front door. It was after midnight. His wife was already in bed. He was a little frightened until he looked out his window and saw his new friend outside on his front porch.

Shorts unlocked the door and just as he was beginning to open it, Derrick, in a panic, pushed his way inside.

"Shut the door!" Derrick said, moving toward the windows.

"What's going on?" Shorts asked.

"Some people are following me."

Derrick peered out the window. He was nervous. Shorts figured he was paranoid.

"Who's following you?" Shorts said.

"Detectives from Zachary . . . They're trying to frame me."

"Uh-huh. For what?"

"Come ride with me," Derrick said. "I'm going to my house."

Shorts was apprehensive but not scared. He liked Derrick. He seemed like a nice guy, and if he needed a friend to ride with him, Shorts would go along. He was that type of guy. But he began to question his judgment once he was inside Derrick's truck and noticed a large pistol in the console. Knowing they were both convicted felons, the thought of getting stopped by police unnerved him.

"You'll go to jail if the police catch you with that," Shorts told Derrick.

"You ain't gonna tell, are you?"

Shorts wouldn't tell. Not for something like that. But he was quick to figure Derrick was not such a wise man for carrying it around.

"I didn't see nothing," Shorts told Derrick and didn't bring it up again.

As the truck pulled onto the road from the driveway, Derrick took off squealing toward Saint Francisville. He sped like fire down the dark and narrow winding Louisiana Highway 68 toward Saint Francisville, driving more than eighty miles per hour in a fifty-five miles per hour zone, keeping his eyes on the rearview mirror.

"Man, slow down," Shorts urged him.

"I told you the police are trying to frame me," Derrick shot back. "They suspect me of murder. . . . But they'll never prove it because they don't have no evidence."

Shorts had learned the code of inmates while in jail, and he knew better than to pry into another man's business. He wasn't going to ask any more questions, but he began to suspect his new friend was involved in something bad. Something big. Derrick was acting too suspicious for an innocent man. He was jumping at his shadow.

"You want a beer?" Derrick asked Shorts when they walked into the Lees' home in Saint Francisville. Shorts, holding up the can in his hand, declined.

"Wait here," Derrick said, as he left Shorts alone in the front living room. "I'll be right back."

Derrick disappeared into a back room. Shorts figured Derrick's wife and children were out of town because he heard and saw nothing of them while he waited. After several minutes, perhaps as much as fifteen minutes, Derrick was back at Shorts's side, walking briskly to the door.

"Let's go," he said.

*  *  *

The next morning was the first Shorts heard about Randi Mebruer's disappearance. He heard it on the news. A woman
missing from Zachary. Blood in her home. Police suspect foul
play. Shorts thought immediately of Derrick. *That's why he
was so scared,* Shorts thought. He felt his stomach knot. *This
man here killed that lady.*

Shorts did not, however, call the police. He did not even
consider it. It needs to be said that relations between the law
and many blacks in the Felicianas is not an open street. The
police do not trust them. And they do not trust the police. Too
many lies and ill feelings have passed between them. Crimes
and criminals are often protected with silence. Victims often
assume they will receive little or no help. And snitches know
too well that the police can't protect them from the bad guy's
brothers, uncles, cousins, and friends who live nearby. So the
idea of reporting Derrick to the police was far from Shorts's
mind. Instead, he told one of the few white men he trusted.


"You know we need to tell somebody about this," James said
after hearing Shorts's story. "We've got to let some authorities
know about this."

"Yeah, I know," Shorts said. "But I'm not going to do it."

James called his youngest son, Joel, who happened to be
an officer with the East Feliciana Parish Sheriff's Office. On
Joel's suggestion, James called the new chief of police in
Zachary, Johnny Wells, that afternoon. The chief wanted to
hear more. The next day, James was at the Zachary police
station talking with Wells and a few detectives investigating
the case.

After telling the police Shorts's story, James learned Derrick was not only already a suspect in Randi's disappearance,
he was also a suspect in the 1992 murder of Connie Warner
and the 1993 machete attack on two teenage lovers in a
Zachary cemetery. Right then, James was convinced, this man
Derrick, who seemed to confess something to Shorts, was
guilty of Randi Mebruer's murder.

Wells and the detectives seemed appreciative of the tip, but as James could see, they were already on to Derrick as a suspect. They did not record or even take notes during the interview. And James never signed a witness statement.

At the time, James thought nothing of it. He just hoped Shorts's story might help in making an arrest. When James left the station that day, he figured he would soon hear from the detectives. But he heard nothing more about the case except what was in the news. Occasionally, he called the Zachary Police Department to inquire about the investigation. All he got was the same refrain: "We're still investigating. We don't have enough evidence to make an arrest." After several months, James assumed his tip never panned out and tried to let it go.

Every once in awhile, though, he would think about Derrick Todd Lee, and he just wanted to kick something. He was sure this man was a killer, and he couldn't believe the guy was getting away with murder.

What James did not know at the time was that Zachary detectives began talking to Shorts right away. Detectives David McDavid and Lewis Banks showed up on Shorts's front porch a few days after James was interviewed in Zachary.

Shorts looked out the window of his home and saw a dark car with tinted windows, obviously an unmarked police car. He answered the door reluctantly. He did not know whether Derrick was watching from next door.

The conversation was short and notably one-sided. The detectives introduced themselves, said they were investigating the disappearance of Randi Mebruer and that they were putting Derrick under surveillance. The gist was they wanted Shorts's help. They wanted him to get close to Derrick, find out as much as he could, try to get him to talk, and then report back to the police.

Nervous and not too willing to get involved, Shorts told them, "I'm not that close of friends with him. I don't think I can help."

The police did not want to take no for an answer. "Try," they said. "We'll get back to you." Before they did, however, Derrick confronted Shorts about the cops' visit.

"I know they came to see you," Derrick said. "I've got a friend in the police department there."

"I didn't tell them anything," Leroy insisted.

"I know you didn't tell them nothing," he said. "Cuz you don't know nothing. You don't know anything about my business. And you never will."

A few days later, the Zachary detectives paid Shorts another visit, this time with an offer.

They would give Shorts money to get close to Derrick, make friends with him. In the weeks that followed, Shorts started spending time with Derrick, riding around with him in his truck, drinking beer at Cat's house, swapping stories about women at her uncle's trailer in the backyard. Police even paid for ribs and slabs of meat so that Shorts could suggest they have another barbecue. But Derrick never spoke to Shorts like he had that one night. Derrick knew how to keep his mouth shut.

Meanwhile, James returned to his quiet life in Jackson. He tried to keep up with Randi's case, but gradually her name faded from the papers and TV news. After several months, then years, passed, it looked like Randi's murder would go unsolved.

James had almost stopped thinking about it when he heard the news about Charlotte Murray Pace's murder and its link to the murders of Gina Green and Pam Kinamore. When he learned of the horrific details of Murray's slaying, about all the blood in her house, and then Pam's kidnapping from her suburban home, James recalled details of the scene at Randi's home. With a shock, his mind went back to Shorts's encounter with Derrick Todd Lee, and the other woman, Connie Warner, Derrick was suspected of killing, of the bloody cemetery attack.

*I know this guy Derrick is capable of it,* James thought. It was just a gut feeling.

But he tempered his thoughts, wondering if he was jumping to conclusions. He did not know about police work. He only knew what he saw on television shows like *CSI,* and what his son, Joel, occasionally discussed about his job. He did not want to presume he knew something that the police did not. He had passed along the tip about Derrick years earlier. The detectives already had the information; James did not see the need to give it to them again.

He remained curious, though. His mind wouldn't stop going over the details. He began discussing his suspicions with Joel, who quickly agreed that Derrick Todd Lee looked like a good suspect in the serial killings. For several weeks in the summer of 2002, nearly every night at dinner, and sometimes at lunch, the father and son rehashed what they knew about Derrick.

Joel had pulled Derrick's record. They saw his arrests as a Peeping Tom, his history of abusing his women, including the time he attacked Cat and nearly beat her to death outside a bar. They knew he had stalked a woman in Saint Francisville, barging into her apartment uninvited. Gradually, the Odoms became more and more convinced Derrick was not only responsible for Randi's murder, but he was quite possibly the man wanted as the Baton Rouge serial killer.

Their talk became so incessant, James's wife got tired of hearing it, declaring one day, "You're driving me up a wall! Either shut up or do something about it."

The two men were right on the verge of doing just that when they learned police in Baton Rouge announced they were looking for a white man.

The Odoms couldn't believe it. Derrick seemed so right as a suspect. They were so sure he was the killer, but the announcement shot that theory right out of the sky. James, however, never removed Derrick's mug shot from his desk, where it had sat since 1998. He was no longer convinced Derrick was the serial killer, but he still believed he was equally as capable of murder.

James also followed every minor turn in the unfolding serial killer investigation, clipping articles on each new murder. Dené Colomb. Mari Ann Fowler. Carrie Yoder. He watched the region sink into mass hysteria. He got to know the faces of the victims' families, particularly Lynne Marino. Every time he saw her on television, pleading with the public to be careful, to look around them, to report anyone they suspect could be involved, he agonized for her. He could see the pain in her face. He admired her strength and her determination to catch

Pam's killer. When she criticized the task force, questioning their investigative skills, he understood, because by the spring of 2003, even he began to wonder if the serial killer task force would ever solve the case.

Then, on March 21, the Baton Rouge police made the stunning announcement that they were not necessarily looking for a white man. New evidence indicated the killer was likely a light-skinned black man or Hispanic.

James was stunned, then angry. How could so many investigators have been so wrong? And then it hit him. This new piece of information was like the last piece of a puzzle he'd been working on for years. Derrick Todd Lee really *was* the perfect suspect in the serial killings. For the next several weeks, he went back and forth in his mind about reporting his suspicions to the task force. He wanted to tell them. He felt so confident Derrick Todd Lee was the killer, but then he would remind himself he was not a cop. He had already given his tip about Derrick to the police in 1998. That was surely on record. The task force must know about Leroy Shorts's night out with Derrick, he figured. Certainly, if Derrick was the killer, James figured he would not be the only one to suspect him. Who was he, after all? A retired grocer. He could already hear the detectives snicker at his theories or usher him out of their office with a dismissive, "Thanks, we'll get back to you."

Even as the days, then weeks passed with no word of a suspect or arrest, and his heart shouted, *Tell someone,* his head told him not to second-guess the investigators. From his son, he knew police often kept information about their investigations to themselves, that he must be unaware of key factors in the case, evidence perhaps that eliminated Derrick as a suspect.

The battle waging inside James came to end in late April when he saw Lynne Marino again on the news urging people to report anyone, anything suspicious, however vague it might be, to the police.

"If it wasn't for her, I don't think I ever would have said anything," James says now.

Still wary of task force ridicule, however, James wanted to speak directly to the detectives working Randi Mebruer's case. Since they would already be aware of Derrick Todd

Lee's background, James believed he would have an easier time sharing his suspicions.

He put his son, Joel, on the job of finding out who was leading Randi's investigation. Within a few days, Joel went to lunch at a Zachary pizzeria with a prosecutor, James Piker, from the Attorney General's Office. The two worked criminal cases together and spent most of the lunch discussing their strategies.

But midway through the meal, Joel changed the subject.

"Don't you have a woman missing from around here?" Joel said.

Joel knew the Randi Mebruer case was a sore subject for both the Zachary police and the Attorney General's Office because her murder was still unsolved after five years.

Piker knew the case was still open, but he wasn't aware of its status.

"My dad believes he knows who killed her," Joel said. "And he thinks the guy is the serial killer."

"Dannie Mixon's the guy to talk to," Piker told Joel. "It's his case."

Piker promised to call Mixon that afternoon and tell him to check in with Joel.


The next day, Mixon called Joel. He wanted to hear about what Joel knew. At first, Mixon thought Joel was talking about a friend of Mike Mebruer.

After four years of investigating, Mixon told Joel he was confident Mike Mebruer had plotted to kill his wife and that he was helped by his best friend.

Joel interrupted him. "No, this guy's name is Derrick, Derrick Lee," Joel said.

Derrick Todd Lee. Of course, Mixon knew the name well.

Joel recounted for Mixon the information Leroy provided years earlier.

Being an old cop, having investigated countless murders, followed hundreds of thousands of leads, some that looked rock solid but led him nowhere, and some that looked weak only to reveal a killer, Mixon knew not to dismiss anything too quickly or fall blindly for a good lead. But *this* was interesting.

What's more, he had never heard it before. Mixon says he had not seen a written report on James's tip, and no Zachary officer had ever told him about the information.

"When can I meet with your daddy?" Mixon asked Joel.

Mixon was out at James's farm a day or two later. He's a talker, and if he isn't stopped, he'll go on for hours. When he met James, Mixon wanted to make sure James knew that all the evidence in Randi's case, albeit circumstantial, pointed to Mike Mebruer as the best suspect.

"I want to tell you up front, Mike Mebruer killed this woman," Mixon told James. "I've been on this case for four years. Mike Mebruer hasn't farted without me knowing about it."

Mixon told James everything he knew about Mike: He was a womanizer who cheated on Randi, a mooch who left his first wife with three kids and no money. Randi left a $30,000 life insurance policy that still had his name on it. He failed a polygraph. And the FBI's profile of the murder suggests the killer was her husband. Mixon seemed to be trying to convince James that no one else could be a suspect.

"Look," James interrupted Mixon. "I don't see how this concerns me. You've obviously made up your mind and don't want to hear what I have to say, so I've got to go back to work."

James was about to get up, disgusted with the meeting.

"Wait. Wait. I do want to hear what you have to say," Mixon said. "Tell me . . ."

James settled back into his chair and began telling the story Shorts had relayed to him so many years earlier. He watched Mixon as he spoke. Slowly, as James described Derrick's panicked late-night drive to his home in Saint Francisville, Mixon's eyes lit up, his demeanor stiffened, his interest piqued. The aging detective began scribbling fast in his notebook. He was more curious than ever when James finished talking.

"Where can I find this Shorts?"

Joel drove to Leroy's house and asked him to come to the East Feliciana Parish Jail for an interview. He assured Leroy he was in no trouble, that they only needed his cooperation. Leroy trusted Joel, so he agreed.

The interview started out rough. Mixon prides himself on his abrasive style, especially with criminals. In an interrogation, he goes at the subject hard. He wants to test their version of reality. How strong is it? How confident are they in their story? Lies tend to crumble under pressure, and Mixon wanted to make sure he was getting the truth.

He was quick to throw Shorts off kilter by teasing him about his last name, dubbing him "Shorty." Then Mixon demanded to know how Shorts got his information. Why would Derrick trust him so much?

"Were you there when it happened?" Mixon asked bluntly.

This was not Shorts's first encounter with police. His arrest record is a long one, although his crimes are petty. He has a marijuana habit that gets him in trouble now and again. But he recognized a pit bull interrogator when he saw one, and he had heard many tales in jail about stubborn, vindictive cops who were good at frame jobs. He certainly wasn't going to get trapped into a murder.

"I didn't have anything to do with it," Shorts said. "And I don't know nothing about this. I don't have anything else to say."

He was shutting down, clamming up. He had agreed to talk, not to get harassed.

He got up to go. He was already out of the room by the time Joel caught up to him.

"Look, we're not trying to jam you up on this," Joel said. "We just want to know what this boy told you, word for word."

Joel promised to protect him, promised to make Mixon back off. Reluctantly, Shorts sat back down and completed the interview, telling Mixon everything he wanted to know.

Mixon says he had already entertained renewed suspicions about Derrick when he learned the task force was looking for a black man, but hearing Shorts's story put the fire under his ass.

"That's what made me go after Derrick immediately," Mixon said. "This was the crowning blow."

He turned 180 degrees around and again focused on Derrick Todd Lee, not only for Randi's murder, but for the serial killings in Baton Rouge and Lafayette.

Mixon reexamined Derrick's file. He had Derrick's conviction record from years earlier, but now Mixon took a closer look at when Derrick was behind bars. And more importantly, when he was out on the street.

There it was in front of him, in black and white. On the date of each of the killings, Derrick was free. He was out cruising the streets.

All Mixon needed now was one solid piece of evidence to test his theory.

He needed Derrick's DNA.

# CHAPTER 37

# The Subpoena

Mixon called Kurt Wagner, who left the Attorney General's Office in 2002, to return to help with the renewed investigation of Derrick Todd Lee. Mixon wanted to put together solid, irrefutable probable cause to collect Derrick's DNA. But it would be tricky since no DNA profiles had ever been developed from evidence in Randi Mebruer's case.

The investigators focused on what they did have: One, Derrick's own admission that he was in the vicinity of Randi's house in Zachary at the time she disappeared. Two, his record as a Peeping Tom and burglar in Zachary. And three, the simple fact that he was not behind bars at the times of the Zachary murders of Randi Mebruer, Connie Warner, and the serial killings in Baton Rouge and Lafayette.

The strongest, newest evidence—at least for Mixon—was Shorty's story about Derrick's late-night visit on the day after Randi disappeared. Shorty's allegation that Derrick was talking about a missing woman before Randi's story hit the news was enough, Mixon believed, to warrant probable cause.

On May 5, Mixon and his assistant investigators Todd Morris, Chris Ribera, and Zachary Detective Ray Day drove to Clinton, Louisiana, and presented their request to Eighteenth Judicial District Judge George "Hal" Ware in Clinton, which is the parish seat of East Feliciana Parish and the location of its courthouse.

The meeting quickly turned sour for the investigators. Judge Ware would not sign the order. Ware agreed investigators had probable cause, but he rejected their request because he thought Mixon was seeking the wrong type of legal authority to obtain the DNA.

Mixon was asking for a subpoena, not a warrant. Legally, Ware believed the subpoena request ought to proceed through a hearing, allowing both sides—the cops and Derrick—to present their arguments. Otherwise, the subpoena could be challenged later in court, and any evidence collected with it could be thrown out as illegally obtained.

Ware had had legal problems in the past when he issued a subpoena for an inmate's blood sample, and the sample was found inadmissible in court.

Ware suspected Mixon's subpoena might be too weak and easily challenged, allowing Derrick to fight the order in court. A warrant, however, was more powerful than a subpoena and would require Derrick to submit on the spot.

Ware suggested the investigators check with their lawyers before proceeding.

Mixon was pissed. He stormed out of the judge's office, cursing as he left the building. He had worked hard putting together the seven-page motion requesting Derrick's DNA.

Mixon disagreed with the judge. His motion for a subpoena had received the OK from lawyers in the attorney general's criminal department. And he certainly did not want a hearing. If Derrick learned they were trying to obtain his DNA, he could take off, disappear.

Mixon and Morris and Day drove back to the East Feliciana Parish Sheriff's Office, where they had met Joel earlier that morning. They again gathered in Joel's office. Morris called the attorney general's legal department and told the lawyers of Ware's objections. They were so close to possibly, finally obtaining the one piece of evidence they needed to put Randi Mebruer's killer behind bars. No one wanted to let him slip away again on a legal technicality.

The attorney general's lawyer, Julie Cullen, once again said the subpoena was sound. She argued the judge should have no qualms about issuing the order without a hearing. No one, she said, should be worried about the decision being overturned.

For the second visit to the judge's chambers, Joel agreed to go. He had a good working relationship with Ware, and the detectives thought he might help sway Ware's opinion to their side. When they arrived, the investigators explained to Ware that their lawyers said they were on safe legal grounds. They were confident they wanted a subpoena.

"You want me to sign it or not?" Ware asked.

"Yes," Mixon said. "We're sure."

"OK, I'll sign it."

By midday, Mixon had his court order to collect Derrick's DNA, and a small army from the Attorney General's Office, Zachary police, and East Feliciana Parish Sheriff's Office to go get it. Their first stop, the closest stop from the courthouse, was Consandra's apartment. No one was home.

One of Mixon's assistants, Todd Morris, called Zachary Detective David McDavid and asked him to drive by Derrick's house on Highway 61. A few minutes later, McDavid spotted Derrick's red Ford Explorer in his driveway.

The investigators sped toward Saint Francisville, but before they arrived, McDavid called to say Derrick left the house with his children and was driving to the Chevron gas station a quarter mile south. McDavid tried to follow Derrick from the station, but Derrick's speedy driving eluded the officer in Saint Francisville.

The investigators, driving six separate cars, split up, each going in a different direction to stake out Derrick's known haunts: Consandra's apartment, his mother's house on Blackmore, and his house on Highway 61.

Less than ten minutes later, Mixon and Ribera saw Derrick

speeding south on Highway 61 in Saint Francisville. They followed him to his house.

They pulled into the driveway behind Derrick's Explorer. As he and his kids piled out of the truck, Ribera and Mixon got out and identified themselves as attorney general's investigators.

"We need to get your DNA," Mixon told him. "We've got a court order."

"Let me see it," Derrick said.

Morris was carrying the subpoena, and he was still on the road from Jackson.

"One of our men has it, and he's on his way," Mixon said. As they stood outside, Derrick's son and daughter played in the yard. Mixon spoke with Derrick about them, asking their names and ages, keeping Derrick calm.

A few minutes later, Day pulled into the driveway.

"This is Detective Day from the Zachary police," Mixon said. "He'll be the one swabbing you."

Derrick seized up.

"No way," he said. "I don't want nothing to do with the Zachary Police Department. You ain't gonna pin that murder on me."

"Fine," Mixon said. "Ray, step back to your car. I'll do it . . ."

Morris arrived moments later with the subpoena. When he handed it over, Derrick appeared to read it.

"Is this it?" he asked. "Where's the order?"

The order had been filed under seal at the courthouse, Morris told Derrick, to protect his privacy, so no one would know he was being swabbed.

"You can get it later," Morris said.

Derrick did not protest.

"Would you mind stepping inside your residence so we can obtain the DNA swab?" Morris asked him.

"Let's do it right here," Derrick said.

They were standing in his driveway on a busy highway in front of his children.

"Derrick, let's do it in private," Mixon said. "Put your kids in the truck. They don't need to see this."

Derrick agreed, told his children to stay in the Explorer for a few minutes, and led Mixon, Morris, and Ribera inside. He sat down on the sofa, while Mixon snapped on latex gloves, and then Derrick politely opened his mouth to allow Mixon to swab inside both his cheeks.

When they were done, the investigators thanked Derrick and cleared out. The task was strangely anticlimactic. They regrouped at the truck stop just down the road, where Mixon asked the local officers to keep an eye on Derrick until the DNA results came back.

The next day, Day submitted Derrick's DNA to the crime lab. On the intake sheet he filed it under the Randi Mebruer case, but when he signed the form, he told the evidence officer at the crime lab to let analysts know they could compare it to the serial killer's DNA.

Then the waiting began. The crime lab was swamped with DNA samples to test in the serial killer investigation, and task force submittals took priority, so Derrick's swab was placed on the shelf to wait its turn.


Derrick, however, was not going to waste any time. When Jackie arrived home from her job at the U.S. Post Office on May 5, Derrick told her the police had been to the house that afternoon.

"They took my DNA," he said.

"What for?"

Derrick said he could not find the paperwork investigators gave him, but he said it was about the missing woman in Zachary. Police were still trying to pin it on him, he complained.

"I'm not going to spend the rest of my life behind bars," Derrick said, telling his wife they needed to leave the state.

Jackie called her aunt in Detroit. Joann Chandler could hear worry in her niece's voice.

Something big is about to blow up down here, and the media is going to be a madhouse about it, Jackie told her. "I want to get Derrick Jr. and Doris out of here."

When Chandler asked for details, Jackie said she would explain later.

"Do you have a place we can come?" Jackie asked. "Until I can get up on my feet?"

Jackie was pacing through the house on the cordless phone.

Derrick Jr. was trying to listen in on the conversation. He had been uneasy since the troop of police showed up at the house that day. He didn't know what was happening, but he could tell by his mother's anxiety that it was serious.

A little later, Derrick called the family into their living room. He sat down with Derrick Jr. and Doris and explained they were moving. He was pulling the children out of school, and they were leaving the state.

Derrick Jr. remembered the conversation vividly: "There's too much stuff going on around Baton Rouge," Derrick told his children. "People being killed, the truck stop being robbed, and drugs."

Derrick was going to Chicago to find a job and save money to buy a house and new furnishings, while they stayed with Jackie's relatives in Detroit. The two cities are close, Derrick told them, so he would visit them soon.

Derrick Jr. watched as his father packed his luggage the next day. He stuffed four pairs of shoes into one of Doris's old book bags and neatly folded a blanket, zebra tie, black leather coat, a white dress shirt, several pairs of pants, boxers, and socks into a large black leather bag. He also packed a toothbrush and toothpaste, several pieces of jewelry, a watch, and a pair of leather work gloves.

While he sifted through his closet, Derrick gave Derrick Jr. two of his high school jackets, including his old West Feliciana band jacket.

When Derrick was finished packing and zipped up his bags, he told his children, "It's time to go . . . I'll miss you . . . Take care of yourselves."

The family piled into Jackie's Hyundai—the Red Ford Explorer had been repossessed that same day—and drove to Derrick's mother's home on Blackmore to drop off the kids. Derrick Jr. and Doris got out, and Derrick hugged them goodbye. Then Jackie drove Derrick to the Greyhound bus station in Baton Rouge.

Nobody had much time to miss him. Two days later, the family reunited at the same Greyhound bus station. Derrick returned carrying the same luggage, and he did not mention finding a job in Chicago.

They drove to the house on Highway 61 that afternoon and began cleaning out their belongings. With the help of Florence and Coleman Barrow and other relatives, the family loaded their furniture, clothes, and other possessions into Coleman's truck and Derrick's utility trailer.

Instead of renting a storage unit, though, the Lees dispersed it among Derrick's sister, nieces, and mother for the time being. Four televisions, including a large screen TV, were taken to Derrick's sister Tharshia Fontenot's trailer home down the street from the Barrows. Kitchen items, a few chairs, and lamps were delivered to Derrick's niece's trailer, which is next door to Tharshia's home.

The three family beds, along with bedspreads and sheets, plus a bedroom dresser, a refrigerator, an outdoor table, and several garbage bags of clothes were taken to the Barrows' house. Derrick's tool box and four pairs of leather work gloves were placed in a storage shed on the Barrow property.

Their sofa was thrown in a Dumpster at the Chevron station on Highway 61 below the Lees' house. Leftover old clothes were dropped off at the Salvation Army.

That night, on May 8, Derrick Jr. and Doris spent the night at Tharshia's while Derrick and Jackie spent the night elsewhere. The next morning, the children walked over to the Barrows' house, where Derrick was saying his good-byes again.

He was off to Chicago again.

Florence hugged her son tightly.

"I love you," she said. "Don't get yourself into anything up there."

Just before he walked out the door, Derrick pulled his son aside.

"You need to be the man now," Derrick told the thirteen-year-old. "Take care of your momma and sister . . . Be good and don't get into any trouble . . ."

Then he left with Jackie, who drove him to the bus station in her Hyundai, which was still stuffed with garbage bags of the family's clothes.

* * *

When she returned to the Barrow house, the children helped her unload the car, packed the clothing into suitcases, and placed the luggage into the Barrows' van. The family slept at Tharshia's home that night, and the next morning Coleman drove them to the Greyhound station, where they boarded a bus for Detroit.

In Detroit, Jackie explained to Joann that police investigating a missing woman had taken Derrick's DNA. She did not elaborate, saying only that Derrick had nothing to do with it.

Joann was not so sure. She never liked Derrick. She had met him only a few times at family gatherings in Arkansas and on an early visit in Detroit. She quickly assessed that Derrick was a womanizer. She did not think he was good for Jackie. He was too good at "running a game on her," she said. He showed his wife no respect, giving his home number out to other women. The calls became so frequent, Jackie had to put a privacy block on the line. Joann believed Derrick was too good at lying and particularly talented at spending Jackie's inheritance. In less than five years, Derrick had burned through the $250,000 settlement Jackie received after her father's accidental death.

Although she and her husband were suspicious about Jackie's sudden appearance on their doorstep, Joann did not push her for details. Jackie said Derrick would be visiting in a few days—on Memorial Day—and Joann hoped to get more of the story then.


Back in Louisiana, investigators were still waiting for the results of Derrick's DNA analysis. Since the swabs were submitted, a week went by, then two.

Joel Odom was getting antsy. As Mixon requested, he was regularly driving by Derrick's house, and he did not like what he saw on May 8.

He called Day. "Derrick's packing up his home," Odom said. "He's moving."

West Feliciana Parish Sheriff Ivy Cutrer, likewise, informed the Attorney General's Office that Derrick was moving his possessions out of the house and looked like he was planning to leave.

Day told Odom he'd call the crime lab and ask that the swab get some priority. But the days continued to pass with no news from the DNA analysts.

# CHAPTER 38

# The Final Link

When the news broke that the serial killer was likely a black man, Saint Martin Parish Sheriff's Detective Arthur Boyd could not quiet his gut feeling about the brutal attempted rape and murder case he was working in Breaux Bridge.

Diane Alexander had been attacked in her home July 9, 2002, the same day authorities in Baton Rouge announced the first DNA link between the murders of Gina Green and Murray Pace. Saint Martin Parish police reported the case and its similarities to task force investigators in late July or early August of that year, but at the time, detectives believed the serial killer was a white man, so they took no further interest in Diane's case.

Now everything had changed. From the beginning, Boyd suspected Diane's case was linked to the Baton Rouge killings. When Dené's murder in Grand Coteau was linked to the serial killer in late December 2002, Boyd became even more convinced.

He and Lafayette Detective Sonny Stutes, who was on the task force, stayed in touch over the next several weeks about Diane's case and its similarities to the Baton Rouge murders. Without DNA, however, the task force could not officially link Diane's attack to the killings. And that meant Diane's witness account, her sketch of the assailant, and the description of his car would not be used to assist in catching the serial killer.

Boyd needed evidence. In late January, Booker at the Acadiana crime lab began reexamining several pieces of evidence submitted for Diane's case, including the dress and swabs from light switches, the back door lock, the phone book he touched, the phone cord, and a rape kit. But the only solid DNA profiles Booker could find belonged to Diane and her family. Once again, the attacker was like a ghost. Despite the brutal physical nature of the attack, he seemed to have left not a shred of his DNA.

Four days after the task force announced the serial killer's DNA revealed his race, however, Boyd got a call from Stutes. The information Stutes offered was to be kept in close confidence because the results were preliminary.

Booker had located some suspect DNA on Diane's dress, a deteriorated and faint strand that revealed only a few loci, nothing close to the thirteen needed to make a complete profile. But the DNA marker at one of the loci was remarkable.

"What caught my attention was the twenty-two," Booker said later.

The "twenty-two" was the rare genetic marker at the VWA loci. The same rare genetic marker found in the serial killer's DNA.

No DNA analyst worth a dime, however, would claim a match based on such a weak and small number of similarities. The evidence was no good for a court of law, no good even for an arrest. The possibility that the DNA belonged to another person was too high.

So when Booker spoke with Boyd about it, she told him she could not make a link between Diane's case and the serial killings.

Boyd was not willing to accept the killer did not leave more of himself behind. Evidence of his existance *had* to be there, somewhere. He suggested Booker go back to the dress again and try swabbing around the neckline, where he knew the attacker's hands were struggling to wrap a phone cord around Diane's neck. Boyd figured if the attacker had sloughed off any skin cells, the most likely place they would fall was around the collar of the dress.

The task was difficult. Diane was beaten so badly around the face and head, her blood drenched the front and top of the dress. When Booker tested the swabs she collected off the denim, most of the DNA belonged to Diane. Her blood cells on the dress outnumbered any of the attacker's skin cells by huge proportions.

For weeks, Booker continued to swab the dress in a determined hunt for a microscopic hint of DNA. Then on May 14, she struck gold. She found suspect DNA on the dress that revealed five markers matching the serial killer's DNA.

The sample still did not have the complete strand of thirteen loci, which is required for a match, but it had enough to create a high probability that the DNA belonged to the serial killer. And it certainly meant that Boyd could not eliminate the serial killer as a suspect in Diane's case.

That same day, Boyd met with Stutes to compare details between Diane and Dené's cases. By 4:30 that afternoon, Boyd was taking a call from Baton Rouge Police Sergeant Ike Vavasseur with the task force who wanted to know more about Diane's case. Vavasseur also told Boyd that the FBI profiler Mary Ellen O'Toole was on her way to the area to discuss Diane's attack.

Three days later, Boyd took Vavasseur and O'Toole to the mobile home where Diane was attacked. He provided Diane's account of what happened and her description of the attacker. Boyd then shared the complaints of two local women: one who was frightened by a black man who walked into her home in June 2002, and another who said a black male exposed himself to her at a Beaux Bridge Taco Bell around the same time period.

On May 18, Vavasseur asked Boyd to set up a meeting between the top brass at Saint Martin Parish Sheriff's Office and the task force investigators. The next day, Boyd, Saint Martin Sheriff Michael Patin, Major Butch Dupuis, and Lieutenant Guidry drove to Baton Rouge to discuss whether Diane's case should be included in the task force investigation.

At the time, O'Toole expressed an interest in interviewing Diane and the other two suspected victims. O'Toole spoke with the two local women on May 19 and agreed their cases seemed to be linked to the serial killer, but she needed to hear more from Diane.

On May 22, at a Holiday Inn Express in Henderson, Louisiana, O'Toole interviewed Diane for four and a half hours. When O'Toole emerged from the meeting, she met with task force investigators, and a decision was made to release information to the media about Diane's case and its possible link to the serial killer.

The following afternoon, Friday, May 23, the task force called a press conference at the Lafayette Parish Sheriff's Office.

"We think this is a significant development in this case," Lafayette Parish Sheriff Mike Neustrom told the crowded room of reporters. "It's another piece to the puzzle."

It was a huge piece to the puzzle—the biggest break so far in the investigation. Finally, after a year of hunting a faceless killer, the task force had a sketch of the man they believed was responsible.

The suspect's face and the description of his gold Mitsubishi Mirage played prominently at the press conference, but his behavior got the most talk time.

Investigators called him "disarmingly charming." Someone who did not appear threatening to the women who opened their doors to him. He was clean-cut, nice-looking, and friendly. The ruse he used to get inside Diane's home began like a typical encounter that happens hundreds of times a day all across Louisiana.

The image of the killer, which was once nebulous and exaggerated by terrified imagination, was suddenly solid, and the reality was just as frightening. From Diane's description, he turned instantly from a pleasant stranger into a hurricane of violence—no provocation, no warning signs, just a sudden and stunning bolt of monstrosity.

Most people assume cold-blooded killers look dangerous, that we can spot them a mile away. Some killers do make the

hair on the back of our necks rise. Some reek of violence as
they walk by. It's easy to see they are on edge. The look in
their eyes is wildfire, a challenging call to *Just try it*.

But serial killers often blend right in. That's their camou-
flage. The only way to become a serial killer is to avoid getting caught at least for the first few times. Like a leopard uses
its spots to hide in the bush, a serial killer must shield his
true intentions from his prey. He must ensure his victims
don't suspect an attack is moments away. Perfecting their
hunt, serial killers get good at slipping past their victims' de-
fenses. By the time the women realize they are in danger, it's
too late.


With the release of the sketch, all of southern Louisiana was
on the lookout for the man in the gold Mitsubishi.

In Baton Rouge, the image of the suspect looked dis-
turbingly familiar to Murray's neighbors who saw a suspicious brown-skinned man staring at her town house the day
before and morning of her murder.

In Saint Francisville, when Collette saw the image, she
burst into tears. She knew Derrick Todd Lee's wife drove a
gold Hyundai that looked just like a Mitsubishi Mirage.

"It's him," Collette told her new husband.

Her previous tips to the police about Derrick were dismissed. Now she would not give up.

She immediately called her brother, who knew how to get
in touch with an investigator on the task force. Collette did not
want to go through the task force tip line again.

Her brother told her the investigator would call her back
the next morning. She did not want to wait.

That night, she called 911 and asked to be connected with
police in Breaux Bridge. She was patched through to the Saint
Martin Parish Sheriff's Office. She left a message.

Ten minutes later, her phone rang. Saint Martin Parish
Sheriff Major Butch Dupuis was on the line. He wanted to
hear everything she had to say.

"I told him, just check out Derrick Lee, and you're going to
have your man," she said.

After hearing her story with Derrick, his description, his

criminal background, the car his wife drove, Dupuis was quick to recognize the lead and thanked her.

The next morning, early, Lieutenant Tommy Rice with the task force called Collette's brother, Terry, with a warning to pass on to Collette.

"Tell her to be careful," he said.


Collette was not the only person calling the police about Derrick Todd Lee. The press conference in Lafayette ended about one p.m. By two twenty-four p.m., the tip line was already taking its first tip about Derrick Todd Lee.

The tip sheet e-mailed to the task force read:

Thinks she knows the person because of a description of the car, a gold Mirage. He was Peeping Tom before. She thinks his name is Todd Lee. He is from Saint Francisville. He is always in and out of jail. His wife had the type of car they are describing. Not long ago, he was charged with a crime similar to breaking in. Call her if you need more information.

The next tip came in at 6:16 p.m.:

The caller works for a local sheriff's office. He knows someone that has a past criminal history for stalking women from the Saint Francisville area. His name is Derrick Lee, about 5'10". The suspect made the comment that he had killed a woman he was dating before. The suspect fits the sketch. He's a light-complected, black male. He had a small gold car at one time. He keeps himself really clean, keeps his hair short, thin mustache, and he has a muscular build.

The next came in the following day at 5:41 p.m.:

He was looking at the picture of the man on the front page of the *Advocate*. His name is Derrick Todd Lee, and he lives in Saint Francisville. He has a history of being a Peeping Tom and as the prime suspect in a double homicide in Zachary. Randy Metz with the West Feliciana Sheriff's Department can tell you more about this case.

Another tip came in a few hours later at 10:22 p.m.:

He is calling to report a man that fits the description of serial killer. This man has a gold Mirage that is wrecked in the front, and the man that tried to rape a woman in Breaux Bridge had a gold Mirage that was wrecked in the front, too. He is the exact same man in today's paper except that his lips need to be a little bit bigger. His name is Derrick Todd Lee, and he used to live on Highway 61 right after you pass the truck stop called Southern Belle. The car is parked in front of his mother's house in Saint Francisville on Blackmore Road. His whole family lives in that area, and he never moved out of the house but just disappeared with his wife and kids.

The tips entered the conveyor belt of investigative data. Soon they would be assigned detectives for follow-up, but Derrick's DNA was already at the crime lab. His cotton swabs had been waiting in line with hundreds of other suspects' swabs to be analyzed. In fact, on May 23, DNA analyst Natasha Poe had already begun testing Derrick's genetic code.

DNA tests can be done in less than six hours if rushed, but the crime lab did not have Derrick's test on high priority, so his was in a system that would take a few days for each step of the process.

Poe planned to let Derrick's and several other samples run through the DNA analysis machines over the weekend. On Sunday, May 25, Poe, who was going off duty, stopped by the lab to hand off a pager to another lab analyst who was coming on duty. Usually the lab staff handed over the pagers on Monday mornings, but since that Monday, May 26, was the Memorial Day holiday, she and the other analyst agreed to meet Sunday afternoon.

Poe had been running errands all day with her one-year-old daughter, who she had in tow at the lab. When she arrived, the other analyst was not yet there. While she waited, Poe decided to go check on the DNA samples she had already begun running.

During the previous several months, she had examined hundreds of DNA profiles submitted in the serial killer case.

She almost had the serial killer's DNA profile memorized from comparing it to others so often. Usually, she needed only to look at one or two markers before finding a mismatch and ruling out the suspect.

On that afternoon, however, when she glanced at the DNA profiles she was running, she noticed that rare marker twenty-two at the VWA loci. She had never seen it in any profile *ever* besides the serial killer's DNA. But now she was looking at a suspect's DNA—a real person's DNA, someone with a name and a face and a known location, someone who the police had tracked down and swabbed.

She sat down to take a closer look, to make a full comparison between the suspect's DNA and the serial killer's DNA. She went down the thirteen loci. Each one matched. She took a deep breath. She went down the list again. Her heart was racing.

By now her coworker had arrived, and she asked him to take a look. He, too, confirmed a match.

Then she called her boss.

"I got a match," she said.

# CHAPTER 39

# Hunting the Hunter

On Sunday, May 25, Joel Odom was in a deep sleep when the phone rang about eleven thirty p.m.

"What are you doing?" Zachary Detective David Mc-David's voice was bubbling with big news.

"I'm sleeping. What's going on?" Joel was groggy, just coming to.

"You need to get up and get dressed and get down to the OEP building right now," McDavid told him.

*OEP building?* Joel thought. Then it hit him. *The Office of Emergency Preparedness building—the serial killer task force headquarters!*

"What's going on?" Joel asked again.

"I can't get into it over the phone . . ." McDavid said.

"Is this about what we did three weeks ago?"

"Yep."

"Did it match all five victims?"

"Just get your butt down to OEP."

Joel had suspected this would happen, but he was not 100 percent sure. As a detective, he had learned not to assume anything without proof. Now it was sinking in like a brick. He felt almost sick, slightly nauseated. He wondered if he was about to vomit or start crying.

He woke up his fiancée and handed her a pistol.

"Here, keep this close and lock the doors," he told her before rushing out to his truck.

On the way down to Baton Rouge, he called his father.


James Odom had been getting impatient. He knew investigators swabbed Derrick on May 5, and he could not understand why the results were not back yet.

"You heard anything about the swab?" James would ask Joel every evening.

"Nope . . ."

The two men again were talking about it over dinner almost every night.

"This guy's going to kill someone else, and they're letting that swab sit on the shelf down at the state police lab . . ." James groused.

When the task force released the sketch of Diane Alexander's attacker on May 23, James nearly lost it. "That's him!" He shouted at the television.

He was sure Derrick was the serial killer. His fuse was burning down. He paced around the house. His gut twisted into knots.

On Saturday, May 24, his wife was fed up with his nerves.

"We're going to the camp," she ordered. The camp is a fishing cabin in Grande Isle, Louisiana, about two hundred miles south, at the isolated swampy end of Louisiana that floats at the edge of the Gulf of Mexico.

James and his wife left Jackson the next day, drove all day, and arrived at the camp by midafternoon. James tried to relax. He was just about to attempt a night's sleep when the phone rang a little before midnight.

He didn't have to answer to know who was calling.

"You don't have to tell me," James said when he picked up the phone. "I know."

"Dad, it matched all five," Joel said. "He killed them all."

James hung up the phone. His wife could tell by the look on his face what had been said. He took one look at her and broke down, sobbing.

All along, the serial killer was Derrick Todd Lee, the man James reported to police as a suspect in Randi Mebruer's case five years earlier. *He should have been stopped then*, James thought. *So many lives could have been saved . . .*

Similar calls were awaking and notifying law enforcement types all over southern Louisiana that night. By midnight, more than one hundred people were crowded into the OEP building, including Baton Rouge Police Chief Pat Englade and Attorney General Richard Ieyoub.

When Joel arrived, investigators wanted to pick his brain about Derrick's whereabouts. The only address task force investigators had at that point for Derrick was his home on Highway 61 in Saint Francisville.

"He's packed up and left," Joel told them. "His house is nothing but an empty shell now."

No one knew where Derrick might be. Joel provided investigators with the addresses of Consandra Green's apartment in Jackson and Florence Barrow's home in Saint Francisville.

Meanwhile, other investigators were at work on writing up warrants for Derrick's arrest and searches of the homes he frequented. At about four a.m., at the request of the task force, Joel called Judge Carmichael, who is a judge in West and East Feliciana Parishes. Investigators needed the judge's signature on the warrants to serve them on Derrick in that judicial district.

"We've identified the serial killer," Joel told him. "We need you to sign some warrants."

"Bring it on up," Carmichael said. "I'll be waiting in my office."

Joel and a state police officer drove forty miles to Clinton, got the warrants, and headed to Saint Francisville, where SWAT teams from several area law enforcement agencies were gearing up behind the River Bend nuclear plant about two miles from Derrick's home.

When Joel pulled into the parking lot between five and six that morning, more than forty cars and trucks were already there. SWAT officers in full olive green uniforms—helmets, AR-15 assault rifles, knee pads, and military style boots— milled around waiting for orders.

The task force also tapped the local West Feliciana Parish police officers to help early that Memorial Day morning.

West Feliciana Parish Sheriff's Lieutenant Archer Lee was called for his advice about how to handle the search warrants, particularly for Derrick's mother's home on Blackmore Road. When officers drove by, they saw Jackie Lee's gold Hyundai with the smashed hood was parked in its front driveway.

Archer Lee is not related to Derrick's family, but he knew them from past experiences with Derrick. Instead of busting through the doors, Archer suggested the task force just watch the house until daylight so he could try to speak with Derrick's stepfather, Coleman, before the police busted inside.

"I know him well enough that he'll tell me if Derrick is there," Lee told task force investigators.

Just before the sun came up, at about seven a.m., Lee called Coleman at the house on Blackmore Road. The SWAT teams had already gone into Derrick's house on Highway 61 and confirmed it was empty. Now they needed to search Derrick's mother's home.

"You need to come outside and talk to us," Lee told Coleman when he answered the phone.

Coleman walked out into the front yard to see an army of police. There were so many police cars parked outside, they stretched almost a block down the street.

Lee explained the house was already surrounded.

"We need to know if Derrick's inside," Lee said.

"Why?"

"He's wanted for the serial killings."

"Really?" Coleman was shocked.

"Who's in the house?"

"My wife, my mother-in-law, two grandkids, and a nephew . . ."

"You need to go in there and get everybody out."

Coleman did as he was told, and the police moved inside to search the house, but they found no sign of Derrick.

* * *

The next stop was Consandra Green's apartment in Jackson. About nine a.m., the SWAT team surrounded the building, positioning men at every window, before storming inside.

While police searched the apartment, Consandra was held in the backseat of a police car in the parking lot. About ten a.m., her cell phone rang. The caller ID showed an Atlanta, Georgia, number. It was Derrick.

"The police are here," Consandra told him. "They think you're the serial killer!"

Derrick immediately hung up, but the caller ID gave police an idea where he was. Within the hour, several investigators were on their way to Atlanta.


Late that morning, the task force called a press conference to release the name and several photographs of Derrick Todd Lee. The news interrupted normal television programming throughout southern Louisiana.

Meanwhile, in Detroit, Jackie was on her way to her uncle Jerome Chandler's home for a family gathering when Jerome received a phone call from a relative in New Orleans.

"The news is saying Derrick Todd Lee is wanted as the Louisiana serial killer," Jerome's relative told him. "Listen . . ."

Jerome listened to the New Orleans television broadcast through the phone. When Jackie arrived at his house a few minutes later, he sent the children out of the room and asked her about what she knew.

"I don't know anything about it," Jackie told him. But she acknowledged that police had taken Derrick's DNA swab earlier that month.

Then Jerome told Jackie what he had learned from his relative in New Orleans and what he heard on the news. Jackie began to cry. She did not want to believe it. She insisted Derrick was not guilty. She told her uncle he was being set up as a fall guy for the murders.

A few hours later, while the family ate dinner in front of the television, the 5 p.m. news broadcast flashed a picture of

Derrick Todd Lee on the screen. The reporter said he was wanted by Louisiana authorities for five murders.

"We've got to do something," Jerome told Jackie.

Jerome took Jackie to the FBI building in Detroit that evening. They spoke to a security guard who said the office was closed. They made plans to come back the next day.

The next morning, at about ten thirty, Jackie got a call from Derrick.

"Have you seen the news?" he said. "Do you know what's going on?"

"Yes, I've seen it," she said. "They say you killed five women."

"I didn't do it . . ."

Then he told her he would not be able to call anymore because the phones were tapped.

"Take care of the children," he said. "I love you all."

Then he hung up.

Later that day, the Chandlers took Jackie to the Patrick V. Mc-Namara Federal Building in Detroit for an interview with FBI agents.

Initially, Jackie said she and the children left Saint Francisville because the bank was foreclosing on their house, but when pressed she conceded they fled after Derrick was swabbed because he told her "something big was going to blow up" on them and that police were going to try to pin a murder on him.

She denied knowing anything about the murders and claimed Derrick was not a physically violent person, although he was verbally threatening, often cursing at her, calling her a "fat, ugly bitch" and telling her no one else would want her. She said he did not beat her, but when pressed she admitted he slapped her a few times.

That afternoon, Jackie and Jerome sat Derrick Jr. down and told him his father was in trouble with the law.

"Pray for him," they told the boy. "And everything will be all right."

Later that night, they turned on the TV and saw a news report that Derrick Todd Lee, the Louisiana serial killer, had been captured.

*Man, they're spreading my name all over the news,* Derrick Jr. thought.

Then he saw a news clip of his father in handcuffs. Derrick Jr. called his mother into the room to see it.

"People think your dad is the serial killer," she explained. "But don't worry about it."

Derrick Jr. was worried. He sat at the Chandlers' computer and searched for more information about the story, but after reading about the murders, he could never believe his father was responsible.

"He's a nice man," the boy told FBI agents. "He always tells the truth about everything. If he had done something wrong, he would say that he did it . . . The truth will be revealed."

Earlier that day, in Atlanta, the city police, the U.S. Marshals Service, the FBI, and a number of Louisiana officers were hot on Derrick's trail. A phone trace narrowed the police search to a gritty, drug-infested area of the city.

Lee's last call to Consandra came from the manager's office at the Lakewood Motor Lodge on Reynolds Drive. But as soon as he hung up, he left the motel and did not return.

By the time investigators arrived at Lakewood, all they got were stories about Derrick.

He had made a vivid impression on the down-and-out residents of the motel. While renting a room with a kitchenette for $135 a week, he was anything but inconspicuous. He did not appear to be hiding from anyone. He was friendly, social and, of course, flirtatious.

Within a few days, he cooked a birthday dinner for the manager, hosted a Bible study prayer session, and bedded more than one woman in his room.

When an Atlanta police officer responded to a complaint at the hotel about a dead, smelly dog rotting nearby, Derrick walked outside to talk with him.

Not all the residents trusted Derrick. More than one woman didn't like the way he tried to give her beer as entice-

ment to visit his room. One female resident caught him staring at her from his room with his door open. He was naked.

On Monday afternoon, worried that he might kill again in
Georgia, authorities released Derrick's picture and last known
location to the local Atlanta media. The news bulletin flashed
across the city's television sets.

A tip came in a little after seven that night. The Atlanta police rushed to where the caller insisted he saw Derrick.

The police pulled up alongside Derrick. He looked just like
the man in the pictures they had in the patrol cars.

They asked for identification. Derrick handed over his license. He did not try to run. He did not lie about his name, and
he allowed officers to cuff him with little fanfare.

Derrick was driven to an Atlanta police station, where several investigators began questioning him about the serial
killings. Derrick did not deny or confirm his involvement, but
he seemed ready to give up the game.

"Ya might as well go ahead and give me the needle," he
said several times. "I spoke to God, and I'm closing the
book."

With the serial killer behind bars, the task force was ready to
celebrate, regardless of their role in Derrick's arrest.

On Wednesday morning, before a wide pool of local and
national news cameras and a crowded room of reporters,
dozens of task force investigators and top city leaders gathered on a stage at the State Police Headquarters in Baton
Rouge to congratulate themselves and praise the "cutting
edge" work of the task force investigation.

Chief Pat Englade barely held back his tears when he
spoke of his pride in the investigation, saying he would want
the same team on the case if his family had been involved. Baton Rouge Mayor Bobby Simpson, arguing that criticism of
the task force had been undeserved, said it was "one of the
most competant task forces" ever put together.

Likewise, Governor Mike Foster, U.S. Attorney David
Dugas, and FBI Special Agent Charles Cunningham all spoke

admiringly of the task force, of the investigators' hard work and the team's smart use of the latest in computer technology.

No mention, however, was made of the attorney general's investigators or the Zachary Police Department. They were not thanked, nor was their role in identifying Derrick acknowledged.

The investigators—Dannie Mixon, Ray Day, David McDavid, Joel Odom, and others who obtained Derrick's DNA—were not even invited to attended.

By Wednesday afternoon, a crush of media and curious spectators gathered near a chain-link fence at the Baton Rouge Metropolitan Airport in view of the runways. They were waiting for an FBI plane to land and the serial killer to make his return to the city. The small plane came in just after one p.m. and taxied toward the airport, stopping directly in front of the cameras. The plane's door opened, and several FBI and law enforcement officers disembarked before Derrick was escorted down the stairs wearing cuffs and ankle shackles. He was also wearing a bulletproof vest.

Driving unmarked police vehicles, detectives slipped past a gaggle of news satellite vans and took Derrick to the State Police Headquarters for questioning. Baton Rouge Detective Chris Johnson, a black man, was given the job of interrogating the most hated man in Louisiana.

Johnson began by reading Derrick his rights: his right to remain silent, his right to have an attorney present, etc.

"Do you understand your rights?" Johnson said.

"Yes."

"Are you willing to answer any questions at this time?"

"No. No."

Johnson, however, wasn't giving up. He continued with his questions, attempting first to connect with Derrick, asking about his family and implying the two had much in common, particularly the color of their skin.

"You and I have a bond for obvious reasons," Johnson said. "I grew up in the hood. Deep, a little deeper in the hood than what you have, man. A lot deeper, so I understand. I seen relatives get killed, close relatives being killed, family, friends . . . So I'm not different, OK? You and I are no different, man."

Johnson explained that police have DNA linking Derrick to five murders: Gina, Murray, Pam, Dené, and Carrie. He told Derrick, who claimed he knew nothing about DNA, that it is irrefutable evidence. And he urged Derrick to fess up to other unsolved Baton Rouge murders he committed.

But Derrick saw right through him.

"Just one black man to another black man," Derrick said. "I know they gonna send you in here trying to talk to me . . ."

And he had no intentions of spilling to Johnson.

"I don't have no story to tell nobody," he said. "Chris, I'm gonna tell you like this here . . . Whatever go on with those five murders . . . I had to answer with me and the man upstairs. Me and the man will deal with it . . ."

No matter how hard Chris pushed, regardless of how he asked the question, Derrick would not give him anything except some highlights of his trip to Atlanta.

"You know, I did get the chance to see something I wanted to see in Atlanta, I tell you that much, I went and stood by the side of uh, Martin Luther King Jr. grave. You know something, I always wanted to do that in my life."

But the murders, Derrick did not want to discuss. He just wanted his trial and to "take his licks."

"We go to court, they come back, they say, 'Lee we give you the death penalty . . .' they can electrocute me up," he said. "They can electrocute me the same day. Like I told you, I done dealed with God, my heart and my mind made up . . . I know I ain't come here to stay . . . I ain't scared to die now. I ain't scared . . . I don't have no fear. I don't have no fear because I been through this, my life is, I been through the rain, I done been scarred, I done been drugged, you know."

He did not even want to make a deal with prosecutors.

"Lee ain't cutting no deal with nobody. I'm gonna tell my lawyer straight up. I'm not cutting no deal . . . I don't even want them people, if they come here, offering me, talking about we got your DNA . . . Don't even offer me no life, I don't want it. I don't want nothing. I'm ready, let me go . . ."

\* \* \*

Yet he still suggested he was framed by Zachary police who took his jeans from him five years earlier during the Randi Mebruer investigation. "They been bothering me for eight or nine years," he said. "I believe he set me up. How I know he ain't just setting me up?"

The closest Johnson got to linking Derrick to the murder victims was when he explained to Derrick that his DNA was found on all of the women. Without admitting he was with them, he implied he had sexual relations with a certain class of woman who would never admit it.

"I done been in the wrong place at the wrong time," he said. "You know, dealing with women, I done slept with some women . . . you're probably gonna say I'm telling you a lie about it, but I can bring some women name up, and you probably go and ask them, say, 'You ever been with Derrick?' They'll tell you no. But I know, and that person know. You know what I'm saying? . . . I've been with some women where they didn't want to get seen, be seen with me on a date, but like, you know what I'm saying. I done been there. I remember women, like, they high society, and then when they was around they friends, they didn't want their friends to know they were dealing [with me]. You know everybody got their little skeletons in their closet, you know what I'm saying. I done been through all that, Chris . . . I done been with some women [who] tell me, [they] say, 'Lord, if somebody see you here . . .' "

As further defense, he argued that the blackness of his skin prevented him from gaining access to the victims' homes.

"First off, what I'm saying is this here. When I read the case, even on TV where I watched, the man got in, they let the man into they house. I'm a black man from the South . . . What average black man you know or what . . . average white lady you know gonna let a black man in they house? I done did concrete work, you know what I'm saying . . . And I done drove a truck and I done got to the house at six and seven o'-clock in the morning. And . . . when they come to the door, it's all, they was always . . . 'Can I help you?' or blah blah blah, they husband come to the door. You hear what I'm saying?"

Johnson pushed Derrick to talk about the other unsolved murders in Baton Rouge, the cases without DNA, saying police would continue to investigate them:

"If it takes us ten years to solve these . . ." Johnson said.

"Old bones will be rotten by then," Derrick quipped.

"Uh, maybe not, you may still be around."

"I won't be around."

He was sure of that.

"You looking at a walking dead man. You know I know these people are gonna kill me, man. I know that."

Feeling persecuted, he gave his life biblical meaning.

"I'm like Job," he said. "Job will say the Lord giveth and the Lord taketh away and that's my belief. That's what I'm gonna [have on] my grave. I feel like I got the whole world on, the whole world looking at me right now. I'm the next O. J. Simpson. I'm the most hated black man in the world right now and you know I ain't lying."

Derrick waxed on about his religious beliefs, how the world of man was wrong, and how his faith in God will save his soul.

"See man will fail. Man gonna always judge you. But see God, the God I serve, I trust in God."

When Johnson asked Derrick what should happen to the serial killer, Derrick avoided a direct answer, again invoking his religious values.

"I don't judge," he said. "I'm a Christian. I don't judge nobody. Before I started getting in trouble with the law, you know they had me on jury duty . . . I said, 'Excuse me, I've got something to say.' Everybody looked at me. I said, 'I can't do this.' [The judge] said, 'Why?' I said, 'Because I can't judge another man . . .'"

The only thing Derrick regretted was the media harassment of his family.

"I don't want my family getting drug through all this shit . . ." he said.

Speaking of his family, however, brought Derrick the closest to an admission.

"The only thing I ask is . . . about my children, that they have a better life and maybe they can keep they nose cleaner than I kept mine. You know, I pray to God on that. You know, don't nobody judge them because of what they daddy may have done."

Johnson pounced.

"What did he do?" Johnson said.

"You know what I'm saying."

"What did you do?"

"I'm talking about . . . you say you got my uh, what that, DNA? You know being judged by DNA right or wrong . . ."

Derrick was still evasive. He talked about how much he loved his children.

"Like I always told my wife, I want my children . . . I tell my son, I tell my daughter, I told all of my children this, I want y'all to, I want y'all to be better than I was. I didn't have much coming up, but my mama and my daddy did the best they could."

Halfway through the interrogation, FBI profiler Mary Ellen O'Toole came into the room. She was introduced to Derrick but did not question him. She only watched the back and forth between Johnson and Derrick.

Occasionally Derrick stopped his conversation dead with Johnson and spoke to O'Toole, twice commenting, "You're a very observant lady."

He was curious about her perceptions of him, initiating this exchange: "So you're the profiler. So how do you see me? I read the stuff on the serial killing. So you been the one to do with the profile? So how you see me?" he said.

"You did read it?" O'Toole said.

"Yes, ma'am. I read it."

"You read the profile?"

"Yes ma'am."

"What did you think?"

"What I think is really you know when I was reading the profile, I really didn't do too much thinking about it . . . It was nothing like, you know, nothing like to affect me . . . But it was, it was pretty touching though. It had some, you know, pretty touching ways to it."

When the interview was over Derrick politely bid her adieu. "Ms. Mary Ellen, it was a pleasure to meet you," he said.

"It was a pleasure to meet you."

"But like I said, if you never meet me no more again, maybe you know . . ."

"You're an interesting man, Todd. It's an interesting case."

"I been told that a lot in my life."

"Well, I think that there are a lot of questions that you have about yourself that have run through your head for a long time."

"That's true."

"And there may come a point when those questions are ones that you want to put on the table and talk about. And if, when that time comes, you get ahold of Chris . . ."

"Ma'am, I ain't gonna . . ."

"This is what we do twenty-four hours a day. It's not just a job, Todd."

"You ever heard the old saying, where a dead dog buried, leave them there? I go by that old theory. I don't have no story to tell."

But he wanted her friendship. "If I go to trial, I'd like for you to be there. And you know, maybe you can write me, or maybe I can write you. I'd like to keep in contact with you like that. You can write me, or I can write you, know what I'm saying . . ."

Derrick's preference for women also entered into his hopes for legal representation. "You know, I'd love a lady lawyer . . . Because they, like, do a better job for you than a man anyway, you know. I don't want no lawyer who ain't gonna fight for me."

The one thing Derrick took pleasure in during the interview was the fact that no one would ever know his story because he would never reveal it.

"The book is being closed. Like I told you, it might be fifteen years from now . . . People gonna always wonder. Wonder."

# CHAPTER 40

# Justice

Justice and vengeance have a long, intertwined history. When wronged, human impulse calls for the wrong to be made right, for the victim to be compensated or avenged in some equitable way. Systems of justice attempt to dole out a fair punishment to the person responsible for the crime. But what is fair when a woman is maliciously slaughtered in her own home and dumped for trash? What is equitable punishment for a man who rapes with such violence he rips flesh and kills by cutting at his victims' throats so deep he nearly severs their heads? How do the families of the victims obtain equal justice to compensate for the nightmarish images they suffer daily and the lost love, companionship, and dreams that died with the victims?

For the families of the murdered, the idea of Derrick continuing to breathe and eat and sleep and walk around on the planet and talk to his mama did not seem just. For them, even death by lethal injection seemed unfair, unequal to the pain and suffering he unleashed.

"We put our pets, animals we love, to sleep with an injection," Lynne Marino told a panel of Louisiana legislators considering, but later rejecting, a moratorium on the death penalty in 2004. "It's too easy."

Much of Baton Rouge certainly felt the same way. The city wanted revenge. Derrick Todd Lee had killed their best and brightest and most beautiful women. He held everyone else hostage in fear for nearly a year: Many believed he deserved the worst punishment possible.

But since torture—a punishment not a few in Baton Rouge offered to inflict on Derrick themselves—was out of the question, the death penalty would have to satisfy the local lust for vengeance. And East Baton Rouge District Attorney Doug Moreau, along with his team of prosecutors led by John Sinquefield and Dana Cummings, promised to bring it about. "The families, the city, needs to know that a strong individual is on their side," Sinquefield said later. "Someone who exudes confidence."

Sinquefield intended to be that guy. Every time he met with the victims' families through the months of pretrial hearings and legal proceedings and delays, he told them the same thing: "We're winning. The verdict is going to be guilty, and the sentence is going to be death."

From the beginning, prosecutors swore they would not offer Derrick a plea bargain. Life in prison was not on the negotiating table. Like Derrick himself said, he was a dead man walking.

In June 2003, Derrick was indicted for the first-degree murder of Charlotte Murray Pace, a charge that carried a possible death sentence. Prosecutors decided to pursue her case first because the evidence was the strongest, but they did not plan to leave the other victims out of the trial. Within an hour of Derrick's arraignment on the charge, prosecutors let the court know they intended to present evidence at the trial from the five originally linked murders of Murray, Gina, Pam, Dené, and Carrie.

Derrick might only be on the hook legally for one murder in Baton Rouge, but all the victims' stories would be told to ensure he was sent to death row.

Anticipation for the trial was building by early 2004, but its originally scheduled date of March 30 was postponed to May 10, then postponed again to September 2. And in a surprise twist in what Sinquefield dubbed Derrick's "serial prosecution," Baton Rouge lost its place at the front of the line to prosecute one of the biggest murder cases in Louisiana history.

In the weeks after his arrest, West Baton Rouge authorities received what was then not-so-surprising news about Geralyn "Sissy" DeSoto's case. A private lab in New Orleans found DNA on Geralyn's fingernail clippings that linked Derrick to her murder.

Initial tests of the clippings conducted by the State Police Crime·Lab found only Geralyn's DNA. But the lab analysts knew the results did not mean the killer's DNA was absent. Rather, they suspected the large amount of Geralyn's blood on the clippings might simply be hiding his DNA.

When conducting typical DNA tests, analysts use a chemical process to highlight pieces of DNA that are then profiled. But the chemical process often will only pick up and highlight the most evident biological material. If the victim's blood on the clippings is so much greater than the few skins cells left behind by the killer, the DNA tests will only find the DNA from the victim's blood.

Hoping to get around this problem, the private DNA lab in New Orleans, ReliaGene, developed a new test that only picks up male DNA—the markers inherited from the father. The test is ideal for female rape and murder victims, whose skin cells and blood often overwhelm their attackers' DNA and prevent investigators from obtaining the attacker's DNA profile. When the new test is used, the female's DNA is eliminated, allowing only the male DNA to show up.

In Geralyn's case, when the DNA from her blood was eliminated, a male DNA profile showed up and matched Derrick Todd Lee's DNA profile.

The results of the new tests, called YSTR, however, are not

as precise in identifying the attacker as a test for nuclear DNA, which can pinpoint an individual exactly.

When the female DNA is eliminated during the test, the resulting profile of the DNA left behind includes only male DNA inherited from the father. And the resulting profile is the same profile of all other males in the paternal line. Meaning the DNA profile developed in the YSTR test is the same profile shared by the DNA donor's father, his father's father, his father's father's father, his father's other sons, the donor's male sons and so on.

So while the results are far better than blood typing in linking a suspect to a crime, they are not nearly as accurate as a full nuclear DNA profile, which is unique to each individual.

Regardless, when West Baton Rouge police had the DNA link found under Geralyn's fingernails in conjunction with the phone call from her home that day to Derrick's former employer, they had enough for an arrest warrant. Later that year, authorities in West Baton Rouge also got a first-degree murder indictment against Derrick in Geralyn's murder.

Prosecutors, however, decided to pursue Derrick for second-degree murder, a lesser charge that does not carry the death penalty as a possible sentence. Second-degree murder trials move faster through the court docket than a first-degree murder trial, so Derrick's trial in West Baton Rouge saw few delays and was set for August 2004.

Then, as the legal machinations across the river in Baton Rouge stalled from postponements, West Baton Rouge Parish, the gritty little parish accustomed to sitting in the shadow of its larger metropolitan neighbors, emerged as the first to get a crack at the Louisiana serial killer.

Sinquefield and Murray's mother, Ann Pace, worried publicly about West Baton Rouge taking Derrick to trial first. They suggested a not guilty verdict would have disastrous effects on the September trial and that even a guilty verdict, with all the expected media coverage, would make it much more difficult, if not impossible, to find an unbiased jury in the city of Baton Rouge.

West Baton Rouge Parish Judge Robin Free and prosecutor Tony Clayton, however, were determined to make the trial date stick in their jurisdiction.

So in the blistering heat of a southern Louisiana August, a

media herd of satellite trucks and sharply suited reporters descended on the tiny industrial town of Port Allen for the local trial of the century.

The West Baton Rouge Parish Courthouse is a two-story faded white columned building built under a pair of 200-year-old oaks. The floors inside are speckled linoleum. The courtroom benches are harder than church pews. And the elevator jerks and creaks like an arthritic old dog. Most days, the biggest case on the docket is a home burglary, and the people attending court are there by judges' orders.

The serial killer trial was the biggest thing to come to town in decades, if not ever. And local authorities took full advantage of it. At the end of the first day of the trial, Judge Free instructed the media on what time to return in the morning to catch a camera shot of Derrick walking into the courthouse, with Free and other local authorities leading the way.

Built like a football player and with matching strategic mind-set, Free isn't the type to sit for long legal ramblings. He's a man who believes in common sense and gut judgments. He trusted jurors when they said they could put out of their minds what they heard about Derrick in the media before making a judgment of his guilt.

Derrick's defense attorney, Tommy Thompson, disagreed.

Media coverage of the serial killer investigation was pervasive on both sides of the river. Only residents in a coma could have avoided the news about Derrick Todd Lee's arrest in the case. The public's level of awareness became clear during jury selection in West Baton Rouge Parish. One after another, with one or two exceptions, potential jurors said they believed Derrick was guilty of killing several women.

Women shared their personal fears felt during the height of the investigation, when they carried mace or a gun, how they were constantly looking over their shoulders and changing their habits to protect themselves. In effect, they, too, were victims, terrorized by the killer.

The men, too, spoke of their concern for the safety of their daughters and wives, how their nerves were stressed by living in the midst of a serial killer.

Despite the obvious signs that almost every juror was personally affected by the serial killer, and their own admission that they believed Derrick was the man responsible, Free allowed them to stay on the jury panel as long as they stated they could put their previous feelings and beliefs out of their minds during the trial and listen only to the evidence.

Legally, that promise, even from people who had previously made up their minds about Derrick's guilt, allowed them a place at the judgment table.

The trial lasted only three days. Prosecutors Clayton and Becky Chustz presented several pieces of key evidence, including the DNA found on Geralyn's fingernail clippings that matched Derrick's DNA from his paternal line. DNA analysts said the match allowed them to rule out 99.8 percent of the black population as donors, leaving Derrick within that 0.2 percent.

In addition to the DNA, prosecutors built a strong case of circumstantial evidence against Derrick:

Derrick was laid off from his job at Dow Chemical on Friday, January 11, and his last paycheck was cut and probably picked up by Derrick on Monday, January 14, the same day Geralyn was killed. He would have to pass right by the entrance to Geralyn's trailer park on his way to the chemical plant. Then there was the unexplained phone call from the DeSoto home to an ExxonMobil employee phone number in Baton Rouge at the estimated time of Geralyn's death.

Diane Alexander testified and identified Derrick as the man who came to her door and asked to use the phone before attacking her.

Prosecutors showed jurors one of Derrick's old knives, a folding buck knife with a three-inch blade that was consistent with Geralyn's wounds. In testimony from Derrick's son, Derrick Jr., Clayton got the young man to admit his father liked to keep his knife sharp, regularly honing it to maintain its razor-thin edge.

Kim Colomb took the stand, too, to testify about the bloody shoe print she found in Geralyn's trailer, the print she was sure the killer left behind after walking through Geralyn's blood.

A pair of Wolverine boots found in Derrick's girlfriend

Consandra Green's apartment, which Consandra identified as Derrick's, had the same bottom tread as the print found in the DeSoto trailer. Derrick's shoes were also the same size as the print left behind.

Derrick sensed he was in a losing battle.

Halfway through the trial, he tried to fire his court-appointed attorney, claiming Thompson had not sought the testimony of people who Derrick claimed would provide an alibi.

"My life is on the line here," he complained in a courtroom outburst. He argued Thompson, the father of four daughters, was biased against him.

Free told Derrick he could not hire another attorney, but if he wanted to represent himself he had the right. Free, however, warned that would not be a smart move.

Derrick settled down and continued the trial with Thompson, whom he would not have to suffer much longer. The jurors were quick with their guilty verdict—less than two hours. A few days after the conviction, Derrick was scheduled to receive his automatic life sentence.

Before Judge Free officially ordered Derrick to spend the rest of his life behind bars, however, Geralyn's family was allowed to confront him with "victim impact" statements.

John Barr walked slowly to the podium set up about twenty feet from Derrick, who was dressed in prison orange and shackled in the jury box.

John took his reading glasses off, folded them carefully, and placed them on the stand next to a sheet of paper he pulled from his pocket. For several seconds, he paused, as if to compose himself, control the rage he no longer wanted to control. He cleared his throat, put his glasses back on, and lifted his gaze toward Derrick. The quiet sobbing of Geralyn's mom was the only noise in the tense silence of the courtroom.

"I raised three girls," John began. "I tried to raise them in a Christian family. Tried to teach them about forgiveness. I loved them more than anything in the world."

Earlier that very morning, John told Derrick, he had searched in the Bible for the right words to say to express his feelings. When he opened his wife's book, he discovered instead a last Father's Day card from Geralyn. It read, "Dad, thanks for giving me the time to teach me the love of God."

Now, as John Barr stood staring at the man he believed to be evil incarnate, he would share with Derrick something about the fear of God.

He read to him from the Bible, Matthew 13:47:

*Again, the kingdom of heaven is like a net thrown into the sea, which collects fish of every kind. When it is full they haul it ashore and sit down to put what is good into buckets. What is bad they throw away. Thus it will be at the end of the age. The angels will go out and separate the wicked from the righteous and throw them into the fiery furnace, where there will be wailing and grinding of teeth.*

John paused again, then suddenly slammed his fist down hard on the podium. The noise boomed through the room, startling even the deputies.

"That's how you got into my daughter's house, huh!" he shouted. "With that smile on your face, talking about God. That's how you got in all those women's homes. She would have let you in to use the phone, believing it to be the Christian thing to do."

John leaned into the solid wood stand that stood between him and the man who slaughtered his daughter. As his words turned fiery, the podium, tilting and jarring toward Derrick, seemed to act as the last piece of civility keeping John from leaping across the courtroom and killing him.

He banged on the podium again; his anger and frustration building, turning his face a bloody red.

"I have to forgive." His voice got quiet again. "But I don't see anywhere where it says *today* I have to forgive. Maybe God will have mercy on your soul, but I don't."

Seated in the jury box, Derrick held John's stare, his face scrunched into a defiant grimace.

John taunted him. "You're a big man, huh, attacking women . . . I never heard of you whipping no man's butt."

Derrick kept his cool. He sat still, never losing eye contact with John. Not once did he look down at his feet or show even a hint of remorse. He was impervious.

"I wish I could talk all day about how sorry you are."

John wanted Derrick to know, to feel how much pain he

inflicted on Geralyn's family, what he took from their lives. He wanted Derrick to recognize the evil, the cruelty, the viciousness and inhumanity of his actions. John wanted to rip the life out of Derrick just as Derrick had done to his precious Geralyn.

"You don't know how badly I want to get closer to you," he said.

But Derrick was a brick wall. John would not get the peace his soul needed from the man seated before him.

"I don't have enough time to tell you how sorry you are," he said. "You have no clue because you have no feelings. You don't have nothing."

His wife, Melanie, Geralyn's mother, approached the podium next. She was in tears before she got to the microphone. She looked at Derrick, whose face seemed to soften just a little. Here was a woman. A mother. His own mother was sitting just twenty feet from him in the courtroom.

Melanie's voice cracked, her sobs drowning out her first word.

"Why?"

Few people in the courtroom, Derrick's family the most noted, got past that question without a knot jamming into their throats. Hard-bitten news reporters wiped at insistent tears.

"Why Geralyn?" Melanie asked again, begging an answer she knew she would not get from Derrick. "Why did God allow such evil to exist in this world? I don't understand why a person like you can function with no heart."

She had so much more to say. She would have liked to shake him for hours until he heard her, really heard her and showed remorse, confessed, apologized. She reached into her faith, her belief that all God's creations have the capacity for good.

"If there is still a heart in that body of yours," she urged him. "I hope God touches it, and you tell the authorities what you have done. Save your family the grief of hearing how evil you are."

But like her husband, she knew he could not give her what she needed. Derrick could no sooner help her understand the pain, the loss, the insanity of the reality she faced every day, than bring her daughter Geralyn back to life. And Melanie was trying to accept that cruel fact.

"I have to believe you will not have an answer that can satisfy me," she said. "Those answers must come from God."

Before she walked away from what might be the only moments she would ever have to confront Derrick, she left him with a message, a message that may not provide true justice, but certainly gave her hope for vengeance.

"Your two-and-a-half-year reign of terror on Geralyn and her family ends today, and hers begins on you today." Melanie shot the words at Derrick as if casting a spell. "When you close your eyes at night, as you lay in your cell, I pray her face and all the faces of all of your other victims burns in your memory until you are forced to face the pain you have caused all these families."

Geralyn's sister could not bring herself to stand before Derrick, but she asked prosecutor Becky Chustz to read her letter to him. It began simply: "I want you to know that I hate your guts . . . I hate you, Derrick Todd Lee, for taking my beautiful sister."

In closing, she wished him good riddance for all eternity.

"You will scream for mercy from God while you burn in the everlasting pit of hell."

When the testimony was complete, Free sentenced Derrick to life. The outcome to Geralyn's trial, however, was only an appetizer for what everyone was waiting to see: the blockbuster proceedings in Baton Rouge when Derrick would not only face a first-degree murder charge but also the death penalty. That was what the families wanted. Nothing else made sense.


Few doubted Derrick would be convicted in the Baton Rouge case, and most assumed he would receive the death penalty. If such a penalty is available, the argument went, Derrick's murders were surely the type to warrant a death sentence. No one could imagine how he could avoid the needle.

The surprise came halfway through jury selection.

Court watchers would not have been shocked if Derrick's defense team claimed he was insane. Derrick's father had been diagnosed with schizophrenia and manic depression and had spent years in mental institutions. Arguing Derrick inherited similar problems did not seem farfetched. But Derrick's lead defense attorney, Mike Mitchell, avoided that defense. Instead, he and his cocounsel Nelvil Hollingsworth and Bruce Unangst, argued Derrick was mentally retarded.

The claim, if proven, would not exonerate Derrick of the crime, but it might allow him to avoid the death penalty. Just one year earlier, the U.S. Supreme Court had ruled that executing a mentally handicapped convict was cruel and unusual punishment.

In essence, Derrick's defense attorneys hoped the jury would decide Derrick was too stupid, too unconscious of his actions, to be put to death.

But Derrick's intellectual capacity—or lack thereof—would be determined only after the guilt phase of the trial. As in most states, death penalty cases are done in two parts.

The first phase is called the "guilt phase." This is the meat of the prosecution, when prosecutors present evidence to prove the defendant is guilty and defense attorneys try to refute it. If the defendant is found guilty of first-degree murder, then the process moves into the next phase, the "penalty phase."

In the penalty phase, the jury must determine whether the defendant should be executed for the crime. To that end, prosecutors present evidence for why the defendant is irredeemable and deserves to die, while the defense argues for mercy.

Penalty phases, for those who have never sat through them, are emotionally charged, intense proceedings. The victim's family testifies about their loss, their heartbreak, the nightmare they have lived since the murder. Then the defense puts the defendant's friends and family on the stand who beg to save their loved one's life.

The sense of death is palpable. Any theoretical ideas about the death penalty become quaint when the decision whether to order someone's death becomes real.

During the guilt phase of Derrick's trial the jury heard irrefutable DNA evidence linking him to the murders of Murray, Gina, Pam, Dené, and Carrie. Derrick's DNA was found in places that could not have been accidental or coincidental.

His semen was found on Murray's cervix, in Pam's vaginal

cavity, and from swabs of Carrie's and Dené's genital area. Derrick's blood was also found on the rug in Pam's bedroom and on Gina's shirtsleeve at the back of the elbow.

The testimony from lab scientists was complicated and dry and long, but the bottom line could be summed up with one figure: 1 in 3.6 quadrillion. Simply put, that was the chance the DNA found at all five murders belonged to a man other than Derrick.

But prosecutors did not rely solely on the DNA. They had an eyewitness.

Diane Alexander was the only known survivor of Derrick's attacks, and nothing could stop her from identifying him from the witness stand. She stared straight at Derrick, her eyes steely with a confident righteousness. "That's him right there."

"Are you sure?" Cummings asked.

"Beyond a shadow of a doubt. I'll never forget that face."

Her words were supported not only by the DNA found on her dress that linked Derrick to the attack but also by the long piece of phone cord Derrick used to strangle her.

Saint Martin Parish Sheriff's detectives had collected the cord, which Derrick had cut while inside her mobile home, as part of the initial investigation in hopes of finding the other end to match the piece. But it wasn't until after Derrick's arrest that investigators realized the other half of the cord was already at the crime lab.

When Pam's body was found at Whiskey Bay in July 2002, crime scene technicians collected several pieces of potential evidence from the surrounding area: beer cans, trash, etc. They also found a phone cord a few feet from Pam's body.

More than a year later, when Diane met with the murder victims' families to share the details of her attack, she mentioned the phone cord. Pam's family immediately remembered the cord found at Whiskey Bay.

Lynne Marino called Saint Martin Parish prosecutor Chester Cedars, who was pursuing Derrick for the attempted rape and murder of Diane. She suggested he compare the two pieces of cord.

A few weeks later, at the Acadiana Crime Lab, analyst Mark Kurowski was examining the two cut ends under one of his favorite comparison microscopes, looking to see if they were once one piece.

"They're a textbook match," he testified. "They fit together like puzzle pieces."

Three days after Derrick cut the phone cord at Diane's house and wrapped it around her throat, trying to kill her, he tossed it into the swamps with Pam's body.

The cord tied him to both crimes: Pam's where he left his DNA and Diane's where he left a witness alive.

The jury took less than an hour and a half to find Derrick guilty as charged. A sigh of relief and vindication whispered through the courtroom. Derrick's mother, wife, and sisters remained silent. Sheriff's deputies later escorted them out of the courthouse and through the crush of news cameras and reporters' microphones. They had no comments.

The victims' families were satisfied, but not happy. No amount of justice would bring back the women they loved so dearly. Derrick's conviction would never fill the void he created in their lives. Even his death would not bring them peace.

The penalty phase began the next day. Casey Pace, Murray's dad, was the first to take the stand.

"Murray was a bright, beautiful person," he began. "She was ambitious. She was hardworking, fun-loving, an athlete, and she was funny . . . One of the things I miss most about her is her laugh. When she laughed, she lit up a room."

He held back the tears as he recounted all of Murray's attributes. But the one that he always admired most was her wisdom.

"Murray was ambitious. She wanted to excel in everything she did. She wanted a career, but unlike so many of the rest of us, she figured out early on that the most important thing in life is friends. No matter how hard she worked, she made time for her friends. She was a people collector. She brought people together."

Murray's older sister Sam remembered Murray's "spirit was too big for her body to contain. She radiated vibrant beauty."

Sam is the scientist in the family. The daughter who was more interested in her books than her clothes.

"Murray was always working on me, making sure I was dressed in a manner she approved of," Sam said. "She took me shopping."

Losing Murray left Sam feeling empty. For months after Murray was killed, Sam would wake in the morning and for a few precious seconds, she would not remember Murray was dead.

"Everything would be OK," she said. "That doesn't happen anymore. It's never going to be OK again. I won't have a sister again."

When Ann took the stand, she told the jury she never escapes the pain.

"There is no peace in sleep," she said.

Every holiday, every birthday, every family gathering that is supposed to be joyful is marred by sadness and their loss.

"It's changed the world for me," she said. "It's a more frightening place than I ever thought it could be. It's like I'm a soldier coming back from war without body parts. You know you're not dead, and you keep going, but you're missing things that you can never have back."


Derrick's defense attorneys in turn put Tharshia Fontenot, Derrick's sister, on the stand. She immediately began crying, almost hysterically.

"On behalf of my family, my mother, my dad, my entire family, for the Pace family and all of y'all, we are so sorry for y'all's loss. And I promise you there's not a day that goes by—before this happened I could remember one New Year's Eve the pastor called me to pray. And I prayed for the families and the victims of this serial killer. And even when Derrick was accused of this, I never stopped praying for y'all. Never. And daily I pray for y'all . . . And we are just so sorry and I am so sorry for your loss and the hurt and the pain. We are sorry. I'm sorry. My family is sorry for your loss."

She did not, however, admit or acknowledge or apologize for Derrick's guilt. As instructed by the defense lawyers, she attempted to give her brother, a certified murdering monster, a sympathetic human face.

She spoke of their time together as children, playing at home, using sheets to make forts, camping outside, climbing trees, and walking through the woods. She remembered his playing with his train set he got for Christmas as a boy and riding horses. Normal kid stuff.

Under cross examination, however, she was forced to admit she filed charges against her loving brother in 1989 when he broke into Florence's trailer and threatened to "whup her like nobody ever had."

But Tharshia stressed that despite Derrick's blowups, he was a generous, fun, and kind person.

"He's always been there for me," she said. "Whenever you need him to do something for you, he'll do it. His friends, if they would call on him for a favor, he would do it for them. He was real personable. He often had cookouts for friends. Even elderly people, he helped them move stuff. When our grandfather was sick, Derrick took him to dialysis. He used his own gas and money to drive him to Baton Rouge."

The jury was stoned-faced. The twelve men and women appeared unmoved by Tharshia's litany of Derrick's fine qualities. They had seen the crime scene photos of his less humanitarian work. They saw pictures of Murray's eyes stabbed out. They looked at Pam's throat slit wide open and her body eaten away by rot and maggots. They had seen Gina lying dead in her bed with bloody tears to her genitals and Dené's beaten and unrecognizable face. They had witnessed the bruising Derrick left deep inside the most intimate parts of Carrie's body.

And they had heard from Diane Alexander about Derrick's other personality, the side of him that attacks women at their most vulnerable, the anger in him that unleashes a vicious, inhumane violence.

It would take more than cute childhood stories to win this jury over.


Defense attorneys hired two expert witnesses to testify about the intelligence and psychological tests they recently conducted on Derrick.

Psychiatrist Sarah Deland, who works at the same state mental hospital where Derrick's father was institutionalized for several years, and an LSU professor of psychology, Drew Gouvier, agreed Derrick's IQ marked him as mildly retarded.

"He came across as someone impaired . . . as slow," Deland testified. And she suggested he might have sustained brain damage as a child from two separate head injuries.

In her tests, Derrick showed difficulty remembering chronology, recalling most events in his life happening "five years ago," even if they occured ten or twelve or one year prior.

He repeated himself often. He had trouble repeating a series of numbers. Most people can remember seven digits in a row, like a phone number, after the numbers are recited one time. Derrick had trouble remembering five. Same with repeating the series of numbers backwards. Most people can recite five of the numbers, but Derrick could do only two.

When she tested his abstract thinking abilities, she asked how an apple and an orange were similar. He responded correctly that they are both fruit. But when she asked how a river and an ocean are similar, he was stumped for a few minutes, taking a long time to say they are both water.

"You think he could tell you the difference between Whiskey Bay and the Atchafalaya River?" Sinquefield demanded from Deland on cross-examination.

Deland did not have an answer. "I don't know."

She refuted suggestions that Derrick might have been faking stupidity to save his life, arguing that on the contrary, Derrick seemed to want to impress her with his smarts and personality.

"He appeared to be putting forth his best effort," she testified, adding, "I will try to trip people up because I want to know whether they are telling the truth or not, and I didn't find any of that."

In a standardized intelligence test, Derrick scored a sixty-five on the Weschler Adult IQ scale, Gouvier testified. A score below seventy is one criterion for labeling someone mentally retarded. The other criterion says the low IQ score must be accompanied by a deficiency in social and adaptive behavior. And Gouvier determined Derrick was deficient in a number of ways, particularly in his inability to control his impulses.

From interviews with Derrick, his sister, his wife, and mother, Gouvier decided Derrick was a bad communicator, had no self-direction, was incapable of organizing his life, and had a serious anger management problem. One area Derrick showed no impairment, Gouvier noted, was in mobility.

Ultimately, Gouvier rested his reputation on his opinion that Derrick legally qualified as mentally retarded.

His testimony immediately drew severe criticism from the victims' families and others in the public who cringed at the idea that a LSU professor, a member of the university where so many of the victims attended school, would argue in Derrick's defense.

In the months after the trial, Gouvier's professional opinions were questioned by colleagues. The university's administration warned him that he was in a precarious position, bringing bad publicity and ill will onto the university. Ultimately, he was forced to hire a lawyer, fearing his job might be at risk.

The jury, however, did not buy the fumbling dumb serial killer story. Prosecutors brought in their own expert, psychologist Donald Hoppe, who was almost chuckling when he stated Derrick Todd Lee "is absolutely not mentally retarded."

Hoppe reviewed the same evidence and test scores as the defense team, but came to a different conclusion, noting that IQ test evaluations can be subjective, particularly the assessment of the person's adaptive behavior and life skills.

During Hoppe's testimony, Sinquefield brought forward several written tests Derrick passed when he obtained his commercial driver's license and pipe fitter certifications to work at the chemical plants.

Deland suggested Derrick paid someone to take the tests for him, but she conceded the signature on the tests looked just like Derrick's.

When Derrick's former coworker and boss testified, describing Derrick's ability to read a blueprint and quickly figure out complicated pipe fitting schematics, the jury looked tired and well past ready to go back into their room for a fast deliberation on his fate.

Before releasing them, Sinquefield assured the jury Derrick did not qualify for a retarded man's free pass from the death penalty.

"Reserve that finding for the truly mentally retarded people who truly deserve that exemption."

The jurors took just an hour and a half to make their decision final. The courtroom was silent when their sentence for Derrick was read. The words "death penalty" landed like a touchdown for the home team. Muffled cheers and high fives and thankful hugs spread through the audience of victims' families. They had won.

Prison guards awaiting the verdict grabbed Derrick out of his seat and ushered him quickly from the courtroom.

His mother yelled to him, "I love you, son. Always."

Tharsia shouted, "I love you, Todd."

Derrick struggled with the guards as they pushed him through the courtroom's back door. He shouted over his shoulder in a desperate, hurried voice about DNA swabs and being framed and crooked cops.

Over the din, Pam's brother, Ed Piglia, shouted back, "Oh, shut up . . ." as Derrick's voice disappeared down the hallway.

# Afterword

In the months after Derrick's arrest, the Zachary police made a stunning announcement. Derrick's DNA was found on evidence collected from Randi Mebruer's home in April 1998.

A pink trash bag left on the cement floor of Randi's carport, right next to several pools of her blood, was the key to finally solving her case. Derrick had left behind some of his semen.

In 1999, when analysts from the Louisiana State Police Crime Lab finally tested the evidence from Randi's house, they located semen on her comforter and blood on several items, including a number of pink trash bags that the abductor apparently used to drag or carry her out of the home. In the crime lab report, the analyst noted that police could obtain DNA tests—which would require the use of a private lab—on the blood and semen for further identification purposes.

DNA tests on the trash bag, however, were not conducted until 2003, after Derrick's arrest, more than five years after he had become a suspect in Randi's murder.

Zachary police try to explain this as a clue missed because of the lack of DNA testing available at the time. The bags were dusted for fingerprints, which provided nothing solid. But DNA tests were expensive and not often used by Louisiana police. That was why they also did not obtain a DNA profile from the semen on the comforter until 2002, after the serial killings began. The results matched to Randi's new boyfriend at the time.

Looking back, the need to test the evidence for DNA seems like a no-brainer. But at the time, the detectives were still operating in a pre-DNA mind-set, when many police investigators were still trying to solve cases without the help of magic and foolproof genetic identification markers. It is not an excuse, it is just a fact.

Tragically, the fact is Derrick Todd Lee could have been arrested for Randi's murder years before he began his killing spree in Baton Rouge and Lafayette. But it was not the first or the last time he slipped through the cracks. Derrick was as good at evading capture as he was at killing. He had the devil's evil luck on his side for many years.

Ultimately, that luck ran out.

Randi made seven victims linked to him by DNA. Today police and prosecutors are more confident than ever that Connie Warner is one of Derrick's victims, as well as the two teenagers attacked in the cemetery. He is also the top suspect in the murders of Eugenie Boisfontaine and Christine Moore.

Many friends and families of the victims are counting down to the day when Derrick will no longer walk this earth. They know continued legal wrangling over Derrick's appeal will last years. His new defense team will argue he did not get a fair trial in the Baton Rouge region, that the jurors were biased because they had too much exposure to the case through the media. The lawyers will also continue to push Derrick's mental retardation, hoping the courts will let him slide past the death penalty.

Yet the families remain confident that one day, in the not too distant future, they will drive up to Saint Francisville, pass by Derrick's old house on Highway 61, and continue down the rural back roads along the Angola Highway to the Louisiana State

Penitentiary. They will be able to take a seat in the viewing room and watch as the guards escort Derrick to the death table.

They do not know how they will feel watching the execution of the man who killed their loved ones. No doubt they will look for remorse on his face, maybe they will hope to see fear in his eyes, a similar look that he must have seen in his victims' eyes before their deaths. The experience might satisfy the families; it might not. They might feel justice served, or they might not.

But one thing is not in doubt: the victims' friends and families will still feel the pain of their loss. Living without their loved one hurts every day. Living with the images of that loved one's murder, their final painful and horrifying moments, is excruciating. For the victims of Derrick Todd Lee—the ones who are still alive to suffer the loss—life is never again the same.

The tears come often and unexpectedly: When a friend rejoices about her daughter's marriage engagement or a job promotion. When birthdays and holidays roll around. Or simply when morning brings reality back in focus.

"Like most men, I spent a lifetime trying to hide emotion from the world," Casey Pace said more than two years after his daughter was killed. "When you lose a child, you can't do it anymore. I learned how to cry . . . I've learned what heartache truly means."

Since the murders, many of the victims' families have found new purpose in their grief.

Lynne Marino has stayed active publicly, promoting victims' rights through the New Orleans–based Victims and Citizens Against Crime. Ann Pace, a former flower child and anti–death penalty activist, has testified at several legislative panels and conferences, discussing her personal conversion to becoming a supporter of the death penalty. Lynda Yoder is working politically in Florida to promote awareness and improved law enforcement of sex crimes. Gina's sister Amy Sanders has become active in an association that raises money for DNA testing of rape kits and other crime scene evidence that is currently sitting idle on crime lab shelves around the country. The Colombs have started a fund in honor of Dené to promote reading, one of Dené's great loves.

The victims' families have also tried to stay in touch, to remember the big events in each other's lives, and call on the birthdays and the hard days that mark the anniversaries of death.

"We're a family," said Tracy Bryan, Connie Warner's daughter. "I would give anything not to be a part of it if I could have my mom back, but it's good to have them."

# APPENDIX A

# FBI Serial Killer Behavioral Profile Released September 3, 2002

The following offender profile is provided by The Behavioral Analysis Unit (BAU) which is a component of the Federal Bureau of Investigation's (FBI's) National Center for the Analysis of Violent Crime (NCAVC) which is located at the FBI Academy, Quantico, Virginia.

Criminal profiling is a process now known as "criminal investigative analysis." Profilers, or Criminal Investigative Analysts, are highly trained and experienced FBI Agents who study every behavioral and forensic aspect and detail of an unsolved violent crime scene in which a certain amount of psychopathology has been left at the scene.

Psychopathology is an offender's behavioral and psychological indicators that are left at a violent crime scene as a result of his physical, sexual, and in some cases verbal interaction with his victim(s). A profile, or criminal investigative analysis, is an investigative tool, and its value is measured in terms of how much assistance it provides to the investigator.

Baton Rouge law enforcement and the FBI recognize that it is not typical to publicly release any portion of a profile in a serial homicide investigation.

However, it is the opinion of the FBI's Behavioral Analysis Unit (BAU) that there are persons in the Baton Rouge area who know this offender and may even suspect he is responsible for the deaths of Gina Green, Charlotte Murray Pace, and Pam Kinamore. Identifying what the BAU believes some of the offender's key personality and behavioral traits, gleaned from the three crime scenes, may give the person who knows him, whether it is a co-worker, family member, or friend, the confidence to contact law enforcement. It is important to note that no one or two traits or characteristics should be considered in isolation or given more weight than the others. Any one of the traits, or several, can be seen in people who have never committed a crime. Instead, these behavioral traits and characteristics should be considered in their totality.


Based on the age range of the victims and their physical appearances, the age of this male offender is estimated to be somewhere between 25 and 35 years of age. However, no suspect should be eliminated on the basis of his chronological age.

This offender is physically strong and capable of lifting a weight of at least 155–175 pounds. Crime scene information indicates a shoe size of approximately 10 to 11.

His socio-economic situation is likely average or even below average for the Baton Rouge area. In other words, his finances would be tight. His employment is likely to be in a job which requires physical strength, and does not involve significant or regular interaction with the public. He does not have a certain amount of mobility either from his employment, lifestyle or both.

These homicides occurred on two Fridays and a Sunday. It is possible that on these days this offender was not accountable to anyone, unlike the rest of the week where he was accountable due to his employment or for some other reason.

This offender appears to have developed limited information about the three victims—before the homicides. Because he put himself in a position to see them, observe them, or even casually run into them prior to the assaults, he would have obtained information about where they lived, and something about their patterns of behavior. However, it is important to point out that following these women could have involved merely "spot" checks which would not have raised the women's level of suspicion or awareness. This offender may also have perceived more of a "relationship" with these women than what was there. He may have even "bragged" to other co-workers, other male friends, about having different relationships with certain very attractive—well off—women, without identifying these women specifically.

This offender wants to be seen as someone who is attractive and appealing to women. However, his level of sophistication in interacting with women, especially women who are above him in the social strata, is low. Any contact he has had with women he has found attractive would be described by these women as "awkward." He might demonstrate an overt interest in certain women, complimenting them, etc., in an effort to get closer to them. However, he may misperceive the intentions of some women who are "nice" to him because they don't want to hurt his feelings. His misperceptions might cause him to think there could be more to their "friendship" than what the women perceive.

It is likely this offender spends a significant amount of time watching women and following those in whom he is interested. Whether he is at work, at a bar, on his days off, alone or with others, he watches women. At times, this behavior could be excessive and something he engages in to the exclusion of other daily activities. Watching women and following them would be exciting for him. When questioned about it, he would defend this behavior and attempt to normalize it by telling others, "I just like women."

This offender does not just follow women from a distance and it is possible he will attempt to interact with them. He has interacted with other women in the Baton Rouge area that he has not killed. However, his low-key style would not have caused suspicion. What may draw attention to him is when his watching and following women becomes obviously inappropriate. He may be so intent on watching them, he can become almost oblivious when he "crosses the line," and they finally notice him or even confront him about it. Persons who know this offender would likely be aware of his behavior and probably have made comments to him about it. He would deny his behavior is inappropriate.

Women who have been or will be questioned by investigators may not even think to mention this individual because he seems so harmless. The women he follows, watches, or interacts with may not even be aware of him because he "blends in" with the community and his physical appearance is normal. He may come across to some women as a "nice guy" who might have tried to get a little too close too soon, but otherwise is a non-threatening person. He may go out of his way to be helpful to women in an effort to get closer to them. This veneer of harmlessness is his shield of protection from suspicion.

This is a person who will not handle rejection—real or imagined—well, particularly by women, and he will become angry, sullen, and determined to retaliate.

There are behavioral aspects of each of the three assaults which are considered very high risk for the offender. This includes home intrusions at times when people are around, or could return home and find him. This high-risk behavior exposes this offender to being identified or even apprehended. However, he does it anyway because it is probably enjoyable for him and adds to his sense of thrill and excitement. People who know this offender will recognize his propensity to engage in behavior which is high risk, to live on the edge—even in normal, everyday activities.

This is an "impulsive" individual. When determined to do something, he disregards the consequences of his acts. However, his impulsivity should not be confused with lack of planning. This impulsivity has likely brought him to the attention of law enforcement in the past, even if for seemingly minor offenses, including trespassing, breaking and entering, and peeping. His decision to attack each of the three women when he did may have been spontaneous or impulsive. However, because he had knowledge of these women's schedules and lifestyles, it would have lessened the "recklessness" of having made a spontaneous decision.

The BAU believes that this offender lost control during the

assault of Charlotte Murray Pace. Losing control would have angered him. He does not like losing control, and he would have been noticeably angry and agitated for some time after the Pace homicide. People around him would have seen this agitation and will recall any disparaging remarks he might have made about Ms. Pace when her homicide was discussed—either by others or in the media. He would have appeared very interested in media reports following the homicide.

If the offender was accountable for his time on the day Pace was murdered, and he had to return to his normal schedule, his distraction would have been very noticeable to others around him. However, if at all possible, he would not have returned to his normal schedule, and his absence from that schedule would have been noted by others.

People who know this offender, know that he hates losing control—even in everyday situations. But when he does, he becomes very agitated and upset—and blames others for what happens.

This offender is determined and mission oriented. Even under stress he is able to complete his assaults on his victims—which was his intention when he entered their residences. This ability to be cool under pressure is also a trait that those who know him have seen in the past. At times, when others are upset, and unable to function, he will appear unaffected and detached.

This is a determined individual who likely became upset at certain times in the past twelve months since the death of Gina Green on Sunday, September 23, 2001. People who know him or were around him specifically during key critical times will be aware of his anger and would have seen his agitation. People should pay particular note of these times, which are outlined below.

(1) Following the death of Charlotte Murray Pace on Friday, May 31, 2002, this offender would have likely behaved in a very angry and agitated manner for a period of time. News reports and other mention of Ms. Pace and what happened to her would have precipitated his making particularly disparaging remarks about her, even blaming her for what happened.

(2) On July 10th, when it was made public that the Green and Pace homicides were connected through DNA, this offender would have again felt agitated and angry and seemed preoccupied. He might have asked those around him seemingly casual questions about the reliability of DNA analysis and how DNA is obtained. He would also make disparaging comments about law enforcement; for example, they were unable to solve these murders because whoever is responsible is too smart to get caught.

(3) This offender did not want, nor did he expect for Pam Kinamore's body to be found. On Tuesday, July 16, 2002, when it was announced that her body was found near the Whiskey Bay Exit off Interstate 10, he would have been noticeably upset—agitated, angry, and preoccupied. Those around him may recall his having made comments that there was no way the Kinamore murder was connected to the other two.

This offender may have even returned to the Whiskey Bay area—to the scene where he left Kinamore's body—because he was so perplexed about her having been found. This return to that area may have appeared to have been for "legitimate" reasons, for example he was "curious" about what the area looked like.

This offender has followed this investigation in the media. His attention to the media reports would be inconsistent with his prior behavior about current events in Baton Rouge, in which he displayed little interest. On Friday, July 12, 2002, two days after the announcement that the Pace and Green murders were connected by DNA, Pam Kinamore is taken out of her home. It is likely this change in his MO is a direct result of his having learned about the Pace-Green connection through the media.

If involved in a relationship with a woman, or living with a female, (mother, sisters, etc.), he can become unpredictably moody, volatile and abusive. These women would know this side of him and be afraid of him. They would also likely describe him at times as being cold and without empathy.

This offender may have given "gifts" to women in his

life—even at times when there was no apparent reason. These gifts could have been wrapped as though they were new, and may have seemed strange to the receiver, because they did not reflect personal "taste" or it was something they neither wanted nor needed.

This offender will be very interested in the release of the "profile" information today. While on the outside he may try to appear very disinterested, he will in fact feel very anxious that some of his own traits as identified by the FBI might make him suspicious to others. Since the Kinamore homicide this offender has felt less anxious and concerned about being arrested. His level of confidence has increased over time and things have returned to "normal" for him. However, the release today of some of the offender's traits and characteristics will raise his anxiety level back up and also produce some paranoia in him. The offender now knows that he has made mistakes before, during and after the commission of these crimes, but he cannot go back in time and fix them. These mistakes make him vulnerable. In addition to the mistakes he has made, this offender will likely be very concerned about people around him who might suspect him. He will be concerned that once they read this profile they will recall specifically his agitation and anger at the critical times identified above. He will wonder about comments he might have made in the past concerning these homicides and the victims, and to whom he made these comments. This paranoia will continue for a while, particularly since he does not know what the entire "profile" says about him, and he does not know what will happen next in the investigation as a result of the release of this information. If he is still in the Baton Rouge area he may be tempted to leave at this time—at least temporarily. However, he is concerned about how his absence would look to others.

# FBI Serial Killer Behavioral Profile Released January 17, 2003

**Addendum for Trineisha Dené Colomb Homicide**

The following addendum is being provided to the original assessment which was released in September 2002. It is based on a review of information to date regarding the abduction and murder of Trineisha Dené Colomb. Should additional information become available, this addendum could change or be modified.

1. Trineisha Colomb's vehicle was seen at approximately 1:30 p.m. on Thursday, November 21. Her vehicle, a black 1994 Mazda MX3 was parked, keys in the ignition, along Robbie Road in Grand Coteau. People were working and conducting normal business in this area during that period of time. As in the three other homicide cases, this is very high-risk behavior for the offender. He could not control who saw him, who recorded his license plate number, or noted his description.

2. The offender drove with the victim in his vehicle for approximately thirty miles to a very specific location in Western Lafayette off of Renaud Drive. Even though there were other locations much closer, the offender chose to "risk it" and drive the distance to the Renaud Drive location.

3. The area off of Renaud Drive is a residential, farming, and light industrial area. There are any number of people around during the day conducting normal business. It is also an area used by hunters and four-wheel drivers. There would be a randomness to when someone might be in this area, working or recreating. However, this offender felt comfortable enough in spite of this activity, to take Trineisha there. This offender is familiar with this specific location, and knew about it beforehand.

4. Trineisha's body is found approximately 250–300 yards off of the roadside in a moderately wooded area, which is extremely muddy and difficult to traverse. It would have been difficult for him to walk this area while controlling the victim.

   (a) The actual site where the attack occurred and where the victim was ultimately found provided concealment for him and emphasizes how well he knew this area. The offender did not want the victim's body to be found and made a concerted effort to prevent that from happening.

   (b) His knowledge of this location comes from living, visiting, or working in this area.

5. On Sunday, November 24th, Trineisha Colomb's body was found, and on Monday, December 23, it was announced that evidence was obtained to link her homicide through DNA to the other three victims in Baton Rouge. The offender would have been noticeably upset after these announcements. Those close to him, a friend or a relative, would have noted this behavior.

6. Because of the high-risk and impulsive behavior seen in this crime this offender made mistakes, which he cannot go back and fix. His only way of monitoring the progress of the investigation and assessing the mistakes he made is to

follow the media reports. People close to the offender would be aware that between November 21st and 24th, and again on December 23 when the announcement was made regarding the DNA, this person was paying very close attention to the news, which might be out of character for him.

7. This crime occurred on a Thursday in the early afternoon. The offender probably was not accountable for his time on that date, giving him the opportunity to complete the abduction and homicide. If he was accountable for his time, the person to whom he was accountable would be aware of his unscheduled absence.

8. This offender has attacked women either in their homes, or, as in this case, outdoors, exposing himself to any number of risks. He took Pam Kinamore and Trineisha Colomb to secondary locations after abducting them. These secondary locations were both outdoors and a significant distance from the abduction site. His selection of secondary sites may be based on the fact he lives with others and could not take the victim to his "comfort zone."

It is the opinion of the Behavioral Analysis Unit of the FBI that this offender lives with and/or works with other people who will recognize the following personality traits believed to be associated with him. The following behavioral traits should be considered in their totality.

a. Impulsive—Acts suddenly and seemingly without thought or deliberation; tends to disregard the consequences for his behavior and actions.

b. Angry—These attacks involve a very unique type of violence. It is an unprovoked violence. This tendency to act out aggressively toward someone, without any apparent reason, has been witnessed by others who live or work with him. He has likely been involved in any or all of the following: domestic abuse, workplace violence, random assaultive behavior, threatening behavior, etc. People who know this offender may be intimidated by him because of his erratic, spontaneous temper.

c. Lack of empathy—There is an obvious disregard for these victims. This offender is concerned about being caught. His coldness and lack of regard for others would be noted in other areas of his life, especially by family members who have been hurt by his lack of concern. His emotions are usually shallow and even inappropriate at times.

d. "Following Behavior"—This offender has the ability to follow women and watch them while not being noticed or alerting them. When the opportunity presents itself, this person is prepared and willing to act out—in spite of many risks. He engages in this following behavior a great deal of time.

e. Need for high risk—Thrill: These attacks, including the most recent one, contain a very distinct high-risk aspect which is unnecessary to the commission of the crime. This suggests this offender may have a need for risk and thrill even in other areas of his life and he will engage in activities which satisfy this need.

# TRUE CRIME FROM BERKLEY BOOKS

## A BEAUTIFUL CHILD
*A True Story of Hope, Horror, and an
Enduring Human Spirit*
by Matt Birkbeck
0-425-20440-5
**The tragic, true story of the girl-next-door's
secret life.**

## UNBRIDLED RAGE
*A True Story of Organized Crime, Corruption,
and Murder in Chicago*
by Gene O'Shea
0-425-20526-2
**Two cold case agents solve the mystery of the
40-year-old murder of three boys in Chicago.**

## ON THE HOUSE
*The Bizarre Killing of Michael Malloy*
by Simon Read
0-425-20678-5
**The true story of the murder of a New York City
drunk at the hands of thugs who had taken out
an insurance policy on his life.**

## HUNTING ERIC RUDOLPH
*An Insider's Account of the Five-Year Search for the
Olympic Bomber*
by Henry Schuster with Charles Stone
0-425-20857-5
**The definitive story of the hunt for the elusive
suspect in the 1996 Atlanta Olympic bombing.**

PENGUIN.COM

b327

# Penguin Group (USA) Online

*What will you be reading tomorrow?*

Tom Clancy, Patricia Cornwell, W.E.B. Griffin,
Nora Roberts, William Gibson, Robin Cook,
Brian Jacques, Catherine Coulter, Stephen King,
Dean Koontz, Ken Follett, Clive Cussler,
Eric Jerome Dickey, John Sandford,
Terry McMillan, Sue Monk Kidd, Amy Tan,
John Berendt…

You'll find them all at
**penguin.com**

*Read excerpts and newsletters,
find tour schedules and reading group guides,
and enter contests.*

Subscribe to Penguin Group (USA) newsletters
and get an exclusive inside look
at exciting new titles and the authors you love
long before everyone else does.

**PENGUIN GROUP (USA)**
us.penguingroup.com